Back on the Road to Serfdom

Culture of Enterprise series

Back on the Road to Serfdom

The Resurgence of Statism

Edited by
Thomas E. Woods Jr.

ISI
BOOKS

Wilmington, Delaware

The Culture of Enterprise series is supported by a grant from the John Templeton Foundation. The Intercollegiate Studies Institute gratefully acknowledges this support.

Library of Congress Cataloging-in-Publication Data

Back on the road to serfdom : the resurgence of statism / edited by Thomas E. Woods Jr.
    p. cm.
    Includes bibliographical references and index.
    ISBN 978-1-935191-90-2
    1. Economic policy. 2. Welfare state. 3. Free enterprise. 4. Welfare state—United States. 5. United States—Economic policy. I. Woods, Thomas E.

HD82.B2145 2010
330.12'6—dc22   2010046027

Published in the United States by:

ISI Books
Intercollegiate Studies Institute
3901 Centerville Road
Wilmington, Delaware 19807-1938
www.isibooks.org

Manufactured in the United States of America

Contents

Introduction   vii
    Thomas E. Woods Jr.

Economic Policy and the Road to Serfdom:
The Watershed of 1913   1
    Brian Domitrovic

Hamiltonianism: The Origins of the Modern State   17
    Carey Roberts

The Modern Welfare State:
Leading the Way on the Road to Serfdom   35
    Per Bylund

The Origins of the Crisis   55
    Antony P. Mueller

The Dangers of Protectionism   73
    Mark Brandly

Entrepreneurship and Government   93
    Dane Stangler

The Cultural Costs of Corporatism:
How Government-Business Collusion Denigrates
the Entrepreneur and Rewards the Sycophant   111
    Timothy P. Carney

Contents

It's Not the Markets, It's the Morals:
How Excessively Blaming Markets Undermines Civil Society   131
     John Larrivee

Religion, the Market, and the State   155
     Gerard Casey

The Road to Cultural Serfdom:
America's First Television Czar   171
     Paul A. Cantor

Notes   189

About the Contributors   221

Index   225

Introduction

Thomas E. Woods Jr.

It was not difficult to predict a major consequence of the Panic of 2008: disparaging the market economy and the free society is now more chic than it has been in half a century. In light of recent events, the argument runs, only a hopeless naïf would champion these things. What we need now is greater supervision by our public servants, and less adherence to the discredited dogmas of the past.

Just how much the free market was in fact responsible for the crisis, or the extent to which government itself and its central bank may have been the culprits (and thus whether the "free market" could have been to blame in the first place), is the subject of one of the essays in this volume. The unifying theme of this book, though, is the brute fact that a shift toward statism is indeed occurring, and that it will not end happily. History is littered with foreign and domestic crises that became pretexts for the expansion of government power, and the present instance appears to be no exception.

When we argue that the winds are blowing in the direction of an ever-larger role of the state in American life, we must be careful not to imply that prior to 2007–8 a broad consensus in favor of the free market and against state coercion had taken root. Even during the 1980s, when free-market ideas were said to be sweeping the country, the net effects were modest. Larry Schwab makes a persuasive case in his overlooked study *The Illusion of a Conservative Reagan Revolution* that the transformation that was supposed to have overtaken America during the 1980s was rather more limited than either liberals or conservatives have been willing to admit. There is little evidence of a lasting ideological shift among the population, and government grew rather than shrank, with the federal budget doubling over the course of the decade.

The failure of conservatives to make significant inroads into the federal apparatus was symbolized by the Contract with America, the series of proposals Republicans promised to support on the eve of their off-year landslide in 1994. What was portrayed as a bold array of policy initiatives was in fact a timid and insignificant list of changes that would have left the federal apparatus for all intents and purposes unchanged. The Brookings Institution correctly observed: "Viewed historically, the Contract represents the final consolidation of the bedrock domestic policies and programs of the New Deal, the Great Society, the post–Second World War defense establishment, and, most importantly, the deeply rooted national political culture that has grown up around them."

The GOP Pledge of 2010 promised to eliminate an unspecified $100 billion from the federal budget at a time of skyrocketing debt, record deficits, and a budget approaching $4 trillion. History seemed to be repeating itself.

In mid-2010, though, F. A. Hayek's 1944 book, *The Road to Serfdom*, soared to the number-one slot on Amazon.com; in a single week it sold, incredibly, upwards of forty thousand copies. Although not the radical libertarian tract its critics claimed at the time, it had a profound effect on many readers, who found in it an intelligent critique of central planning and its effects on individual liberty. Was it a sign of the times that interest in a book like this would suddenly be revived? Had a critical mass of the American public grown concerned that their own country faced a watershed moment in its history involving freedom and the state?

That remains to be seen.

Introduction

Hayek never expected his small book to become an international sensation, or to wind up on lists of the seminal works of the classical liberal canon. Prior to the book's release, Hayek had been a professor at the London School of Economics, where he earned a reputation as one of the world's great economic theorists. His work developing the Austrian School's theory of the business cycle won him the Nobel Prize in 1974, four decades after he wrote it. His works in economics were technical and difficult for a lay audience, though, so the popular reception of *The Road to Serfdom* added a new dimension to his career.

The genteel Hayek dedicated his book "to socialists of all parties"—people he believed were guilty of nothing more than intellectual error. He proceeded to state his case firmly but without acrimony or invective. (If anything, he may have been too accommodating, conceding that certain interventions in the economy were acceptable or even desirable.)

Some of Hayek's book can seem dated today, since few now call for state ownership of the means of production or for the kind of central economic planning to which his criticisms apply—a welcome development for which Hayek himself may take some share of the credit. The problems we face stem from the mixed economy, as opposed to the fully socialist ones that Hayek criticized. All over the world, the impossible promises governments have made to their populations are beginning to unravel. Millions of people have arranged their lives in the expectation of various forms of government support that will be mathematically impossible to provide.

Aggravating this problem are the demographic trends at work across the developed world, which faces an aging crisis that will strain its welfare states to the breaking point. (As *Foreign Policy* magazine reported, "The global population of children under 5 is expected to fall by 49 million as of midcentury, while the number of people over 60 will grow by 1.2 billion.") At the very moment that some Americans are calling for a single-payer health-care system in the United States, pointing to the alleged successes of such systems in Europe, the finance ministers of those countries privately concede that of course those programs are going to implode, and that the collapse is only a matter of time.

What the rising generations across the developed world are facing is a genuine road to serfdom. They will have to work harder and longer than did their parents just to tread water, if they can find work at all in artificial economies battered by years of "stimulus" and misdirected resources. Retirement will seem like something out of science fiction. And to add insult to injury, they will be putting in this effort on behalf of transfer programs that are going to collapse anyway—Social Security, Medicare, pensions, and so forth.

The economic consequences of an expanded government presence in American life are of course not the only outcomes to be feared, and this volume considers a variety of them. For one thing, as the state expands, it fosters the most antisocial aspects of man's nature, particularly his urge to attain his goals with the least possible exertion. And it is much easier to acquire wealth by means of forcible redistribution by the state than by exerting oneself in the service of one's fellow man. The character of the people thus begins to change; they expect as a matter of entitlement what they once hesitated to ask for as charity. That is the fallacy in the usual statement that "it would cost only $X billion to give every American who needs it" this or that benefit. Once people realize the government is giving out a benefit for "free," more and more people will place themselves in the condition that entitles them to the benefit, thereby making the program ever more expensive. A smaller and smaller productive base will have to strain to provide for an ever-larger supply of recipients, until the system begins to buckle and collapse.

We should recall, though, that when the French classical liberal Frédéric Bastiat spoke of "legal plunder," he was not thinking exclusively of the use of state power to expropriate the rich on behalf of the poor. He was thinking of all forms of state violence employed to benefit one group at the expense of the rest of society. The greater the scope of the state over the economy, the more entrepreneurial energy will be misdirected into lobbying for special privileges and loot, and less into ongoing efforts to please the consumer.

The more functions the state usurps from civil society, the more the institutions of civil society will atrophy. Once supplanted by coercive government, tasks that people used to perform on a voluntary basis come to be viewed as impossible for civil society to manage in the absence of government—even though civil society did indeed perform these functions at one time. This spiritless population comes, in turn, to look for political solutions even to the most trivial problems.

The more the market is supplanted by a system of crony capitalism, the more the very phenomenon of profit appears disreputable. How, apart from some grant of privilege or other underhanded means, could someone have grown wealthy? Journalist Hedrick Smith, in his study *The New Russians*, found that this was the effect of decades of Communism—anyone who seemed to be prospering became a target of suspicion and envy. Entrepreneurship can scarcely function in such an atmosphere.

Spanning history, economics, religion, and the arts, the essays in this collection constitute both a warning about and a corrective to these trends.

Back on the Road to Serfdom begins by considering how we got here. Brian Domitrovic leads off with a look at what happened in the twentieth century to give the federal government such broad sway over the economy. In examining this development, he shows that the historical record is clear: the more the authorities try to steer the economy, the more erratic it becomes.

Carey Roberts goes back even earlier than Domitrovic, to the era of the American Founding. He traces the present resurgence of statism to the seminal conflict between Thomas Jefferson and Alexander Hamilton, and sets forth a refreshingly revisionist account of Hamiltonian economic policies, which Americans are expected to revere as self-evidently sensible and wise.

Per Bylund then looks beyond America's shores to show how the welfare state became the dominant model of government throughout the Western world. He also punctures the myths of the welfare state that Americans have been lectured about for decades. A native of Sweden working on his doctorate in the United States, Bylund reveals that the so-called Swedish model is hardly a dream for modern civilization.

In so doing, he rules out the default position of so-called progressives, which is to claim that large welfare states are compatibile with long-run prosperity, and that there is nothing about the American situation that higher levels of wealth confiscation cannot solve. Moreover, he demonstrates that the welfare state harms not only the economy but also individual liberty and civil society.

With Domitrovic, Roberts, and Bylund having established the broader context for the government's accelerating intrusions into the economy, Antony Mueller looks at the more immediate causes of the recent financial crisis. His essay is a valuable corrective to the standard account of the economic downturn that has fueled so much of the recent resurgence of statism. Professor Mueller's interpretation of the crisis, which is informed by the Austrian School of economics, also accounts for why the proposed remedies are likely to prolong the economic malaise in those countries adopting them.

Since the financial crisis began, free trade has come under withering attack across the political spectrum. While some of the older arguments in favor of domestic protection continue to be made, new arguments have recently been added to the traditional arsenal. We hear repeated claims these days that unhampered trade is not in fact mutually beneficial, and that although the overall number of widgets may indeed increase under free trade, the interests of the working classes in the developed world are grievously harmed. Mark Brandly uncovers the flaws in these arguments in his robust defense of the international division of labor.

Dane Stangler discusses another vital element of the economy and society that is threatened by state encroachment: entrepreneurial activity. When we understand what entrepreneurship is, we realize how foolish it is to expect the state to foster it, except perhaps by removing barriers to economic activity.

Tim Carney's essay builds on an area in which he has made such important contributions: the relationship between government and big business. The superficial account with which American schoolchildren are familiar conceives of these two forces as antagonists. Both theory and history suggest that the true nature of their interaction is rather more interesting, and often involves collusion against the public interest rather than the righteous regulation of private malefactors by wise public servants.

Western religious leaders have as a rule been scandalously naïve about the nature of the state and sanguine about its expansion. Two of our essayists subject the unexamined premises behind these arguments to critical and fruitful scrutiny. John Larrivee deftly responds to some of the more common criticisms of the free market that may be heard in religious circles. Such criticisms, he shows, undermine the role of values, faith, and civil society while opening the door to more government intervention. In the next essay, Gerard Casey of University College Dublin considers whether some Christians' social-democratic views of wealth redistribution, the state, and the market are justified in light of tradition and the Bible

The University of Virginia's Paul Cantor, who attended Ludwig von Mises's seminar at New York University in the early 1960s, has done much groundbreaking work on markets and the arts, a tradition he continues in the final essay of this volume. Here he explores the bureaucratization of culture, and finds that this form of government planning, just like all the others, grossly oversimplifies the phenomenon it is attempting to control, and involves the hopeless task of substituting top-down direction for the spontaneous and dispersed origins of real culture.

Americans are taught a great deal of civics-book nonsense about the nature of the state, the benefits it confers, and the unbearable difficulties we would face without its careful custodianship of society. In reality, Americans are ruled by a patchwork of self-perpetuating fiefdoms, which beneath a veneer of public-interest rhetoric seek to pursue their own power and resources.

There is, one would think, another way for human beings to live than this. Ironically, it is government itself that is about to teach that very lesson. When its grandiose schemes and promises inevitably unravel, all that will be left is civil society managing its own affairs, the very thing we have been taught to believe is impossible.

Economic Policy and the Road to Serfdom:
The Watershed of 1913

Brian Domitrovic

We are perhaps apt to forget that during the Cold War, it was generally conceded that the Soviet Union had a higher rate of economic growth than the United States. Given that the United States accounted for nearly half of world output in 1945, the logic held that it did not have room to grow like the other nations of the world, which collectively accounted for the other half. Starting from a much lower base—and having gained an empire—the USSR surely could expect greater economic expansion than the United States.

There was no more confident advocate of this position than the postwar world's premier economist, Paul A. Samuelson. Samuelson touted the growth record of the USSR in his book *Economics: An Introductory Analysis*, the leading economics textbook of the era, and he said the same thing as adviser to those in power. When John F. Kennedy was running for president in 1960, Samuelson wrote to the Democratic candidate, *"America has definitely been falling behind not only with respect to the USSR, but with respect to most of the other advanced countries of the world.* For years, our production has been growing more slowly than that of Russia, Western Germany, Japan, [and a host of other countries]" (emphasis in the original).[1]

1

JFK offered no resistance to this point, and few others in Washington did either. By the 1980s, the CIA's national estimates held that the USSR's economy, which had been at mass famine levels four decades prior, was now half the size of that of the United States. The Soviet Union's rates of growth had been so much higher than those of the United States, according to U.S. intelligence, that the two economies were possibly on a path of convergence.[2]

Then, in 1989, an official in the USSR's national accounts bureau named Yuri Maltsev defected to the United States and revealed that by good standards of measurement, the Soviet economy stood at only *4 percent* of the U.S. total. After the Soviet state collapsed two years later, investigations by the World Bank, the International Monetary Fund, and the Organization for Economic Cooperation and Development concluded that the Soviet economy had been only half as big as the CIA reckoning, reaching about a fourth or a fifth the size of the U.S. economy. Maltsev stuck with his number, and soon he was joined by dissenters from within the Western statistical bureaucracies, such as William Easterly at the World Bank. An old rule of thumb in the face of two clusters of professional estimates is to split the difference. Applying the rule in this case, we can say that the Soviet economy peaked at about one-eighth the size of the American economy.[3]

Although the economic failures of the centrally planned Soviet state are now well documented, no less a champion of the free market than F. A. Hayek expressed doubts that free-market capitalism was superior to planning when it came to total output and standards of living. In *The Road to Serfdom* Hayek wrote:

Which kind of values figure less prominently in the picture of the future held out to us by the popular writers and speakers . . . ? It is certainly not material comfort, certainly not a rise in our standard of living or the assurance of a certain status in society which ranks lower. Is there a popular writer or speaker who dares to suggest to the masses that they might have to make sacrifices of their material prospects for the enhancement of an ideal end? Is it not, in fact, entirely the other way round?[4]

The Road to Serfdom was a warning that collectivism is a temptation of the most serious sort, in that it had the ring of a good trade. In exchange for civil liberties, which is to say a high degree of personal, familial, and community autonomy, submission to a centralized state stood both to eliminate social inequality and to bring material well-being if not affluence.

This is one of the great overlooked aspects of *The Road to Serfdom*: Hayek is careful to argue for the market not on the grounds of what it may produce in terms of standards of living. Rather, he urges that yielding to the market will make us better persons, though it may make us economically poorer. Under "individualism," we will develop good values and habits "which are less esteemed and practiced now—independence, self-reliance, and the willingness to bear risks, the readiness to back one's own conviction against a majority, and the willingness to voluntary cooperation with one's neighbors."[5]

This defense of individualist over collectivist values is the book's strongest suit. But history has shown that the actual road to serfdom not only leads to the uncivilized value structure of which Hayek wrote so eloquently. It also debilitates living standards, despite Hayek's fears that there were *legitimate* reasons to be tempted by collectivism.

We should be careful not to fall into the common trap holding that economics is inevitably the science of trade-offs—a trap that snared even Hayek. He felt compelled to write *The Road to Serfdom* "to the socialists of all parties" because he believed that material well-being and social equality were plausible results of collectivism. Hayek's conclusion was perhaps not unreasonable at the time, given that the ascendant Nazi Germany was achieving a higher rate of economic growth than the less collectivist Britain to which he had fled. But in fact, such benefits are not plausible. More importantly, preparing the ground for collectivism at all may well introduce the slippery slope toward impoverishment more quickly than we think.[6]

Today, more than sixty-five years after the publication of *The Road to Serfdom*, the United States seems to be taking alarming steps in the collectivist direction. To understand where this path leads, we need not look at something so manifestly disastrous as the Soviet economy, whose history is one of privation, supply-demand disconnect, constant rescues by foreign capital, and unsustainability tantamount to simple preposterousness. America's own history, while blessedly bereft of analogues to the Soviet experience, is itself quite clear about what happens when nods are made in the collectivist direction. For an investigation of the course of American economic history since the Civil War reveals a remarkable truth: *all* periods of prosperity in the United States have coincided with decided efforts to keep collectivist inclinations at bay, and *all* periods of economic weakness have occurred in the context of dalliances with collectivism—that is, with efforts to impose governmental management on the economy.

The frightening truth is that if America's leaders do not understand this history, our government may only double down on economic policies that have caused trouble in the past.

The American Economy: Potency and Act

The most significant fact about the past century and a half, treated as a statistical run, is that it had an inflection point. This was the one-third mark, 1913. Before that year, the macroeconomic performance of the United States, by the main measurements, was regular and strong. After that point, however, extended contractions and bouts of new, unfamiliar negative side effects—namely, unemployment and inflation—emerged rather out of the ether.

The most impressive half century in American—arguably world—economic history was that which followed the Civil War: the nearly fifty years from 1865 to 1913. The American economy expanded at a yearly rate of 3.62 percent from 1865 to 1913. By way of comparison, from 1913 to 2008 (also a peak-to-peak period), the American economy grew at 3.26 percent per year. The difference of about four-tenths of a percent per year proved enormous. Had the United States maintained the trend that held in the half century after the Civil War, it would now be about half again richer than it is now, in the second decade of the twenty-first century.

Macroeconomic performance is generally judged on two criteria: growth and "variation." Variation refers to the degree of steadiness of growth and of macroeconomic ill-effects, above all unemployment and price instability. Here again, the era of the Robber Barons is the shining one. The greatest decades of economic growth in American history were the 1870s and 1880s, when the economy expanded by two-thirds each time. There was one significant recession in this period, in 1873. It was overwhelmed so soon and so comprehensively that the 70 percent real growth gained in the 1870s amounts to the largest of any decade in the peacetime history of the United States.

As for the "panic of 1873" of textbook lore, that year brought a big drop in output, with people thrown out of work. The episode was a function of the incredible depreciation of the dollar that had been undertaken in the Civil War, when (following decades of price stability) the Union government printed greenbacks so quickly that the dollar suddenly lost half its value. After 1865, the U.S. government pledged to restore the value of the dollar against gold (and consumer prices), but doubts about this led to speculative investments to hedge the uncertainty and ultimately produced the asset crash of 1873.

In the wake of the 1873 bust, however, the dollar slowly reclaimed its value, just as the U.S. government had pledged. The price level declined by 1.4 percent per year on average for the next two decades, such that by the 1890s, a dollar saved before 1860 achieved its original purchasing power. As for unemployment, the term was not coined until the tail end of the century for a reason. The United States was importing tens of millions of immigrant workers on account of labor shortages given the growth boom.

President Barack Obama's first chair of the Council of Economic Advisers, Christina Romer, owes her professional reputation to her bringing to light these realities in her doctoral dissertation at MIT in the 1980s. Romer found that the era of the American industrial revolution (and by her analysis the trend held until 1930) was so superior in terms of growth and variation—growth was high; recessions were rare, shallow, and short; prices changed little as employment boomed—that it effectively defined the kind of results that governmental macroeconomic management should aspire to. The irony was that there was precious little macroeconomic management at all for most of this era. We can say with statistical precision that there has never been a golden era in American macroeconomic history like the 1870s and 1880s.[7]

There were two other significant recessions in the half century after the Civil War. These occurred in 1893 and 1907. Both cases correlated to governmental overtures to introduce macroeconomic policy. In 1890, the United States signaled that, despite having attained the very price level that had held for decades before the Civil War, as well as having watched growth cruise at more than 5 percent per year for the long term, it was now going to monetize a new asset, silver. The prospect was of too much currency in the economy (1873 redux), and the markets quickly swelled and crashed. The recovery from 1893 stayed tepid while President Grover Cleveland spent his term trying to end the silver lark. Aggregate output was flat from 1892 until the next election year, 1896; in the latter year, free-silverite William Jennings Bryan succeeded Cleveland as Democratic nominee for president. The strong recovery began only when, with the election of Republican William McKinley in 1896, the United States committed to dropping the program for the extra silver money. Overall, growth was slower in the 1890s than it had been in preceding decades—33 percent for the decade, a typical twentieth-century number. But from the year McKinley was elected until 1907, growth came in at 4.6 percent per year, approaching the 1870s–1880s standard of 5.2 percent annually. This is tantamount to saying that the real trend of yearly growth in the post–Civil War period was not 3.62 percent, but something like 5 percent per year—because 5 percent held as long as the government stayed out of the way.

In 1907, there was another market crash and recession, only this time a strong and sustained recovery did not follow. The recovery, such as it was (3.3 percent growth per year until the 1913 peak), was haunted by a new prospect: that comprehensive new tools allowing governmental intervention into the economy would be put in place. Immediately in the wake of J. P. Morgan's famous settling of the markets in the fall of 1907, measures were introduced in Congress to create a federal reserve (or central banking) system that would be the first line of defense in any future crisis. In addition, the push for a federal income tax, which had died in the courts in recent years, gained renewed momentum.

Both of these massive means of governmental intrusion in the economy, the Federal Reserve and the income tax, were finally established in the same year: 1913—our inflection point.

Even though the mild recovery after 1907 occurred before 1913, its characteristics actually may have owed themselves to 1913. Capital is known for looking to the future to take a gander at prospective returns. Had there been no prospect of the Fed and the income tax in the wake of the economic events of the fall of 1907, there may not have been a recession at all, let alone a weak recovery. For if 1908 had brought a recovery on the order of nearly 5 percent annual growth as had been initiated in 1896, we would not even call the 1907 event a recession. There were episodes in the 1880s where growth dipped and assets were sold, but the recoveries were so quick and so big that the down periods do not register to the naked eye. It is not out of the question that this fate was in store for the economy had the 1907 crash not been met with calls for a Fed and an income tax.

This, of course, is a hypothetical point, but there is no shortage of historical evidence that is consistent with it. Christina Romer calculated that the recovery in industrial production from the 1907 event proceeded according to recent precedent until 1912. As for anecdotal evidence, there is one delicious piece: J. P. Morgan's will. When Morgan died in 1913, the moneyed class expressed shock that his declared assets amounted to only $118 million. Andrew Carnegie—whom

Morgan had bought out in 1901 and who was worth some $400 million—felt tricked, feeling that Morgan had posed as one of the top set's own all those years. Yet in view of the major macroeconomic reforms proposed in the wake of 1907 (which included an estate tax that would be made law in 1916), it is possible, even likely, that the aging Morgan rearranged his assets such that only a fraction was manifested in his estate—in which case he would have displayed the talent at which "trusts" came to be so proficient in later decades, as the estate tax hit 55 percent. This story is but one indication that high-powered capital was gamely rearranging itself as the nation's economy braced itself for the onset of 1913.[8]

The Variation Era

Perhaps the most forgotten period in American economic history is the eight years that followed the creation of the Fed and the income tax in 1913. From 1913 to 1921 the growth rate came in at just 1.4 percent per year. The period included two long recessions: one beginning in 1913, in which that year's level of production was equaled only two years later (and with the assistance of military production that did nothing for living standards); and another from 1919 to 1921 that was simply the worst depression the nation would ever suffer outside of the 1930s. "Unemployment" quickly joined the parlance; people scrambled to measure the phenomenon, and the consensus was that it stayed in the high double digits in the latter recession. And then this novelty: the price level went up by 110 percent from 1913 to 1920, and then swerved down in the year following by 25 percent. Strikes swept the land, since wages had no hope of keeping up with the unprecedented inflation, and the new income tax system hit persons making as little as $1,000 a year ($11,000 in today's terms).[9]

Before 1913, there had been at most only shadows of government fiscal and monetary policy, and the United States had cruised at its 5 percent per-annum rate of expansion, with the price level making small oscillations around the antebellum number. But after 1913, the government used its new macroeconomic policy tools to the hilt. Immediately after its creation, the Fed arranged for a doubling of the money supply—this in the face of a manifest recession. The inevitable result was the doubling of the price level. As for income taxes, the first top rate, upon passage of the Sixteenth Amendment in 1913, was 7 percent. In four years' time, it was up elevenfold, to 77 percent. Meanwhile, someone whose income merely kept up with the inflation engineered by the Fed—that is, someone who saw no *actual* gain in income—could be pushed into the stratospheric top tax bracket, since the progressive tax brackets were not adjusted for inflation. (This is the phenomenon known as bracket creep.) The investor class soon adjusted away from entrepreneurship and into tax shelters. Morgan's will had been a sign.

Then there was the recovery—perhaps the most famous recovery in American history. The Roaring '20s that followed 1921 aped the bygone era very well: 4.7 percent yearly growth through 1929, unemployment gone, and a price level that barely moved. The government's macroeconomic policy posture during this period is unmistakable: the Fed expressly got out of the business of trying to undo the 1913–20 inflation via a commensurate massive deflation; and the marginal rate of the income tax was cut by 52 points. In other words, fiscal and monetary policy retreated.

How we have ever associated the onset of the Great Depression with a "crisis of capitalism" is anyone's guess. In fact, the years 1929–33 brought historic governmental intrusions in the economy. In late 1929, the Fed resumed its 1920–21 efforts to reclaim the 1913 price level by appreciating the value of the dollar. Deflation held at 9 percent per year from late 1929 to early 1932, blowing away the gentle deflation standard of the post-1873 years that had seen constant, rapid growth. Over the same interval, the marginal income tax rate jumped by a magnitude of one and a half, to 63 percent. Severe deflation and confiscatory taxes led to a capital strike, with savage unemployment being the inevitable result. And this is not to mention the Smoot-Hawley Act of 1930, which raised tariffs to record levels, cut foreign trade in half, and convinced the world that convertible currencies—and indeed international economic cooperation—were no longer useful.

In other words, fiscal and monetary policy extended their scope and sway as never before. In turn, real conditions in the United States became as horrendous as any developed country had experienced since the dawn of the industrial age.

All of this macroeconomic intervention occurred during the Herbert Hoover administration, *before* Franklin Roosevelt took office and instituted his New Deal. Under FDR, the Fed and the U.S. Treasury actually dropped the misguided deflationist policy. By raising the gold redemption price 75 percent, to $35 per ounce, the government effectively announced that the United States would never strive to appreciate the dollar again. It remained an open question whether the U.S. government would strive to depreciate the currency, but in point of fact it did not. The consumer price index from 1934 to 1940 mimicked the band of oscillation that had prevailed in the era of the Robber Barons: small moves around par.

But while the Roosevelt administration reversed course on monetary policy, it only built on Hoover's fiscal policy. FDR increased the marginal tax rate even more, sending it up to 73 percent—nearly triple the rate that had supervised the Roaring '20s.

This mixed record on monetary and fiscal policy produced a mixed recovery at best. Output did go up slightly during this period, and by 1939 it finally returned to the 1929 level (adjusting for population, which grew at a tiny rate). But instead of posting a peak-to-peak growth rate in output of 4–5 percent per year, as had been usual before 1913, the New Deal recovery—not the *mot juste*—was nil peak-to-peak.

From 1940 to 1944, gross domestic product (GDP) boomed in the United States as living standards collapsed. We should not be detained by the aggregate output, or even the employment, statistics of the World War II years if the topic under consideration is economic recovery. The amount of goods and services produced for the real sector hit bottom with the war. Government/military goods, which are not real goods, became the exclusive specialization of the American economy in this period. Calling the 1940–44 run tantamount to a recovery (let alone a great one), as is so often done, is one of the great misnomers of modern economic history.

Consider two pertinent questions about this period. First, given that employment rebounded massively during the war, but that pay for those employed had to be saved on account of the shortages, did that saved pay retain its value after the war? And second, was the GDP boom of 1940–44 consolidated and built on as the economy cycled into real production?

The answer to the first question is that the saved pay did not retain its value, meaning that one cannot really hold that there had been a true return to full employment during the war. From 1944 to 1948, the United States experienced inflation of 42 percent (the Fed had been expansionist again), devaluing savings accrued before that time. Moreover, redemptions of U.S. war bonds (where so much of workers' pay had gone during World War II) were taxed at one's marginal income tax rate, and rates were jacked up across the board, the top one reaching 91 percent. Therefore, when World War II employees redeemed the bonds after the war, the World War II employer—the government—recovered much of what it had laid out in pay to its workers. A conservative estimate is that given inflation and taxes, the average World War II worker lost half of his or her pay to the government. In economic terms, this means that World War II solved the unemployment problem of the 1930s only half as much as is commonly supposed.

As for the second question, GDP fell precipitously from 1944 to 1947, by 13 percent, as prices soared. This was a clear indication that the growth of the war years was artificial. Nonetheless, living standards improved, as the real sector made huge inroads into the government's share of economic production. Then a transition hit: the postwar inflation stopped. This occurred because the U.S. government focused on its commitment to the world made at the 1944 Bretton Woods conference that it would not overproduce the dollar so as to jeopardize the $35 gold price. And when Republicans won control of Congress in 1946, they insisted on getting a tax cut; they finally passed it over

President Harry Truman's veto in April 1948. The institutions of 1913 had signaled a posture of retreat.

That is when postwar prosperity got going. From 1947 to 1953, growth rolled in at the old familiar rate of 4.6 percent per annum, as unemployment dived and prices stayed at par except for a strange 8 percent burst just as the Korean War started.

Taxes were still high, however, with rates that started at 20 percent and peaked at 91 percent. When recession hit in 1953, a chorus rose that they be hacked away. But for the eight years of his presidency, Dwight D. Eisenhower resisted these calls for tax relief. Despite the common myth of "Eisenhower prosperity," the years 1953 to 1960 saw economic growth far below the old par, at only 2.4 percent, and there were three recessions during this period. Monetary policy, for its part, was unremarkable. Once again the coincidence held: unremarkable monetary policy and aggressive tax policy led to a half-baked result.

Much ink has been spilled on how the JFK tax cuts of 1962 and 1964 were "Keynesian" and "demand-side." Whatever we want to call the policy mix of the day, in the JFK and early Lyndon B. Johnson years, fiscal and monetary policy clearly retreated. Income taxes got cut across the board, with every rate in the Eisenhower structure going down, the top from 91 percent to 70 percent, the bottom from 20 percent to 14 percent. And monetary policy zeroed in (at least through 1965) on a stable value of the dollar, with the gold price and the price level sticking at par after making startling moves up with the final Eisenhower recessions. The results: from 1961 to 1968, real U.S. growth was 5.1 percent yearly; unemployment hit peacetime lows; and inflation held in the heroic 1 percent range before the latter third of the period, when it began creeping up by a point a year. The real effects inspired slogans. If four decades prior had been the "Roaring '20s," these were the "Swingin' '60s" and "The Go-Go Years."

At the end of the decade, however, the government loudly signaled a reversal in fiscal and monetary policy. The Fed volunteered that it would finance budget deficits, and LBJ pleaded for and got an income tax surcharge, soon accompanied (under Richard M. Nixon) by an increase in the capital-gains rate on the order of 100 percent. This two-front reassertion of fiscal and monetary policy held for a dozen years. The nickname eventually given to that period, in view of the real effects, was the "stagflation era" (for stagnation plus inflation). From 1969 to 1982, real GDP went to half that of the Go-Go Years, to 2.46 percent; the price level tripled (with gold going up twenty fold); average unemployment roughly doubled to 7.5 percent; three double-dip recessions occurred; and stocks and bonds suffered a 75 percent real loss. It was the worst decade of American macroeconomic history save the 1930s, and it inspired Christina Romer to write a dissertation.

Paul Volcker took over the Fed chairmanship in 1979. He was determined to stabilize the dollar (given the recent 200 percent inflation) at least against prices, if not against gold and foreign exchange. He ultimately did this well enough with the support of the Ronald Reagan administration. The average inflation rate for the period after 1982, and beginning strongly in that year, was about a third of what had prevailed in the 1970s—3 percent as opposed to 9 percent. The monetary authorities even came to announce that they were pursuing "inflation targeting." This retreat in monetary policy was once again coupled with Kennedyesque tax policy, with all rates getting reduced substantially, and most of the brackets eliminated in the bargain. "The Great Moderation" became the term coined to describe the 1982–2007 period, where annual growth came in at 3.3 percent, with seven-year runs at 4.3 percent in the 1980s and 1990s. There were only two recessions in this period, both mild. GDP growth got in the tightest band ever recorded since quarterly statistics began in 1947. Average unemployment went down to half the stagflation level.

Finally, with the "Great Recession" of 2008–10—which even with its five down quarters of GDP growth and 10 percent unemployment does not equal the extent of the 1980–82 double-dip recession—monetary policy has declared its everlasting intention to be relevant again. Taxes are set to rise by statute in 2011, and by commission after that so as to cover federal spending 50 percent larger than we are accustomed to. Once again the series is maintained. A growth stoppage along with variation coincides with the rearing of the heads of fiscal and monetary policy.

Business versus Busy-ness

The post-1913 period of American economic history is a world of fits and starts, at least until the Great Moderation which dissipated with the government bailouts of 2008–9. In contrast, the pre-1913 era has an integrity, a statics, with patterns that hold for a long time. Its story is easier to relate. Variation, when it came in that bygone time, coincided with the weird appearance of a shadow, that of an overseer seeking power to bend things to a different course.

The era of the Robber Barons was one of business, perhaps the most supreme there ever was. The post-1913 era—the macroeconomic era, the era of policy—was rather one of busy-ness. Economic performance shed its regularity and constant peak nature in favor of previously unheard-of growth swings, so much so that a clamor started to measure that very thing, and to do so quarterly.

In the canons of macroeconomics, fiscal and monetary policy are supposed to bring "stabilization" to an economy. That is, policy will smooth out the cycle of boom and bust and reduce the parameters of inflation and unemployment. Advocates of macroeconomic policy have long conceded that there will have to be trade-offs in exchange for these benefits. Lower growth will be the price for smoothness. Some unemployment or inflation will have to exist at the expense of the other.

And yet from a simple statistical perspective, it is clear that the macroeconomic era gave evidence not so much of trade-offs as diminutions *across the board*. Growth was both smoother and higher in the pre-1913 era. Unemployment and inflation not only did not exist inversely to each other; they did not exist at all.

What have been the costs of having macroeconomic policy? Recall that the real growth trend of the pre-1913 era was something like 5 percent per annum, not the recorded 3.62 percent. The unusual breakdowns in the long peak-growth runs in that era occurred when the government attempted to introduce macroeconomic policy. This means that the real output lost to us since 1913 is not 50 percent, but 500 percent. Had we grown at 5 percent annually since 1913, instead of at the 3.26 percent that in fact happened, we would be *five times* better off today.

We can remonstrate that correlation is not causation. Perhaps fiscal and monetary policy had nothing to do with the sub–Gilded Age performance of the economy since 1913. Perhaps their absence had nothing to do with the impressiveness of economic performance before then. After all, other things were at work. Maybe so. But we can say one thing for certain. The correlation is fact. Every period of sustained peak economic activity in the United States since 1865 has correlated to the nonexistence, or the blanket retreat, of fiscal and monetary policy.

Although correlation is not causation, the United States will be foolish and reckless to maintain current policy in the face of its unambiguous economic record. Macroeconomic policy, as much as any outright push toward collectivism, is on the record as putting us on the road to serfdom. And if we think there is a high bottom which will always catch us in our mistakes, we are indulging an optimism not based on the lessons of history.

Hamiltonianism:
The Origins of the Modern State

Carey Roberts

Here then was the real ground of the opposition which was made to the course of administration. Its object was to preserve the legislature pure and independent of the executive, to restrain the administration to republican forms and principles, and not permit the constitution to be construed into a monarchy, and to be warped, in practice, into all the principles and pollutions of their favorite English model.

—Thomas Jefferson, *Anas*

A distraught Alexander Hamilton confronted the newly appointed secretary of state, Thomas Jefferson, shortly after his arrival from France in 1790. According to Jefferson, the beleaguered Hamilton appeared weakened from weeks of political wrangling. What brought Hamilton, President George Washington's secretary of the treasury, hat in hand to Jefferson's side was public finance. After years of war and a failed experiment with one federation, American political leaders embarked upon another experiment with another federation. This time, Hamilton and his supporters thought, things would be different. This time the new government would exercise indirect control over the nation's financial resources in a bid to support the burdensome public debt remaining from the War for Independence. And this time, public debt would be turned into a public blessing.[1]

Hamilton's scheme involved a great many smaller plans that would come together in a transformative climax during the first several months of the Washington presidency. Jefferson and his fellow Virginian James Madison, the floor leader of the House of Representatives, stood in the way. Hamilton did not have the votes in Congress to pass his proposal to restructure the country's public finances, and public opinion seemed set against him. More importantly, Hamilton's vision stood against what most learned Americans thought they knew about public debt and finance. Judging from the public reaction, which was nothing less than the creation of the first American party system, Jefferson and Madison were hardly alone in their concerns.

By the mid-1790s, Hamilton's plans had backfired in unkept promises, failed expectations, and mistaken consequences. Hamilton's reputation suffered throughout most of the nineteenth century, and the political party led by men who idolized him—the Whigs—failed to garner permanent public support. Yet by the twentieth century, Hamilton's reputation had recovered; indeed, it flourished after World War II as historians, intellectuals, and business leaders championed Hamilton as a prophet of industrialization and the unforeseen architect of a financial *Pax Americana*.[2]

Admittedly, from the standpoint of the twenty-first century, one can hardly mistake Hamilton's foresight. But it should also be noted that in history, as with all human endeavors, there are many paths that we may take, some of which may reach the same destination with fewer hardships. The path toward the creation of the modern American state was not linear as some would suspect, but neither was it merely thrown off course by the Progressives in the early twentieth century. It began in the Founding era itself. At a time when the national government has become a dominant presence in the economy and the broader American society, we must revisit the contrasting visions of Alexander Hamilton and Thomas Jefferson to understand the formation not only of the early American republic but ultimately of the sprawling, interventionist state we know today.

Hamilton's Bailout

By the end of the American Revolution in 1783, the United States rested in an economic quagmire of inflation, depreciated treasuries, insufferable public debt, and mounting financial repercussions in the private sector, notably in land values and foreign trade. Throughout the War for Independence, the Continental Congress had inflated away the real value of money by increasing the supply of money in circulation many times over. People did not believe that Congress could ever pay off its debts and "IOUs" at face value. Merchants and farmers seldom accepted the notes at face value regardless of how strongly they supported independence. Even those forced to accept Congress's debt instruments usually traded them at a fraction of their supposed value. In other words, inflationary pressure forced people to exchange more Continentals and debt certificates for a diminishing supply of goods. The value of nearly all assets in the United States sank.

Detractors of the first U.S. constitution, the Articles of Confederation, most often attributed its weakness to its inability to pay off the Revolutionary War debt, which was estimated to be at a massive £165 million in 1783.[3] States raced to extinguish their debt burdens. Several states, such as Virginia, went so far as to pay off their public debt at the depreciated market value determined by speculators, who traveled across the states trading for as many debt instruments as possible, paying only a fraction of their face value and hoping for a windfall if Congress ever paid off the debt in full. Other states followed Massachusetts, which set up rigid plans to finance its debt at face value by levying high taxes and, when these went unpaid, foreclosing on personal property. (The tax revolt normally attributed to Daniel Shays in Massachusetts reflected the violent ends to which property holders resisted high taxes for the payment of public debt.)

Concerns about paying off the national debt became so intense that creditors began lobbying the state governments to furnish relief when Congress could not. By 1786, three states—Massachusetts, New York, and Pennsylvania—commenced funding payment on nearly one-half of the national government's existing debt.[4]

All of these responses clearly show that Americans did not accept public debt as a permanent fixture of politics. Rather, they saw it as something to be eliminated as quickly and as fairly as possible. Americans looked upon their government's debt as a means of enslavement, not as a form of liberation or as a path to future prosperity.

This American animosity to public debt was entirely in keeping with the broader Anglo-American intellectual inheritance within which most of the Revolutionary leaders, Framers, and Founders thought. The issue of public debt had come to the fore in England as the modern state emerged in the seventeenth century. When Parliament restored the Stuart family to the English throne in 1660, the family treasury was exhausted. King Charles II relied instead on his family's vast land claims in North America to reward supporters and settle old debts. By the end of the century, available crown lands became scarce—hence the new solution of public debt and a system of state-sponsored banking.

Ensuring the stability of the English throne and settling internal disputes was not the only problem facing late seventeenth-century English leaders. Managing foreign affairs proved more expensive than domestic concerns. The minor wars and skirmishes associated with maintaining an empire required vast sums of money to field troops overseas and sustain the imperial navy. When taxes would not suffice, borrowing from future generations was the next best thing. At the turn of the eighteenth century, borrowing from investors became the source for the English government's power and prestige. The national government could wage war by issuing public credit to be liquidated after the war either through taxes or booty. Coordinating the credit would be the Bank of England. The bank's directors were legally bound to lend to the state all that it asked; in exchange, the bank's notes would be the legal tender of the country. The state got immediate revenue; the bank got long-term financial gain. Once the war was over, the government repaid its loans and the bank continued to make profits by issuing its notes as legal tender and privately lending to corporations, individuals, and other banks.

Above all, in the minds of most Englishmen, public debt existed for the specific purpose of waging war. At the same time, however, such debt was a *temporary* measure—a necessary evil—to be paid off as soon as possible.[5]

The issue of public debt proved crucial to the development of British republicanism, which profoundly shaped American ideals about representation, self-government, and independence. In fact, eighteenth-century republican advocates concerned themselves primarily with public debt in their criticisms of the British government. It was the Bank of England and the inflationary bubble it created in the Caribbean Sea during the 1720s that first garnered the attention of John Trenchard and Richard Gordon, who authored the treatises collectively known as *Cato's Letters*, which were popular on both sides of the Atlantic. Sir Robert Walpole's long-term direction of the British government was attacked because of perceived connections with the Bank of England. Even the biting satire of Jonathan Swift had as much to do with public finance as it did with Swift's insight into human nature and English politics. Criticism of parliamentary administrations, the Hanoverian kings, and the Bank of England rang loudest when public debt remained unpaid. Government indebtedness might be justified in dire circumstances, yet even then, critics insisted that great care must be taken to ensure that it did not become a means for the politically well-connected to enrich themselves at the public's expense.

But when Alexander Hamilton became secretary of the treasury in late 1789, he advocated a form of public finance that deviated sharply from this Anglo-American standard.[6] Hamilton took office as Congress faced a number of financial problems, some of which the Philadelphia Convention of 1787 specifically had been called to resolve. The first bill passed by the new Congress established a mildly protective tariff that provided steady revenue for the new national government. The other principal source of revenue came from the sale of western lands, transferred to the federal government under the Articles of Confederation. And yet a steady revenue stream did not bode well for creditors and foreign merchants. Exporters and planters still faced steep interest on bills of exchange used to facilitate foreign trade. Southern planters hated the system of factoring and debt required to maintain trade in staple agriculture. Eastern merchants feared that the country's poor credit rating made too many inroads into their profits by raising the cost of trade. Combining these burdens with those generated by the new tariff meant that commercial men and planters faced a significant problem.

Building on the concerns of merchants and planters, Hamilton issued a series of official reports from 1790 to 1791 calling for the creation of a neomercantilistic system upon which to stabilize the country's economy—a system of government debt, a quasi-central bank, an expanded monetary base, and modest controls on trade.[7] The most important, Hamilton's Report on Public Credit, came in January 1790. In it he offered a choice of remedies, but the one that he hoped to achieve—and that Congress ultimately accepted—involved paying off the principal of foreign debt using present tax revenue and, more controversially, having the federal government fund the total domestic debt at par rather than at the much depreciated market value. He issued a second report in late 1790 on a national bank, followed by reports in 1791 advocating the establishment of a mint and ways to encourage domestic manufacturing.[8]

Led by Hamilton's political supporters and future leaders of the Federalist Party, Congress followed with a plan to restructure the country's entire public debt called "funding" and "assumption." Funding involved financing the old congressional debt instruments and IOUs at full face value by exchanging them with new treasury securities. Congress then assumed the Revolutionary War debts of the states and funded them also at full face value with the new treasuries. To make regular payments on the new issue, Congress passed a series of federal excise taxes on property and consumable items such as alcohol— hence the dreaded whiskey tax. By erecting the first Bank of the United

States, Congress became the principal investor and deposited much of the Treasury's specie there. The bank then pyramided its notes on top of the specie deposits on a fractional-reserve basis, meaning that the bank lent out many more notes than it had in specie.

Given that the old debt instruments still circulated as means of exchange and savings, the new securities may have nearly doubled the money supply of the United States. To this were added notes of the Bank of the United States as well as those of new commercial banks that pyramided notes either on their own assets or on loans taken from the Bank of the United States.

In effect, Hamilton and the Federalists absorbed the heavily depreciated "toxic assets" of the 1780s and artificially (that is, politically) reinflated their market value beyond what the American economy could support. It was a bailout, but only for specific interests and specific states. Speculators who took advantage of the depreciating value of congressional and state debts enjoyed a considerable return on their investments. States with outstanding debts like Massachusetts and South Carolina benefited, but states like Virginia that had gone to great lengths to pay off debts did not. Americans in general faced a two-pronged blow. First, the expanding money supply caused double-digit inflation, especially in the settled areas of the East. Second, they paid higher excise taxes on consumable goods and property.

Scholars have long accepted Hamilton's financial genius and attributed to him the country's financial salvation at a time of great uncertainty. Public credit improved, foreign trade soared, a stable currency was established, and the country's financial elite became happily tied to supporting and strengthening the national government. Modern scholars especially approve of the establishment of a national bank and the use of its notes as a national tender. Gone were the days of hard currency and the debilitating effects of a limited money supply. Thanks to Hamilton, so the story is often told, an increased monetary base also increased the rapidity of exchange and ignited the American economy. Without Hamilton, the United States would have remained a barren, provincial, agrarian island set apart from the modernizing influences of Great Britain.

And yet one could hardly call Hamilton's efforts a stroke of monetary genius. In financial crises throughout American history, attacks upon free economic exchange have been justified as a means of "saving capitalism" or the like. Upon closer inspection, the actions of Hamilton and the Federalists did more to centralize the power of the national government than any event since the American Revolution—and in the process they shaped the rise of the centralized, modern state. Edmund Burke was not far off the mark when he contended that "the revenue is the state."

The most immediate result of the Hamiltonian financial experiment was the Panic of 1792. Throughout the country rapid inflation commenced in the early 1790s and misled entrepreneurs into believing that the economy and consumer demand could easily support new production and investment. Large sums of the new money and loans supported by the Bank of the United States and subsequent commercial banks flowed into real estate schemes, transportation companies, and extravagant boondoggles. Not surprisingly, Americans could not provide enough demand to sustain the "boom." As with any boom, investment poured into the next "sure thing" with little attention to risk. In this era, the bubble pertained to land development and transportation companies, including the Yazoo land schemes of the Old Southwest and the Foggy Bottom land company organized to settle the area around present-day Washington, D.C. These and many other land and transportation companies fell into bankruptcy by the late 1790s, taking with them the fortunes of several leading American financiers and Federalist leaders. Robert Morris, the financier of the Revolution and one of the wealthiest men in the Western hemisphere, spent the final years of the 1790s in debtors' prison—not far from his Philadelphia residence, which he had loaned to the federal government to serve as the president's mansion. James Wilson, the leading nationalist at the Philadelphia Convention, died in North Carolina fleeing from his creditors. Henry Lee, Patrick Henry, and other leaders of the Revolution or the Federalist Party grappled with financial ruin by the end of the decade.

In short, the smartest men did not prosper under Hamiltonian finance. The wealthiest men made mistakes. The inflationary economy misled entrepreneurs into making risky investments that did not promote economic prosperity. But that was not all. No examination of Hamiltonian finance is complete without a serious consideration of its political and social consequences.

The Jeffersonian Reaction

The Hamiltonian financial agenda stirred the turbulent political atmosphere of the 1790s. Hamilton and his supporters insisted that they intended to extinguish the national debt and moved to pay off the foreign portion as planned. But many in the fledgling opposition questioned the Federalists' intentions. The Bank of the United States operated as a quasi-central bank. Its shares were owned by the federal government and foreign investors while the bank's notes circulated as legal currency. But the bank also supported loans to the federal government as well as to smaller commercial banks that fed the boom times of the early 1790s. The bank's fractional-reserve lending practices compounded the inflationary tendencies of Hamilton's full funding of the domestic debt at face value.

The bank's establishment and operation raised a number of constitutional concerns. At least two members of Washington's cabinet, Thomas Jefferson and Edmund Randolph, voiced such concerns, and in Congress, James Madison knew that a federally chartered bank was unconstitutional, since he had specifically proposed such a power at the Philadelphia Convention, only to have it voted down. President Washington requested his cabinet to provide their reasoning on its constitutionality. The subsequent arguments by Hamilton and Jefferson serve as the earliest examples of how opposing political factions would either loosely or strictly interpret the constitutional powers of the federal government. Even then, the constitutional questions raised about Federalist finance were part of a much larger picture.[9]

The opposition to the Washington administration soon formed a political party, creating the first American party system. Hamilton's financial schemes were the fuse that ignited outrage and consternation. The economic and constitutional logic used to support the schemes caused reflective anti-Federalists and Jeffersonian Republicans to publish a number of important pamphlets and newspaper articles examining the basis for the new Constitution and raising questions about how to best govern such a large country.

In this regard, Hamilton's reasoning for why the Bank of the United States was constitutional or why Congress should support his financial agenda kept open the debate commenced in Philadelphia in 1787 about the nature of government and the relationship between liberty and political power. It also provided the context for Jefferson and his followers, most notably John Taylor of Caroline, James Monroe, William Branch Giles, Nathaniel Macon, and Albert Gallatin, to hone their ideas and present a coherent platform on which to build the Republican Party. How this occurred illuminates an alternative side to the nationalist tradition in American history. At its heart, the contest between Hamilton and Jefferson, or Federalist and Republican, represented competing ideas of nationalism and different directions down which American politics would venture through modernity. In a sense, both sides hoped to "modernize" the American state, but along radically different paths.

The Jeffersonian Republicans saw themselves as the true inheritors of the British constitutional tradition. Jefferson and his followers believed that Americans inherited from British constitutionalism a political and legal system in which no single institution should be supreme over all of society. Institutions were equal in that they covered different spheres of life that sometimes overlapped. Within those spheres, powerful institutions should be further divided according to their purposes. Religious institutions could be divided into denominations, governments separated into different branches, and even agriculture diversified (none did this better than John Taylor). James Madison's June 6 speech to the Philadelphia Convention and his now famous

Federalist No. 10 outlined this sentiment in detail. For the Jeffersonian Republicans, the social nature of human beings made them prone to collapse upon each other, jeopardizing their interests in the process. Their writings and speeches are filled with exhortations against "consolidation" in all aspects of human society.[10]

Resisting social consolidation required determining its cause. In the 1790s, in response to Federalist finance, John Taylor of Caroline made the Jeffersonian case. Social consolidation occurred because the wealthy, seeing the providential and inevitable dispersion of their wealth, used political institutions to artificially consolidate it. Their manipulation of politics to pursue their "monied interests" enlarged the scope of political power, which in turn fostered greater consolidation of society in general, as other interests competed to determine whose interests were protected. As the state grew in power, it naturally absorbed the attention of everyone until all spheres of life fell under its direction. This process required the perpetuity of public debt, which was issued to the benefit of "monied interests" and largely owned by them. It also required expanded government services and protections to artificially enhance the wealth of select groups; in the 1790s this merely meant protecting manufacturers from foreign competition, granting privileges to certain forms of trade and agriculture, and providing legal bankruptcy protections.[11]

The Jeffersonians insisted that public debt distracted American voters from realizing their real interests. In the same way that entrepreneurs viewed market prices as indicators for investments, production, and consumption, the Jeffersonians believed that taxes acted as a pricing mechanism for government. If taxes were high, people would realize that the state was growing in power and should be further limited. If taxes were low, but people were miserable, then greater political protections ought to be provided and paid for. With public debt, however, governments expended more than they took in from taxes. People could be easily misled into thinking that the power of the state, normally concomitant with taxation, remained limited.[12] In keeping with the pre–Revolutionary War tradition, if public debt meant war, it most certainly meant power. In the minds of men like Taylor or future secretary of the treasury Albert Gallatin, its continued presence meant that political power had exceeded its natural limits. Even the Quasi-war with France (1798–1800) did little to persuade the Jeffersonians that a growing national debt was necessary.

On another front, the role of public debt brought to mind the extravagance, if not decadence, of the British monarchy and the political corruption of Parliament in the mid-eighteenth century. While the Federalists used religious labels in their attacks on Jefferson and his followers, the Republicans used terms reflective of their experience with the English crown. "Monarchists" and "monocrat" became favored disparaging appellations. Surely some of the Republican writers seriously believed that the Federalists wanted to create a true monarchy, and other Republicans played up suspicions in the mind of the wider populace. But for Jefferson to label John Adams a "monocrat" did not mean he believed that Adams wanted to invite George III to retake the reins of government. Instead, the charge of monarchy referred to those who wished to surround political institutions with pomp and pageantry or other trappings that distracted people from attaching their sentiments on the basis of interest. Public debt, which distracted people from the real cost of government, fell neatly into this category.[13]

Ironically, Hamilton's quest for stronger economic consolidation divided the country politically and socially. His economic nationalism not only combined various opposition groups and factions into a serious rival to Federalist power but also sparked tax revolts, nullification movements, and partisan literature and newspapers, not to mention pivotal congressional debates over the nature of the Union and its government. Whatever economic accomplishments Hamilton may have achieved, they came with political and social costs—not least for his Federalist Party. In the pivotal election of 1800, the American people turned to the Jeffersonian Republicans.

But the Hamiltonian experiment was not dead, as it turned out.

Booms, Busts, and Bailouts

Despite the public's rejection of the Federalists, the elevation of a new political party to national office in the early 1800s did not end the cycle of boom, bust, and bailout. Republicans proved as adept at it as the Federalists or the future Democrats and Whigs. Most notably, the exigencies of the War of 1812 brought Hamiltonian reasoning back to the fore in American politics.

At the close of the War of 1812, both Republicans and Federalists argued in favor of measures to relieve the hardships of the fateful Embargo and Non-intercourse Acts of 1808–11 in addition to the devastation caused by the war. Fighting the war had left the federal government broke, and financiers and public creditors like John Jacob Astor, who invested heavily in the government's wartime financial instruments, stood to lose their fortunes. Once again, Congress corrected its financial mismanagement with a bailout. Congress passed the Tariff of 1816 ostensibly to provide temporary relief for New Englanders and those in the South hurt by the embargo. The same year Congress chartered the second Bank of the United States (Congress had let the first bank's charter expire in 1811). Just as had occurred in the 1790s, inflationary effects of the bank produced an unsustainable economic boom. The inevitable crash followed in 1819.

Once again, those financiers who suffered the most called upon Congress to assist them in the form of higher tariffs and subsidies for transportation improvements—hence the birth of the "canal mania" of the 1820s. At the state and local level, the same process continued with a cycle of unsustainable boom, bust, and calls for immediate relief through public finance well into the 1830s. It was not until the 1840s and 1850s that a string of constitutional amendments halted the cycle at the state level.[14]

Observers of the period could argue that all was for the good. The transportation revolution ushered in a new era of industrialization and forever changed the economy of the United States. But such observers fail to admit the financial wreckage of bankruptcy, political corruption, partisan strife, and rapid social migration that followed in the wake of such progress. Those misled by the canal boosters or encouraged by the assistance of public debt did not find consoling the promise of future economic prosperity when they lost everything in the Panics of 1819 and 1837.

In our era of immense and activist national government, the Hamiltonian model may seem as if it was foreordained, but in fact the Jeffersonian political tradition continued to hold back economic nationalism for much of the nineteenth century. Generations of politicians and intellectuals laid out the case for classical liberalism and cultural conservatism, offering an alternative path to achieve national prosperity. A wide array of politicians bolstered this cause, including presidents like John Tyler and Franklin Pierce, as well as numerous senators and congressmen. There was no shortage of political economists to disseminate popular ideas about sound currency, banking, and limited government. They ranged from the editor of the *Philadelphia Gazette*, William M. Gouge of Pennsylvania, to Susanna Cheves McCord of South Carolina, translator of the writings of French classical liberal Frédéric Bastiat. Popular authors such as James Fenimore Cooper, Washington Irving, and William Gilmore Simms provided literary descriptions of what customs Americans stood to lose in the face of politically manipulated economic development.[15]

Perhaps the best illustration of the lingering Jeffersonian tradition occurred on the floor of the U.S. Congress in March 1824 when Philip Barbour of Virginia debated Henry Clay of Kentucky, then the country's leading Hamiltonian and promoter of economic nationalism. Most are familiar with Clay, who, in response to Barbour's challenges, offered one of his early defenses of the American System of government subsidies, tariffs, and central banking.[16] Few remember Barbour, and yet he proved prophetic in his economic reasoning and political acumen.

Barbour's approach to federalism highlights the argument used by most within the Jeffersonian tradition. He claimed that the proper role of national politics was to ensure that everyone and every region of the country "participate equally in its burdens and benefits." The states and their people were "equal" only in the sense that no one group, interest, or institution would reign supreme over all the rest. No entity was too big to fail.

More importantly, Barbour, like many Jeffersonians, questioned the degree to which any politician could accurately allocate the economic resources of the country. No governing official, he said, could possess the same kinds of knowledge that entrepreneurs and consumers use on a daily basis to foster economic exchange. Barbour noted, "Before, then, it can be justified to invoke the aid of government upon this subject, it is incumbent on those who would do so, to prove that government knows better how to direct this desire . . . than the individual citizen themselves."[17] In summarizing his position, he explained that while governing officials may lack the right information, "each individual in his own immediate and separate pursuit has . . . all the information required, in relation to his business. To individuals, then, let us leave it . . . as they have the desire to give their capital and labor the most profitable direction." An economy was not a machine that could be constructed or manipulated at will; it was made up of real people whose decisions to exchange goods and services were motivated by ideas, desires, wants, and needs.

A few days later, James M. Garnett of Virginia summarized the Jeffersonian opposition's consistent plea against the combination of business and government: "The monopolists must secure their ill-gotten gains by strengthening the hands of the government that bestowed them—by increasing its revenue, patronage, powers. The government, on the other hand, must reward the monopolists by an increase of privileges. Thus a reciprocity is begotten between them utterly incompatible with the rights and the happiness of the rest of the community."[18] The economy, in other words, was not something that could be fueled to run in a specific direction or for the long-term benefit of interests exempted from sharing the burden of their own prosperity.

The Jeffersonian argument against supporters of a Hamiltonian regime of economic control, public debt, and political boosterism remained remarkably consistent through the years. Several conclusions can be derived from the presence of Jeffersonian resistance to Hamiltonian policies. First, the presence of a federal political system required Americans to recognize that "equality" was not synonymous with "sameness." Americans were different, and as long as they remained tolerant of those differences and refrained from controlling trade so as to make Americans something else, economic stability and political liberty went hand in hand. Second, the key feature of federalism remained the absence of any sovereign institution with enough power to command authority over all of American society. This applied as equally to federal-state relations as it did to enterprises, religious institutions, or any other of the "little platoons" that composed American society. Finally and perhaps most importantly, only by undermining the American commitment to federalism and genuine cultural and economic diversity could nationalists hold sway over national politics. This last task was not easy to pull off. In many ways, whether in terms of civil liberties for citizens or economic controls over the national economy, the federal government of 1858 was sharply more limited than the federal government of 1798.

But the nationalists did, of course, ultimately triumph, as we know all too well in confronting a massive state apparatus today. The most powerful and lasting legacy of Alexander Hamilton and the Federalists is that they set the standard for future political movements that held in tandem state-sponsored economic development, consolidation of political power, and nationalism. In time a cultural shift took place whereby economic development—or as Washington Irving suggested, the Almighty Dollar—became the measure of all things.[19] Scholars call the cultural ramifications of economic development the "market revolution," a most undesirable term that conveys the opposite of what actually occurred. Nationalists did not champion freedom of economic exchange and an appreciation for market-driven development. A revolutionary change occurred nonetheless, one so powerful that by the twentieth century, much of what politicians and scholars considered "conservatism" was nothing more than nineteenth-century boosterism.

Hamiltonianism

It is a strange form of conservatism given that it is rooted in two revolutionary changes in the early republic: an appreciation for permanent public debt and a gradual cultural shift whereby money became the arbiter of right from wrong.

The Modern Welfare State:
Leading the Way on the Road to Serfdom

Per Bylund

In the twentieth century the welfare state superseded the older type of government, which had only limited authority and narrowly defined competencies. Now it is by far the most common type of regime in the Western world. Although welfare states come in many forms, shapes, and sizes, they all have something in common: each attempts to increase the general welfare and the well-being of its citizens by establishing and enforcing public programs that replace market incentives with government power.[1] In effect, the welfare state relieves the individual of everyday decision-making. This protects the individual from the consequences of making ill-informed choices and promotes equality through a "one size fits all" welfare system and social safety net. The welfare state furthermore strives to provide equal opportunity for all, and a nationwide (if not global) equal distribution of wealth.

Advocates of the modern welfare state see it as a symbol of the great success of large-scale government planning. And to such advocates there is perhaps no better example than Sweden, which has one of the highest tax rates in the world, an extensive public sector, a relatively high level of achieved equality, and "universal" welfare benefits.[2] Sweden is often referred to as one of the richest countries in the world despite having been ruled by a socialist party (the Social Democratic Party) almost throughout the twentieth century. Advocates of the welfare state quickly took to endorsing the socialist country's "Swedish model."[3]

One champion of the Swedish model is *New York Times* columnist (and Nobel Prize–winning economist) Paul Krugman. In his book *The Great Unraveling*, Krugman describes Sweden's recovery from economic troubles in the 1990s. "How did the Swedes manage this turnaround?" Krugman writes.

> Did they Reaganize their economy, adopting an American-style regime of low taxes and winner-take-all markets? In a word, nej. . . . Last year Sweden collected an awesome 63% of GDP in taxes. The Swedish welfare state remains extremely generous, its safety net remarkably far above the ground. If you believe the people who think that America's comparatively trivial tax burden—a mere 34% of GDP!—is an oppressive drag on the economy, you would expect to see the Swedish economy imploding instead of booming.[4]

For Krugman and many others, the Swedish welfare state represents a dream for modern civilization where nobody is left in poverty and everyone enjoys sufficient riches. To some commentators, the Swedish model has become even more attractive since the international financial crisis began in 2008. The reason for this is that Sweden's economic struggles during this crisis have been fairly minor compared to those experienced by many other countries.

But a closer look at the so-called Swedish model demonstrates that the story of the Scandinavian country's supposed success is more complicated than its advocates would have us believe. A study of the Swedish welfare state—from its rise in the twentieth century, to its fall in the 1990s, to its unanticipated return in the first decade of the twenty-first century—provides valuable insight into the everlasting sources of real and sustainable growth in overall wealth and prosperity. It also offers a clear example of how democratic regimes tend to degenerate into huge state systems aspiring to control everyday life, and how such political advances fundamentally harm society's ability to support sustainable growth and generate prosperity for its members. For the welfare state advocate, there can never be sufficient government power, as there is always something in need of correction—and meddling—from "above."[5]

And as Friedrich Hayek recognized when he wrote *The Road to Serfdom*, the bloated government power that inevitably results in a welfare state affects not just the economy but also individual liberty and the very viability of civil society. Indeed, the story of the Swedish welfare state shows how politics is always subject to and restricted by economic law,[6] and how attempts to escape its bounds have detrimental effects on societal structure, social life, prosperity—and even morality.

The Golden Years

While the Kingdom of Sweden, at least according to the lyrics of its national anthem, rests on memories of past prominence, especially its Age of Greatness (1611–1721), the country was economically as well as culturally insignificant for most of the eighteenth and nineteenth centuries. Extensive poverty and merciless rule by both monarch and state church were undoubtedly among the reasons why more than 1.2 million Swedes decided to emigrate to America in the latter half of the nineteenth and the early twentieth centuries.[7]

Things change, however, and Sweden developed from one of the poorest nations in Europe in 1870 to one of the richest in the world by 1970.[8] These "golden years," as economist Andreas Bergh calls them, ensured Sweden's reputation as a socialist utopia combining strong economic growth and high standards of living with extensive welfare programs and a high level of equality. But the economic growth experienced during these hundred years was not the *result* of the rapid expansion of the welfare state; rather, it was the economic growth that financed, and made possible, Sweden's massive welfare state.

Significantly, the substantial growth that Sweden experienced after 1870 was predicated on certain cultural preconditions. At least since the early sixteenth century, Sweden's agrarian population had consisted primarily of freehold peasants. In other words, Swedes were comparatively free men with property rather than serfs working on land owned by the privileged class.

The industrial revolution, however, did not come to Sweden until the 1870s—approximately a century after it started in the United Kingdom. Bergh explains that industrialization could take hold in Sweden only after a number of economy-supporting and institution-building reforms were instituted. In the early- and mid-nineteenth century, Sweden experienced a plethora of political reforms, such as a universal protection of property rights from arbitrary confiscation by the government, and investments in human capital and physical infrastructure, including compulsory schooling and patent laws. As Bergh notes, Sweden's modern patent law—first enacted in 1834 and greatly "improved" in 1856 and 1884—opened the door for Sweden's outstanding innovators.[9] Many of the Swedish inventions at the time were capitalized in firms that to this day are among Sweden's greatest exporters and largest corporations.[10] Likewise, Sweden expanded its railroads and other infrastructure. Such reforms helped increase exports of Sweden's abundant natural resources to industrializing countries. Between 1850 and 1870, with strong demand from trading partners such as the United States, Sweden also removed many trade barriers and began extensive deregulation. This fundamental liberalization allowed for the free movement of people, goods, and capital both within Sweden and across its borders.[11] Moreover, Sweden's liberal (in the classical sense) movement gained great influence in the nineteenth century, making Sweden one of Europe's beacons of liberty.[12]

The institutions Sweden developed in the nineteenth century were generally stable, thanks to the separation of government powers between king and parliament after the end of monarchical power in 1809. As Bergh argues, these institutions provided the prerequisites for a well-functioning capitalist economy. That is to say, the developments of the nineteenth century paved the way for the economic growth of Sweden's "golden years."

Constructing the Welfare State

Stable and growth-supportive institutions are important, but so is allowing the market to solve arising problems efficiently rather than counting on the competence of government regulators. Sweden in the latter half of the nineteenth century was characterized by a generally free market, with classical liberal thinkers, politicians, and activists such as Johan August Gripenstedt and Lars Johan Hierta exerting great influence.[13] Sweden was very far from being a welfare state.

But many liberals at the time feared that the newly won freedom and prosperity might not lead to a general increase in welfare, and that the failure to bring higher standards of living to the working class and the proletariat might cause social unrest. To reduce the risk of a subversive movement that could endanger the free society they had established, and to accelerate the market-based diffusion of prosperity in society, some liberals began to advocate limited social and welfare reforms. The result was an early political orientation toward equality and an egalitarian distribution of wealth throughout Swedish society.

These liberals often worked together with and supported Social Democrats in order to have a basis for continuing to reform government. For instance, Hjalmar Branting, the first Social Democrat to be elected to parliament in Sweden (and later, in the 1920s, the party's first prime minister), was elected with the help of liberals in Stockholm. The liberals established, among other things, the universal right to retirement with publicly funded base pay (1913) and joined forces with the Social Democrats to restrict the normal workday to eight hours (1919) and to limit the right to inheritance (1928). As the Social Democrats grew in popularity, however, they gained sufficient influence to move farther down the road of welfarism. Eventually liberals began working with conservatives to try to keep socialism at bay, but by then it was already too late.

On the foundations laid by liberals, the Social Democrats rapidly expanded the welfare state. They created a "Swedish model," a unique combination of mixed economy, corporatism, universal welfare benefits, and active government involvement through labor market policies.[14] Writing in the *Journal of Economic Literature*, Erik Lundberg notes that this Swedish model generally existed "from the beginning of the 1930s up to the 1970s," which is basically the Social Democrats' hegemonic era.[15] The party dominated Swedish politics for almost a century,[16] and even today it remains the largest party in terms of sympathizers and voters.[17]

Reasons for Success . . . and Failure

It would be a mistake to attribute the success of the Swedish model to the welfare policies of the Social Democratic Party. Sweden became a country of incomparably high taxes and strong government presence in the market, both of which have damaging effects on economic growth. They necessarily affect incentives, thereby causing people to behave in ways that would otherwise not be in their interest. Even if a taxation scheme could be constructed to affect all actors in the economy in a "neutral" manner (which is arguably impossible), using the funds to cover the costs of a government apparatus and its programs would interfere with individuals' comparatively efficient market preferences. Thus it would have a negative effect on economic behavior and lead to inefficient or wasteful investments.

On the other hand, it would be as much of a mistake to say that the Social Democrats played no role at all in the relative success of the Swedish model. The Social Democrats were important for the continued development of Sweden as a modern nation in the twentieth century largely because they were *not* traditional socialists: they took a pragmatic approach to capitalism, consistently supporting free trade and, however limited in extent, allowing for and maintaining institutions supporting businesses and the market (and market solutions in general).

The Swedish government under the Social Democratic Party consistently employed two parallel strategies for achieving prosperity and equality. Like the People's Republic of China, the Swedish government implemented a double system where, on the one hand, the Swedish economy was heavily taxed, regulated, and controlled, while on the other hand the government aided the wealth-creating powers of the market. In Sweden, this was done by focusing most of the taxes and regulations on labor and consumption rather than on production, while allowing businesses to compete in a market left mainly to its own devices within the state's regulatory framework. Consequently, Sweden had the world's highest taxes on individuals and consumption,[18] but it also had a relatively beneficial business climate through a very simplified legal framework and low taxes.[19] As Bergh puts it, Sweden had many wealthy companies but few wealthy entrepreneurs.[20]

During the "golden years," then, Sweden benefited from stable and generally supportive institutions, a well-functioning private property rights system, and a framework in which government was reluctant to interfere with these institutions or to directly regulate economic behavior—while supporting the market through extensive investments in infrastructure and human capital development. Even where government oversaw the process and threatened with legislation, as in the case of labor relations, it generally preferred solutions through voluntary agreement between the parties (in this case, centralized negotiations between national labor unions and national business federations). For this reason, the market was able to function fairly well by establishing balanced "standards" through which it regulated itself. Equally important, while building a massive welfare state, the Social Democrats traditionally were reluctant to engage in deficit spending. Finally, the flourishing international economy in the decades after the Second World War contributed to beneficial economic conditions.

In short, the circumstances simply played out very well for Sweden.

The importance of these circumstances becomes obvious when one considers the type of policies pursued by the Social Democrats throughout the twentieth century. The Swedish model was based on the economic teachings of the so-called Stockholm School, which conceded that it was both possible and desirable to "stabiliz[e] the [business] cycle by means of active fiscal policy," as Erik Lundberg puts it.[21] As such, the school was to a large extent one of many precursors to Keynesianism.[22] But what set Sweden apart, says Lundberg, was the fact that the Social Democrats "endorsed these views at once and made attempts to carry out the expansionary policies which the model required."[23] The initial driving force behind the welfare state, therefore, seems to have been, at least in part, to stabilize the market through expansion of the public sector and thereby guarantee a high level of employment.

Indeed, employment policy has always been at the core of the Swedish welfare state and remains so until this day. The Social Democratic Party was originally formed to defend workers' interests against industrialists (employers), and one of their foremost political aims was each worker's "right" to employment with reasonable pay and an equitable work environment. The social reforms earlier implemented by liberals were along the same lines, and sought to protect those who lost their jobs through, for example, government subsidies to the sickness funds (1891), legally mandated employer's responsibility for victims of accidents at work (1901), and the public retirement pension (1913).[24] Full employment is still a standard to which government is being held, and unemployment, especially high or increasing, is to this day seen as a governmental failure in Swedish political discourse.

Although Sweden's economic growth capitalized on beneficial circumstances, the favorable economic effects could not continue indefinitely as the government dramatically expanded the welfare state.[25] Employment levels could initially be boosted and were kept at a high level because the economic growth financed the increase in the size of the public sector. But as freedoms gradually eroded and the welfare state expanded, the favorable effects on the economy eventually subsided.

Had the Swedish welfarist policies been truly Keynesian, the Swedish government would then have resorted to deficit spending in order to support and strengthen the (artificial) boom and maintain full employment. The Social Democrats' reluctance to engage in deficit spending did not allow for this type of "solution," however, and it turned out not to be needed.[26]

As a small country dependent on international trade, Sweden relied on the state of the international economy and therefore fell victim to recessions and depressions while being lifted up by periods of international economic growth. Since Sweden did not partake in the world wars, the country was well positioned to capitalize on postwar booms and help rebuild countries badly damaged by war by supplying them with products.[27] Under such advantageous circumstances during the "golden years," first through a well-functioning market and later through nonparticipation in the world wars, Sweden invested in and experienced essentially uninterrupted increases in labor productivity—at least relative to other countries.

This increased labor productivity can be explained partly by the welfare state's investments in industry-supporting infrastructure and public-sector services such as higher education, increasing overall human capital. It can also be explained by the real effects of the "solidaristic wage policy," which enforced equal pay for equal work nationally in order to reduce the wage spread and to accelerate the dissolution of unprofitable business firms.[28] By effectively excluding low-productivity labor and firms from the labor market, the Swedish model created comparatively high unemployment levels among youth as well as immigrants and minorities, at least over the past four or five decades. Even people who did not technically show up in unemployment statistics did not pursue traditional employment paths. For example, many young people were gently pushed into "free" (tax-financed) higher education programs to get an (additional) advanced degree while receiving grants and heavily subsidized student loans to cover living expenses. The alternative, unemployment without being eligible for unemployment benefits, would simply be too discouraging for most people. Others were almost forcibly referred to long-term sick pay and early retirement programs, or to other government programs that housed those who were no longer formally available for work (and hence, not unemployed). The Swedish state has used a plethora of government programs to move large numbers of unemployed into other categories. For example, one initiative used fully salaried higher-education programs targeting the development of knowledge or skills officially recognized as lacking in the market.[29] In practice, too, welfare benefits are often made available exclusively to members of the large middle class—not to high- or low-income earners—which forces the rich to supply their own insurances (while subsidizing the middle class).

The circumstances that played out well for Sweden ended with the international economic crisis in the early 1970s. Sweden was, as would be expected, fundamentally unprepared for handling this crisis and the unsound structure of the welfare state led to its downfall. It had for too long and too heavily relied on circumstances playing out to its benefit, circumstances that no longer existed. It could not remain in its previous form without being propped up by relative increases in economic growth. As Bergh explains, the end of the successful Swedish model came as government suddenly began meddling with important capitalist institutions, thereby making them fundamentally unpredictable. This policy-caused uncertainty inhibited economic growth, and, as a result, the public sector was no longer viable. The change in policy from supporting stable institutions to detail-oriented regulation caused a crisis the Swedish model was not capable of surviving.

In contrast, Lundberg attributes the end of the "golden years" to the failure of macroeconomic principles and to problems arising from too high wages, overvalued currency, and a severe weakening of incentives caused by welfare programs benefiting a large part of the population. Lundberg's analysis is more closely related to the international crisis than Bergh's, but the story both analysts tell about Sweden from approximately 1970 to 1995 is the same: this period constituted the fall of the Swedish model, which led to a chaotic financial situation in the early 1990s. Because of poor economic performance during the period,

Sweden fell from being the fourth-richest country in the world in 1970 to seventeenth in 2001.[30]

The Swedish government tried to solve the problems throughout the 1970s and early 1980s by frequently devaluing the currency in order to boost Swedish exports and by expanding the public sector to fight unemployment.[31] These attempts seemed to give temporary relief but only aggravated the structural problems in the Swedish economy and weakened previously stable institutions.[32]

The problems of the welfare state became visible because the international economic situation put strain on the Swedish model. The government's political policies, escalated to try to save the welfare state, revealed the inherent contradiction in the Swedish system: it was dependent on high economic growth to finance a public sector and welfare programs that ultimately placed a burden on the economy. As the public sector grew and the welfare programs expanded, the economy had less opportunity to provide the economic growth needed to prop up the welfare state.

Sweden and the Financial Crisis

The effect of these decades of destructive economic policy was an economic collapse in the early 1990s, which necessitated a shift in policy toward more market and less state. Bergh labels this shift the "return" of the capitalist welfare state—a withdrawal from the recent policies of detailed regulation of economic life, extreme taxation, and frequent policy changes. This is partly true: Sweden underwent great change in the 1990s and early 2000s, but the change seems to have been deeper and more fundamentally structural than Bergh suggests. Not only were taxes lowered and markets deregulated, but the previously universal welfare system was also restructured. Welfare benefits are now available to a much lesser degree: many benefits have been limited; restrictions have been added; and many programs have added private or individualized elements.

These changes slowed down but did not completely reverse the downward trend, as Fredrik Bergström and Robert Gidehag clearly show in a study comparing Sweden to the United States. The study focuses primarily on the effects of economic growth and shows that if Sweden in 1998 had been one of the states, it would have been the poorest in terms of median income (adjusted for purchasing power), making less than 87 percent of the poorest of the fifty states—North Dakota.[33] Swedes as an ethnic group were in the year 2000 approximately as well off as American blacks in 1999 and had an adjusted median income of less than two-thirds of that of American whites.[34]

Comparing the countries in the European Union to the fifty states, the same authors find that most European countries had lower adjusted per capita GDP in 2001 than most of the states. In fact, the United States had consistently higher economic growth in the years 1970 to 2000 than each of the five richest countries in the European Union. It is safe to say that the European countries are in poor shape. The authors summarize their findings by saying, "There are very big differences between the American and European economies." They point out that "a long period of high growth has made the USA far and away the world's richest region" and that "most Americans have a standard of living which the majority of Europeans will never come any where [sic] near."[35]

The poor economic shape of Europe explains why countries such as Greece suffered the recent crisis so badly. Without sufficient economic wealth and with a structurally unsound economy, the burden of the economic strain along with oversized public debt simply became too heavy. What is interesting here is not, however, why Greece and other countries (especially in Europe) were so badly hit by the crisis, but why Sweden was able to get through the crisis relatively unharmed.

The answer lies in the 1990s crisis, Sweden's own depression, which forced the government to greatly reduce expenditure, limit welfare programs, and get the public finances under control. Sweden could remain relatively unharmed by international crisis not, as Krugman would have us believe, because of its high taxes and "generous" welfare benefits. Spending has not been the solution. Statistics from the Swedish National Debt Office show how the national debt has consistently *decreased* as share of GDP since the mid-1990s: from almost 80 percent in 1995 to below 40 percent in 2009—with only a minor increase due to the recent financial crisis.[36] At present, the government has begun to sell many state-owned corporations in order to pay down the national debt further.

The Swedish experiment over the past century shows that a government can take one of two paths: either increase political power, public spending, deficits, and the national debt, and heavily tax and regulate the market—or do the exact opposite. True, the former strategy seemed to work out fairly well for Sweden for decades, but it did so primarily because circumstances played out well and the government consciously exploited the market's wealth-creating power to finance the expansion of the welfare state. As the state grows, however, the house of cards will eventually come crashing down as the weight on top gets too heavy. Swedes learned this lesson starting in the 1970s and especially during the 1990s, and the partial implementation of a stricter economic policy with more limited welfare benefits is what kept Sweden afloat through the recent crisis—although Sweden still has not adopted a policy sufficient for sustaining long-term growth. Other countries are currently having the same experience. The latter strategy, including pushing back government and allowing the market to swiftly correct malinvestments and amend unsound structures, makes crises much more tolerable while providing the working population with sustainable growth and prosperity.[37]

The Welfare State Mindset

The policy aspect is important in the analysis of the Swedish welfare state's rise, fall, and return. One important aspect is still missing, however. To be sure, the economic history of Sweden makes a clear-cut case for economic freedom, showing how big government adversely affects economic growth. But long-term welfare statism has deeper

47

and even more destructive effects—political, cultural, and ultimately ethical. The long experience of a "nanny state" in Sweden has damaged how Swedes view life, liberty, the pursuit of happiness, and the economy.

At the turn of the twentieth century, Swedes were a hardworking, independent people. The major part of the nineteenth century had meant hardships but also an incredible growth in both population and wealth, with which came a sense of self-confidence and self-esteem. To be Swedish, old people still say, is to work hard, take care of yourself and your family, endure any condition—and be proud to have justly earned your independence.[38]

With the newly earned prosperity came a generosity and a willingness to care for those less fortunate. The moral standard of the time was never to be a burden, which included not accepting favors unless absolutely necessary, but also to offer help where needed even if one did not have much to give. The welfare programs suggested and implemented by the liberal and conservative regimes in the late nineteenth and early twentieth centuries conformed with this outlook. A universal safety net and a centralized system to give relief to the poorest in society was probably conceived of as an efficient way of channeling some of society's prosperity to help those in greatest need.

But as the welfare state expanded and the programs became more numerous, the perverse incentives it created became a real problem. As a welfare state increases available benefits, it creates an incentive to seem in need and therefore be eligible for government relief, replacing the incentive to earn a living wage through productive work.

While these changing incentive structures exacerbate the problem, the welfare state society fails to provide a solution. Welfare programs of the state tend to undermine and marginalize individual and private help efforts, especially over time, since it is difficult to convince people to voluntarily donate time and money when everyone is already forced to contribute to the state welfare systems through taxation. This is especially the case when the welfare state reaches a certain size, which suggests that all people should already be taken care of. In fact, it has been shown that government social-welfare transfers tend to "crowd out" private charitable contributions.[39]

In other words, the incentives caused by the welfare state are in direct conflict with the morality of a hardworking people that is confident in its ability to cope. It is not surprising that the mindset and culture of the Swedish people have changed. The older generation of Swedes was independent, took pride in being able to fend for oneself, and was reluctant to ask for help, but that traditional morality was completely destroyed in little more than two generations—what I call the children and the grandchildren of the welfare state. These generations came to depend on public benefits and the concept of welfare rights, and consequently they learned and embraced a new morality.[40]

The children of the welfare state, the baby boomers of the 1940s, were the first generation to be raised in a welfare state society. They grew up when the country was approaching the height of the Swedish model and there was no conceivable limit to what could be accomplished through the public sector; they went to public schools and universities to get degrees that made them a highly productive labor force. They also learned that they had inalienable rights to welfare benefits, and that demanding their share of society's wealth was legitimate behavior. During the international postwar boom, increased demand for government welfare benefits was not a real problem—the growth of the economy could cover most of the expenditure increases.

The universal nature of the Swedish welfare state fits well with what one would expect from a period of high, long-term economic growth. Unemployment was not a problem since there was a general shortage of labor; the middle class grew and poverty was quite a rare occurrence. The welfare state had no problem satisfying popular demand for welfare programs and a social safety net for those temporarily in trouble. Indeed, the public finances were in such good shape that there was no real limit to new, more comprehensive reforms.

The next generation, the grandchildren of the welfare state, were taught what their parents had learned: that there was practically no limit to the benefits that were or could be made available. They were also to a large extent raised in the quickly growing public day-care system and, later, in public schools, while their highly productive parents worked.[41] Erik Lundberg writes about the "outstanding mobilization of women into the labor force" during the 1960s and 1970s,[42] which logically gives reasons for both the expansion of the public day-care system and the number of children basically being raised by the state, spending only nights and weekends with their parents.

It is easy to imagine how the international economic crisis was received by the Swedish population and their political leaders at this time. Not only had the children of the welfare state gotten used to trusting—and demanding—that the welfare state would help them when so desired, but they also came to depend on the state to take care of their children. Furthermore, they believed that their children had a right to at least as many benefits as they had had. This is the logic in a world with high and continuous economic growth—each generation is richer than its parent generation. But this does not automatically apply to government welfare benefits.

It follows that the only possible way forward in the face of crisis would be to continue to prop up rather than reform the system. In order to make Swedish firms competitive in the international market—and thereby boost the economy through exports—the Swedish currency was devalued numerous times in less than a decade. As a result, Swedes became significantly poorer while the grandchildren of the welfare state learned from a very young age that they would always be able to demand assistance from the state.

This generation is now the demanding parents of young children, who are also brought up primarily in public day-care centers and in public schools, and they—as parents—often claim that the state has to take "responsibility" for their children so they can have time for self-fulfillment. It is not uncommon to hear representatives of this generation—apparently deeply insulted by what is expected of them as parents—furiously demand that society relieve them of their too burdensome and time-consuming parental duties. Swedes of this generation tend to rely on the "nanny state" to take care of them; when they in turn enter parenthood, they expect the state to be there to alleviate the burden when so requested. Consequently, the 480 days of paid parental leave (for each child) is considered far from sufficient.[43]

At the same time, this generation is feeling the repercussions of the unsustainable welfare state to which they and their parents have grown accustomed. Unemployment rates for the younger generation have surpassed 25 percent.[44] This generation, furthermore, will have to spend the coming decades paying taxes to finance the retirements of their parents' generation. Recent cutbacks in the public retirement system mean they will be supplying for their parents when public pensions are not enough *and* planning for their own retirements through private pension plans. We do not know what the future brings, but given this generation's poor work ethic, its failure to take responsibility for itself, and the likely necessity of caring for three full generations (themselves, their children, and their parents), the picture is quite frightening.

The new sense of morality became evident in a 2006 broadcast on Swedish state television. The broadcast featured a group of children and grandchildren of the welfare state discussing unemployment and the problems facing young people entering the labor market. This televised discussion reflected a common perception of justice among the grandchildren of the welfare state. Many called for "old people" (that is, those born in the late 1940s, 1950s, and 1960s) to stop working because they were "stealing" jobs from the young. Such a preposterous demand demonstrates the new logic of the welfare state: I have a "right" to a well-paying job, so anyone who holds a good job is in my way and violating this right. Even the national trade workers union espoused this viewpoint, demanding that the state "redistribute" jobs by offering people in their sixties state pensions if they stepped down. In the labor union's calculations, such a stunt would "create" 55,000 jobs for young people.

What we are now seeing in Sweden is the perfectly logical consequence of the welfare state: when handing out benefits and thereby taking away the individual's responsibility for his or her own life, a new kind of individual is created—the immature, irresponsible, and dependent.

The social engineers of the welfare state obviously never considered a possible change in morality and perception—they simply wanted a system guaranteeing security for everybody, a system where the able could and should work to support themselves, but where the unable, too, could live dignified lives without being subject to the generosity of others. Who would have thought that the progressive reforms to secure workers' rights and prosperity for all in the early twentieth century would backfire philosophically and morally?

It should be obvious that nothing came to be as expected; society simply wasn't as predictable as was predicted.

But of course we do know—or should know—one thing for certain: people do what they have an incentive to do. The example of Sweden shows that if powerful but destructive incentive structures are kept in force over time, people's sense of morality will change.[45]

Lessons to Learn

One may wonder how, if at all, a country like Sweden would ever be able to break the cycle of a welfare dependence culture and an ever-increasing welfare state to satisfy the swelling need for benefits and welfare services. The answer is obvious: the kind of society that constitutes the Swedish model is unsustainable because of its inherent contradictions; it will eventually crash under its own weight. The welfare state, it must be pointed out, is dependent on people not using the benefits it makes available to a more than minimal extent. As the system of benefits is expanded, people are expected to *not* do what they have an incentive to do. Instead, people are supposed to have an impeccable work ethic while being taxed to ridiculous degrees; only then is a welfare state at all possible.

But as we have seen in Sweden's case, the welfare state erodes the very ethic on which it depends for success. The fact is that the welfare state not only is economically unsustainable but also changes the mindset of the people it supposedly serves: their incentives are altered, as

52

people are gradually made better off by not working. Tampering with incentive structures eventually has a devastating effect on the economy.

If the economic effects of welfarism are not terrifying enough, consider this obvious truth: the road to serfdom is not complete unless people self-identify as serfs. And people are, we must admit, more than willing to accept serfdom—if they perceive it makes them better off.

The Origins of the Crisis

Antony P. Mueller

The crisis that erupted in the financial markets in 2007 and extended into the real economy came as a shock to many observers. The economy had witnessed steady growth over the previous quarter century, with only occasional, shallow downturns. Pundits, politicians, bureaucrats, and economists searched for answers to why things went wrong. Many diagnosed the banking crisis as the result of "too little regulation." The meltdown came about, some said, because of "Wall Street greed." To certain observers, the collapse represented nothing less than "a failure of capitalism."[1]

But such assessments miss the deeper causes of the crisis. The problems extend far beyond subprime mortgages and the freeze in international financial markets. They can be traced to long-dominant interventionist strategies on the part of governments and central banks. With economic policies, there is often a considerable lag between the time of planting and the time of harvest, between cause and effect. In the case of the recent crisis, the time of planting goes back to the 1960s and 1970s, when the lessons of classical economics were thrown out. A crucial change occurred at that point: a shift away from limited government and sound money and toward favoring governmental control of the economy and an inflationary monetary system. The expansion of the welfare state became the new creed in the Western world; governments adopted Keynesian economic policy, calling for the expansion of government spending and interventionism, as the new orthodoxy; and more and more unsound monetary arrangements were established.[2]

The seeds were sown decades ago, and now we are reaping the bitter harvest.

Most troubling of all, it would seem that the harvest is not complete, for the underlying causes of the financial and economic crisis still have not been corrected. In fact, the situation has only worsened as government has gone to extraordinary lengths to try to "stimulate" a recovery. Massive government spending, excessive increases in the money supply, and artificially low interest rates have exacerbated the problem that was the fundamental source of the crisis: indebtedness. Government spending, trade deficits, and consumer debt have combined to put the entire economic system on the brink—and in trying to pull the economy back, governments and central banks are only making these problems worse.

It is only a matter of time before the financial and economic crisis shows up more prominently as a social and political crisis. The growth of Leviathan has reached a stage where the expansion of state power will become ever more repressive.

What Went Wrong?

In the second half of 2007 international financial markets suddenly began to freeze. From one month to the next, liquidity dried up. Monetary authorities were caught by surprise, as revealed in the 2009 annual report of the Bank for International Settlements (BIS), the international organization that is in charge of global supervision of the banking and the financial markets:

How could this happen? No one thought that the financial system could collapse. Sufficient safeguards were in place. There was a safety net: central banks that would lend when needed, deposit insurance and investor protection that feed individuals from worrying about the security of their wealth, regulators and supervisors to watch over individual institutions and keep their managers and owners from taking on too much risk. . . . Prosperity and stability were evidence that the system worked. Inflation was low, growth was high, and both were stable.[3]

A year earlier, reflecting on the financial turmoil sparked by subprime mortgage problems, the BIS had similarly expressed doubts that anyone could have seen such a collapse coming. The 2008 BIS report observed:

Over the last two decades, much seems to have gone right in the global economy. Inflation has been maintained at very low levels almost everywhere and, until recently, was remarkable stability. At the same time, growth has generally been high, with that in the last four years being the fastest on record. Along with these features, economic downturns in the advanced industrial economies have been so shallow since the early 1980s that they gave rise to the accolade "the Great Moderation."[4]

Trying to make sense of what had gone wrong, the BIS team noted that the theories of economic thinkers Hyman Minsky and Irving Fisher, involving "deteriorating credit standards," were "of particular relevance to current circumstances." But the bank's report did not go much further, saying only that "a number of other prewar theorists warned about the danger of poorly assessed credits leading to asset bubbles, deviations in spending patterns from sustainable trends and an inevitable economic downturn."[5]

This vague assessment does not get to the heart of the matter. It reflects the specific kind of economics that governments and central banks have adopted over the past couple of decades, which holds that everything is fine as long as economies display "growth" and "stability"—that is, as long as gross domestic product (GDP) expands and price inflation seems to be under control. This condition became known as the "Goldilocks economy."

Likewise, the BIS report's claim that "no one" saw the financial collapse coming reflects the economic thinking that prevails among governments and central banks. The fact is that some economists did warn of deep-seated problems in the economy despite evident growth and stability through most of the late twentieth and early twenty-first centuries.[6] Specifically, the Austrian School of economics has long diagnosed the fatal flaws in the modern monetary and political system, maintaining that excessive monetary expansion undertaken by central banks produces unsustainable booms and consequently unavoidable busts. Yet the BIS report never cited the Austrian School or any of its major thinkers, such as F. A. Hayek and Ludwig von Mises.

The Austrian view is quite different from the common belief in surface growth and stability. Austrian business cycle theory holds that the starting point of the crisis cycle is a monetary expansion that produces an artificially low interest rate (one held below the pure market or natural rate). What happens when the money supply is expanded? Available monetary funding of credit-based consumption and investment misleads the individual consumer into thinking that he has sufficient savings to spend on consumption goods, such as housing, and similarly tempts businesses into engaging in more roundabout production projects. But in fact, savings have not increased. Artificially low interest rates actually discourage savings, and thus the combination of these two factors induces malinvestment, or misdirected business projects.[7]

The cycle ends with a bust when businesses realize that there are not enough available savings to complete ongoing projects or maintain finished projects, and when consumers recognize that they cannot sustain their "investments" in the long run. The retrenchment leaves behind a wasteland of unfinished projects and unused or underused capacities, including durable consumer goods such as housing. People now have to realize that the boom was nothing more than a detour to disaster. Along with the economic cost, a psychological effect sets in that makes emerging from the slump even more difficult.

At this stage government stimulus policies no longer work. The so-called multiplier effect, which Keynesian macroeconomic theory promises, goes into reverse. Instead of bringing the economy out of the recession, expansionary monetary and fiscal policies add more debt to the high level of indebtedness that already exists because of the fake boom. The next stage of experimental interventionism produces what economist Robert Higgs named "regime uncertainty," the "institutional discontinuity" that also prolonged the Great Depression.[8] The sequence of stages has advanced from a financial market crisis to a broader economic crisis, and from an economic crisis to a fiscal crisis of government indebtedness. From this point on, the social and political crisis is only a few steps away.

The problem is that the modern monetary system creates precisely the conditions that ultimately lead to bust: monetary expansion and artificially low interest rates. This modern system emerged in the early 1970s, after the Nixon administration ended the convertibility of U.S. dollars to gold. The Bretton Woods conference of 1944 had linked the dollar to gold and thus had established an international monetary system anchored to gold. Yet the more that the U.S. dollar became the global currency of trade, the more this link was disrespected, and the amount of dollars circulating the globe went far beyond the stock of gold at the fixed price. President Nixon officially cut the dollar's link to gold, finally severing the international monetary system from its Bretton Woods anchor. Keynesian economic policy was already dominant by the 1970s, and now that governments were not obligated to maintain currency rates within a fixed value in terms of gold, the demands of modern populist democracy produced a dynamic that drove toward credit expansion and debt accumulation.[9]

It did not take long before the combination of the new inflationary monetary system and government interventionism produced its first disaster: the "stagflation" of the 1970s, marked by unemployment, economic stagnation, and inflation. This economic malaise sparked demand for a new economic policy paradigm beyond Keynesianism, and such a policy guide was found in "monetarism." Advocates of monetarism, the most notable of whom was Milton Friedman, held that inflation was a purely monetary phenomenon, and that central banks should follow a rule such as letting the money supply grow annually at a definite rate (rather than radically expanding the money supply). But as an economic policy concept, monetarism was in some respects even more simplified than Keynesianism. It soon became clear that financial innovation made it almost impossible to realize the monetarist rule and define the relevant monetary aggregate. Despite its promotion of free markets, the monetarist model contained little true classical economics. When monetarists declared, "We're all Keynesians now," it meant much more than an ironic twist.

When Reaganomics—the economics of President Ronald Reagan, which promoted a combination of tax cuts and deregulation—came along in the early 1980s, it failed to reduce government expenditures. Although unemployment fell and Paul Volcker's Federal Reserve (the American central bank) brought down the inflation rate, government deficits began to swell and the public debt increased to new heights.[10] Around this time a new economic policy consensus emerged: that deficits didn't matter.[11] If deficits didn't matter, then debt level didn't either. The exchange rate of the dollar could be neglected, too. The new consensus held that central banks were fully capable of managing the monetary side of the economy.

It was at this stage that the so-called Goldilocks economy became the ideal. As long as price inflation seemed to be under control and crude macroeconomic statistics registered the expansion of GDP, the new paradigm left no room to question the quality of this economic growth (despite the uncertainties that surround such measurements) or what was going on behind the monetary aggregates. This is why policymakers stopped paying serious attention to credit growth and debt accumulation.[12]

The early 1980s introduced another remarkable phenomenon. This period marked the beginning of an unprecedented stock market boom, not only in the United States but also in Japan and Europe. Although the stock boom came to an abrupt stop in Japan by the end of 1989, it continued in the United States and Europe, and spread to China, other parts of Asia, and some Latin American countries. Wealth now meant mainly financial wealth, and financial market quotations for stocks and bonds became global obsessions.

Bailout Economics

The stock market plunge on October 19, 1987, with a one-day decline of 22.5 percent, could have been interpreted as a signal that it was time to reduce consumption, government spending, the trade deficit, and the accumulation of internal debt (domestic government debt) and external debt (the foreign debt of the United States). Yet it turned out differently. A few months before the global stock market crash, Alan Greenspan had become chairman of the Federal Reserve. The morning after the unexpected market meltdown, the new Fed chairman declared, "The Federal Reserve, consistent with its responsibilities as the nation's central banker, affirmed today its readiness to serve as a source of liquidity to support the economic and financial system."[13]

After August 15, 1971, when the United States took the U.S. dollar off the gold standard, Greenspan's declaration of October 20, 1987, is probably the second most important event in the monetary history of the past several decades. Here Greenspan took actions that would characterize his entire rule: as soon as some trouble appeared—and many troubles would appear over the next two decades—he would step in by actively increasing the money supply and cutting interest rates. (Greenspan also displayed a unique talent for soothing the market with words.)[14] Thus began a new period of monetary policy in the United States, a policy which is best called "bailout economics."[15]

While a bailout may be beneficial for the individual case and definitely is so for the persons who receive the bailout money, bailouts have highly problematic systemic consequences. What at first tends to be viewed as a benevolent donation from government will come to be regarded as nothing less than an endowment, a rightful claim on government money if things should go wrong. Over time bailouts produce moral hazard: it is not long before the business community and financial market operators, believing that they are insulated from the risk of financial losses, adopt an aggressive attitude and overexpand their commercial activities.[16] This economic expansion will produce economic growth, but much of it will be driven by malinvestments, which will lead to capital destruction. Thus, the economy that appears to be obtaining new levels of prosperity is actually getting poorer. When the bubble pops, the level of prosperity is lower than it was at the inception of the fake boom.

It did not take long for Wall Street to name the Fed chairman's implicit bailout guarantee. It was called the "Greenspan Put." In the perception of many financial market operators, Alan Greenspan was now the "Maestro," a sort of almighty when it came to bailing out financial markets. After a few years in office, Greenspan assumed almost total rule over the financial markets, with an ever-growing crowd of followers as his true believers.

At that time, it was mainly only Austrian economists who did not get swayed by Greenspan's siren songs, and their warnings remained unheard.[17] The financial media became as enthusiastic as the majority of the stock and bond market operators. Risk awareness began to recede as ever-larger profit opportunities arrived.

The so-called New Economy led to stock market prices that exceeded all conventional measures in terms of price-to-earnings ratios. Initial public offerings by companies that lacked earnings and sometimes even a product (the only thing they had was a business plan) achieved extreme valuations at the stock market and produced billionaires overnight. Of course, hype, gullibility, and greed were involved as well,[18] but these emotions do not fall from the blue sky. Although Greenspan lamented "irrational exuberance,"[19] his Federal Reserve provided a broad basis for such irrationality: liquidity. In one dip in the financial markets after another—from the Asian crisis, to the

Long-Term Capital Management (LTCM) bankruptcy, to the Russian and Argentinean defaults, to the imaginary Y2K computer glitch, to 9/11—Greenspan's central bank lowered the interest rate and opened the floodgates of the money supply.[20] As a result, financial markets moved from one bubble to the next.[21] Prudence vanished in favor of a mentality to "go for it," and soon financial markets discovered the largest bubble of all: the real-estate market.

Global Imbalances

While the United States was ushering in a phase of prosperity, Japan entered a period of enduring malaise. In December 1989 the Japanese stock market began its long decline. Over the next couple of years the NIKKEI index dropped from a height of almost 40,000 points to less than 10,000 points. Two decades later, the index was still below that mark.

In the 1990s Japan performed the biggest experiment of applied Keynesian-monetarist economics—with devastating results. While the Japanese central bank brought down its interest rate near zero, the Japanese government began an unprecedented spending program that lifted the debt ratio to more than 200 percent of GDP.[22] These extremely low interest rates and massive government expenditures did not turn around the economy, contrary to the promises of Keynesian theory. The Japanese economy basically stopped growing. Keynesian policies have utterly failed in Japan; only because of exports did Japan hold on to stagnation instead of plunging into a more severe depression.

In the 1990s a new symbiosis began to emerge between Japanese exports and American imports. While Japan achieved persistent surpluses in its trade with America, the United States accumulated deficits in its foreign trade position and consequently became a net foreign debtor. In accordance with the macroeconomic accounting framework, high Japanese savings rates corresponded with a low U.S. savings rate, which in turn got reflected in the trade imbalances and the accumulation of foreign assets by Japan and of debt by the United States.

Nor was Japan alone in accumulating surpluses. China joined in with a vengeance, flooding the United States with cheap goods.[23] The United States became a consumer's paradise, where credit was easy and goods were cheap and abundant, particularly imported goods. Government finances profited from higher tax receipts that seemed to come from nowhere but reflected the bubble in the stock market. This provided the ideal constellation for China to accelerate its economic rise. The Chinese development model found its crucial counterpart in the American consumer, who never seemed to tire of buying imported goods. China became America's factory, even more so than Japan before. "Borrow to buy" became the new mantra for the U.S. consumer. Overwhelmed by cheap credit opportunities, all segments of the American population went on a consumption spree.[24]

As much as the great American boom of the 1990s was claimed to be the result of America's entrepreneurship, competitiveness, capacity of innovation, cultural dominance, and military pole position, it was also the result of this symbiosis between the United States and its trading partners. As the United States came to be characterized by low savings, high consumption, trade deficits, and consequently accumulation of debt, Japan and China came to be distinguished by high savings, production, trade surpluses, and consequently the accumulation of assets.[25]

For such a pattern to persist over a long time, the international monetary system must have no inherent mechanism for rebalancing. Such a freewheeling system was set in place in 1971 when the last link to gold was cut.

The international monetary system that came into existence in the early 1970s has little to do with the flexibility and adaptability of free markets. On the contrary, in areas like exchange rates and interest rate policy, government and central banks as agencies of interventionism have become even more dominant than under the former system of fixed exchange rates. The Chinese development model is a political project based on exchange rate manipulation and interventionist control over the banking sector and over large parts of the productive economy. By this policy of massive currency management,[26] backed up by domestic economic interventionism, China gained trade advantages that fostered its export industry and laid the foundation for the expansion of the domestic production base. Chinese monetary authorities accumulated a dollar surplus through their interventions in the currency market. This was transformed into capital outflows and showed up as foreign lending to the U.S. government.

A superficial analysis would find that such an arrangement is all pleasure for the United States and all pain for China, and thus it seemed for a long time.

Deficits *Do* Matter

From a certain perspective, it seemed that the imbalance could go on forever. In the accounting framework of the balance of payments, a trade deficit can exist as long as there is an equivalent inflow of capital—as long as the deficit is financed, that is. This thesis was said to hold especially for the United States as the issuer of world's prime currency, the U.S. dollar. While financing of the deficit may be a problem for the rest of the world, the United States would not face such a debt limit. It appeared as if the best of all economic worlds had been found: while the U.S. consumer became ever more prosperous in terms of consumption goods, the Chinese producer got ever richer in terms of international assets, as the owner of U.S. Treasury bills and government bonds and their underlying currency equivalent, dollars.

But this kind of analysis, which has dominated decision making at the U.S. Treasury and the Federal Reserve, is limited to monetary flows and consequently is blind to the long-term structural economic effects of such policies.[27] Trade deficits are not only a monetary phenomenon. Most non-Austrian economists use an extremely simplified concept of capital, regarding it as a homogeneous and clearly measurable entity that can be easily augmented through equally homogenous amounts of investment. Austrian economics recognizes that capital resources are *heterogeneous*; each capital good has a specific position in the overall production process of an economy. Each unit of investment will vary depending on where it comes in the capital structure, the sequence of production from the early stages of the manufacturing of a product until its final stage as a consumption good.[28]

Counter to the mantra sung by politicians, bureaucrats, and many economists that "deficits don't matter," deficits matter crucially in the perspective of Austrian economics. Persistent trade imbalances harm the debtor country's creditworthiness and risk perceptions. Even more so, imbalances affect the capital structures of the countries involved. That is because changes in the pattern of consumption alter the pattern of production. In the natural way of international trade, changes in the production structure take place as countries open up to international trade, and the emerging trade pattern reflects the comparative advantages of the companies involved. Trade imbalances reflect different domestic macroeconomic conditions and exchange rate effects.

A sustainable pattern of trade may well exist for a country that mainly imports goods and exports services, or even for a country that imports goods and services, as long as its foreign investment income (cross-border payments of interest, dividends, and other income on international financial transactions) is sufficient to pay for the imports. Yet it is different with a country that finances its overall imports through debt accumulation because of insufficient domestic savings. There is an inherent limit to this relationship, because over time the share of the negative investment income becomes larger and larger. This means that an ever-increasing amount of foreign financing will be needed even when the share of goods and services in the current account does not change. Typically creditors will notice this discrepancy in advance and the perceived creditworthiness of the debtor country will collapse.

The perception of creditworthiness changes abruptly and drastically in an event-driven recalibration of standards. Suddenly the debtor country needs to generate accepted means of payment through exports and a cut of imports. This requires a massive shift from a trade deficit to a surplus—something extremely difficult to achieve on short notice, given the country's import dependency and the resulting changes to its capital structure.

Could such problems emerge for the United States? As long as the United States can maintain its position as the producer of the dominant international reserve currency, the imbalances may go on. This, however, means that changes in the capital structure will become even more profound. More importantly, as U.S. debt level rises, foreign central banks will begin to diversify their reserve holdings while businesses will search for alternatives in international trade. As a result, the dollar will begin to lose its status as the world's prime reserve and international trade currency. Given the high level of U.S. domestic and foreign debt, there can be little doubt that the move away from the U.S. dollar will accelerate.

Sovereign Debt Crises

Excessive debt not only could be the undoing of the dollar as the world's prime currency; it was also the fundamental source of the financial crisis that began in 2007. The modern monetary system is based on debt. It is an engine of debt expansion—of the public *and* private sectors. Overindebtedness among households is most clearly visible in the real-estate sector, particularly in the United States but also in Spain and some other countries. The debt position of U.S. consumers has become unsustainable. It is illusory to expect a consumption-led economic recovery.

Excessive debt is endemic among governments as well. For 2011, Germany's government debt is estimated to amount to 84 percent of GDP; the United Kingdom's, 91 percent; France's, 99 percent; Italy's, 135 percent; Greece's, 139 percent; and Japan's, 205 percent. For the United States, the figure is 95 percent of GDP.[29] Because of insufficient domestic savings,[30] the United States has lost its status as a creditor nation and has turned into the world's largest debtor nation.[31] And as we have seen, the post–Bretton Woods global monetary system puts the

United States into the unique position of maintaining persistent trade deficits and accumulating international debt beyond sustainable levels.

Worse still, the U.S. government, since the outbreak of the financial crisis, has massively intervened in the private market and taken up positions with financial institutions and major companies that were close to bankruptcy. At the same time, the U.S. central bank has acted massively as a lender of last resort and, along with lowering interest rates practically to zero, has bought up junk papers from the private banking sector and drastically extended its balance sheet.[32] In modern monetary systems, the currency of a country is backed by the assets of the central bank. In the past the largest part of these assets consisted in government debt; because of this, one could say that the U.S. dollar was as good as a U.S. government bond. But as the amount of junk assets held by the American central bank grows, the U.S. dollar itself is at risk of becoming junk as well. With this fiscal expansion occurring in tandem with extremely loose monetary policies, government debt and the external investment position of the United States have reached highly critical levels.[33]

International debt problems extend beyond the United States. In early 2010 Europe was shaken by an assault on the common European currency, the euro. Greece was getting close to default, thereby putting at risk the other so-called PIIGS countries—Portugal, Ireland, Italy, and Spain. In a massive response, the leadership of the eurozone implemented a gigantic bailout program with a credit line of almost a trillion euros.

In Europe, too, massive monetary expansion and low interest rates that temporarily turned into negative real interest after the year 2002 lie at the heart of the debt crisis.[34] Before joining the eurozone, countries like Greece, Portugal, Italy, and Spain had had high inflation rates for decades. In preparation for their participation in the common European currency, these countries had to place their government bonds at yields that were considerably higher than those of the more stable countries in Europe. By adopting the euro as their circulating currency in 2001, these high-inflation countries gained a higher degree of creditworthiness and thus had to pay lower interest rates on their debt. In fact, the interest rate differential between these countries and Germany, for example, disappeared almost completely. The low interest rates and perceived creditworthiness triggered a period of credit expansion in the private and public sectors of these countries.

While some observers took the European sovereign debt crisis as a sign that the establishment of a common European currency was to blame, one should remember that common European currency arrangements were adopted as the consequence of the breakdown of the Bretton Woods arrangement. To achieve deeper economic integration, European countries needed a currency framework that did not depend on the inflationary U.S. dollar.

The Drive Toward Dissolution

Recall the BIS annual reports that tried to make sense of the financial crisis. In saying that "no one thought that the financial system could collapse" and praising the stability and growth that had marked the "Great Moderation," the BIS avoided pointing fingers at itself. The BIS is the central banks of central banks, and its initial reports did not evaluate the role that central banks played in laying the groundwork for the financial crisis. This is strange, because in the years before the collapse, the BIS did warn about interest rates that seemed too low, and in the years since, its annual reports have discussed the importance of low interest rates and extreme credit growth as major monetary causes of the crisis. The 2010 BIS report, for example, observed:

> Previous episodes of low interest rates suggest that loose monetary policy can be associated with credit booms, asset price increases, a decline in risk spreads and a search for yield. Together, these caused severe misallocations of resources in the years before the crisis, as evidenced by the excessive growth of the financial industry and the construction sector. The necessary structural adjustments are painful and will take time.[35]

Then again, the BIS's failure to discuss the role of central banks should not seem that strange at all. For if the chief central bankers did issue a mea culpa, it would amount to their own death sentence. If they honestly described why things went wrong, it would automatically raise the case for abolishing central banking.

The current economic and financial crisis has exposed the modern monetary system as a mechanism of debt expansion whose inherent dynamics move this system incessantly to the limit. The structure of the modern monetary system combined with populist democracy produces an environment where government interventionism blooms and debt expansion flourishes. This dynamic propels the system inexorably to hyperinflation or bankruptcy. Interventionist systems without inherent order drive toward their own dissolution.

The monetary authorities' main concern is deflation, because deflation would mean bankruptcy of the system right away. Therefore, the authorities work as hard as they can to produce more debt inflation. Ultimately, however, the end stage will be the same: bankruptcy. Interventionist policy measures directed at avoiding any recession prevent a repositioning of the economy and thus suppress the correction of past errors. These interventions do not help the economy but instead produce widening distortions of the capital structures. What one or two decades ago could have been corrected by a quick recession will now require a much costlier process of adaptation.

The crisis that began in 2007 is of systemic nature. The U.S. government and governments worldwide have tried to pull the economy away from the brink through costly interventions that have produced more debt. Yet by doing this governments and central banks ignore the fact that is was overindebtedness in the first place, which was the main reason for the outbreak of the financial crisis.

Debt levels of consumers in the banking system and of the public sector have reached such dimensions that we cannot reasonably expect that such debt can be serviced in the future. Unless central banks and governments recognize that the cure they are prescribing is actually the cause of our economic ailments—that, in fact, *they* are the cause of our problems—we will be subjected to ever more costly and repressive government interventions. Leviathan will keep growing, and debt levels will keep exploding.

The current paradigm is simply unsustainable. The longer the state keeps trying to fend off collapse with their disastrous policies, the more cataclysmic that inevitable collapse will be.

The Dangers of Protectionism

Mark Brandly

I n the 1944 book *The Road to Serfdom*, Friedrich Hayek attacked
the movement toward totalitarian, centrally planned economies.
While his book did not directly address protectionist arguments,
Hayek's fundamental argument that central planning is destructive
can be applied to restrictive international trade policies. Hayek was a
proponent of free trade. He opposed the Smoot-Hawley tariff, enacted
at the beginning of the Great Depression, saying that it was time "to
abolish those restrictions on trade and the free movement of capital."
Sure enough, the 1930 Smoot-Hawley Act, which roughly doubled tariff rates, led to a collapse of world trade. While the tariff did not cause
the Depression, it made a bad situation worse.[1]

Eighty years later, with the U.S. economy in the midst of another
economic crisis, we are hearing renewed calls for protectionism.
Included among the government interventions of the Bush and Obama
administrations—bailouts and stimulus spending, massive increases in
government debt, heavier regulatory burdens, and more—have been
efforts to increase government control over international trade. The
Obama administration, for example, has implemented multiple protectionist measures, including a 35 percent tariff on tires imported from

China and a stimulus bill that includes "Buy American" provisions, whereby works projects funded by the stimulus package use only iron, steel, and other goods produced in the United States.

Policymakers and political commentators see times of economic crisis as opportunities to expand the size and reach of the federal government. With the crisis that erupted in 2008, the government's tentacles are reaching into many different sectors of the economy, including international trade. But just as the Smoot-Hawley tariff exacerbated the Great Depression, enacting more trade barriers today will do more harm than good. The benefits of free trade are unmistakably clear, as are the dangers of misguided attempts at protectionism.

The Case for Free Trade

Since 1776, with the publication of Adam Smith's *Wealth of Nations*,[2] economists have repeatedly demonstrated the case for free-trade policies and explained the fallacies in protectionist arguments. Smith concluded that the free-trade "proposition is so very manifest, that it seems ridiculous to take any pains to prove it; nor could it ever have been called in question, had not the interested sophistry of merchants and manufacturers confounded the common sense of mankind."[3] In order to counter the "sophistry" of protectionist arguments, it seems appropriate to restate the case for trade.

According to the classic economic argument for free trade, called the law of comparative advantage, an economy will prosper and use its resources more efficiently if it specializes in the production of goods in which it has a comparative advantage. Every economy, from the individual to a national economy, has the choice of producing good X or other goods. In choosing to produce an additional unit of good X, the economy must forgo the production of other goods. For two trading economies, the economy that gives up the least amount of other goods when it produces good X is said to have the comparative advantage over its trading partners. Goods that are produced at a comparative advantage will be exported and the economy will import the products in which it does not have a comparative advantage. The result of this specialization is that more goods will be available for consumers.

Two observations are useful at this point. First of all, imports represent the benefits of trade and exports represent the costs. A common fallacy is that exports are better than imports and that the key to prosperity is the promotion of exports. To see the problem in this kind of reasoning, consider an economy that is importing cars and exporting wheat. Do the benefits of trade in this economy come from driving the imported cars or from seeing the foreign consumers eat the exported wheat? Of course, the consumption of the imported products is the reward of trade. The cost of trade is the wheat that cannot be eaten by the consumers in this economy, because it must be exported in order to acquire the imports. The purpose of production is consumption, and consumption, not production, is the appropriate measure of an economy's standard of living. Trade, as we will see, increases an economy's level of consumption.

The second observation is that an economy has two ways to use its domestic resources to acquire a product. Consider cars again: a country can build domestic automobile factories and employ its workers and other inputs to build domestically produced cars. Alternatively, it can produce a domestic product—say, wheat—and then trade that for cars. Trade is similar to a technology that converts exports into imports—in this case, wheat into cars. Regardless of which option is chosen, domestic production or trade, the economy is using its own resources to acquire the cars.

Given these two methods of obtaining cars, we must consider when it is more efficient to produce the cars domestically and when is it more efficient to trade for the cars. The answer is clear: when fewer resources are required to produce a car domestically than to produce the wheat that must be traded for the car, domestic production is advantageous. But when it takes fewer resources to produce the wheat needed to trade for the car than to produce the car, it's more efficient to trade for the car. In this second case, the country has a comparative advantage in wheat and reaps the benefit of trade by specializing in wheat production and trading for the products—cars—in which its trading partners have a comparative advantage. Since it requires fewer resources to acquire the cars by producing the wheat than it does to domestically produce the cars, trading for cars frees up resources to produce more goods. Consumers gain in the sense that they have more cars and wheat. Trade increases our standard of living.

Note that these exchanges are mutually beneficial. The trading partner with the comparative advantage in automobile production benefits from specializing in automobile production, exporting cars, and importing wheat. Free-trade policies allow consumers and producers in both countries to reap the benefits of international trade.

This is the famous argument in favor of free trade. Even a "cautious" protectionist, Nobel laureate Paul Krugman,[4] believes that if "there were an Economist's Creed, it would surely contain the affirmations 'I understand the Principle of Comparative Advantage' and 'I advocate Free Trade.'"[5]

We can now understand the dangers of the Obama administration's Buy American policies, which require firms receiving stimulus monies to purchase domestic products and ban them from purchasing certain imports. When firms are prohibited from buying imports in favor of domestically produced goods, they forgo the opportunity to benefit from international trade. Instead of acquiring the goods in the most efficient manner, buying only American goods results in more expensive goods and wastes resources.

Protectionism

Governmental restrictions on international trade, such as tariffs and import quotas, are termed protectionist policies. It is important to note who is being protected and who is being harmed by these policies. Consumers are not benefiting; they are, rather, the victims of this protection. Industries that have a competitive advantage in world markets are not being protected; such industries welcome the opportunity to compete with foreign firms. The industries that are competitively weak, that are at a comparative disadvantage, are the ones that seek protection from foreign competition. The purpose of protection is to limit international competition, thereby harming consumers by increasing the prices of imports, which also results in higher prices for domestically produced products. I must stress this point. A primary consequence of protection is that it harms consumers by raising import prices. Protection transfers wealth from consumers to domestic producers that are not competitive in world markets.

Protectionist policies reduce the benefits of trade. Protection shifts resources out of the industry that has a comparative advantage—think of wheat production in the above example—to the less competitive industry, such as the car industry. The point is that protection helps some industries but hurts other industries. Also, acquisition of the cars occurs not through trade but through less efficient domestic production. Therefore, restricting trade makes a country poorer in the sense that it reduces the overall level of consumption.

In spite of the case for free trade, there is a long history of policymakers' advocating protection. From the country's first tariff act, in 1789, to the protectionist measures of the Bush and Obama administrations, politicians have used protection to pay off politically favored industries. Alexander Hamilton, Henry Clay, Abraham Lincoln, William McKinley, Herbert Hoover, George W. Bush, and Barack Obama all backed protectionist measures.[6] Protection is a method of rewarding political supporters. The steel industry will reward you with votes and campaign contributions, for example, in exchange for restrictions on steel imports. Of course, when policymakers advocate trade barriers, they do not point out the damage that their policies will have on the country. They claim that their policies help the steel industry in particular and the economy in general. Let's consider some of these claims.

Protection to Increase Wages and Create Jobs

In the current crisis, unemployment is high and wage rates are stagnant. An often repeated argument is that protection will create jobs and increase wages. True enough, protection increases employment and drives up wages in the protected industries. But it costs jobs and reduces wages in other industries. When we reduce our demand for imports because of trade barriers, foreign entities lower their demand for U.S. exports. Demand for workers in the protected industries increases—the industries, by the way, that are at a comparative disadvantage—but jobs are lost and wages fall in the industries that have a comparative advantage. Protection is a method of transferring wealth from some sectors of the economy to other sectors. There is no positive effect on the overall level of unemployment in the United States, and wages, on average, are reduced.[7]

This demonstrates one of the common fallacies of protectionist arguments. Many times, the protectionists see the benefits of protection, such as the jobs created in the protected industry, but they fail to see the full effects of restricting trade. Economist Henry Hazlitt sums it up nicely, pointing out that the error in the protectionist argument is "that of considering merely the immediate effects of a tariff on special groups, and neglecting to consider its long-run effects on the whole community."[8]

There is an additional complication from protectionism: as we will see, domestic firms can move some of their production offshore, such as by building factories overseas.

Low-priced Imports

The argument that protection benefits domestic workers is based on the idea that low-priced imports harm our economy. There are several separate arguments that fall into this category. Some protectionists argue that we must protect our industries from competition from cheap foreign labor. Others assert that we must protect ourselves from "dumping," which occurs when foreign firms sell their goods at low prices in order to gain market share overseas. In both cases, the argument is that protection is needed to increase the prices of what would otherwise be low-priced imports.

Those who promote the cheap foreign labor or the antidumping arguments fail to see that low-priced imports are good for our standard of living. Lower prices mean that we can buy more imports, and recall that imports are the benefits of international trade. The best possible situation for the United States would be to have the rest of the world send us imports for free. Of course, other countries would never agree to this, but consider the possibility. Less than 5 percent of the world's population lives in the United States. If the rest of the world would be willing to send us free goods, in perpetuity, we could spend most of our time engaged in leisure activities. Admittedly, our industries would suffer. Our manufacturing would be reduced, but we would get to keep everything we produced domestically. Exporting would be unnecessary. Standards of living would soar. Everyone sees this principle in his or her personal life. Free or low-priced goods increase a household's level of consumption. The same is true for a large economy. We should welcome inexpensive imports.

Paralleling the cheap-foreign-labor argument is the case against foreign export subsidies. Some protectionists complain that it's unfair to have free trade when the trading partner is subsidizing the sale of its exports. For example, a Chinese subsidy on goods imported to the United States reduces the prices of the imported goods. The claim is that such subsidies are unfair to domestic competitors and we therefore need to restrict the importation of such goods. This is a puzzling argument. Foreign export subsidies benefit the economy that is purchasing the imports. When a foreign government subsidizes its exports, it is taking money from its taxpayers and paying its firms to lower the prices of goods exported to the United States. Wealth is being transferred from foreign taxpayers to U.S. consumers. We should welcome these transfer payments. In 2007 the Bush administration pressured the Chinese government to reduce its export subsidies. This policy was misguided. Lowering the export subsidies was a way of taking money out of the pockets of American consumers. Complaints about foreign export subsidies are analogous to retirees complaining that transferring wealth from workers to retirees through the Social Security system is harming the retirees' standard of living.

The idea that we should protect ourselves from low-priced imports reminds me of a statement by Ludwig von Mises, Hayek's brilliant teacher: "The desperate attempts of the advocates of protection to refute the statements of the classical economists concerning the consequences of free trade and protection failed lamentably."[9]

Protection Lowers Wages

While it's claimed that protectionist measures increase the wages of U.S. workers, the opposite is true. Trade barriers have a negative effect on wages. Why is this so? First of all, protection drives up the prices of goods, reducing the purchasing power of workers' wages. This has a negative effect on real wages (wages adjusted for price changes). Workers' wages purchase fewer goods because of the price effects of protection, so protection, on average, makes workers poorer.

Economists generally recognize the benefits of competitive markets. Competitive markets allocate resources efficiently and produce the most highly valued goods and services for consumers. Reducing the amount of competition tends to lead to a less efficient allocation of resources. Every student of the principles of microeconomics is exposed to the explanation that competition drives down prices, increases production, and leads firms to produce the most highly demanded products. The fact that trade restrictions reduce competition is a strike against protectionism. A prominent trade theorist, Gottfried Haberler, argues that imperfectly competitive situations strengthen the case for free trade, since "free trade is a potent antimonopoly weapon."[10] The beneficial aspects of competition and the impact that protection has on the prices of consumer goods need to be emphasized in any discussion regarding trade policy.

In addition, protectionists may overlook the link between wages and productivity. Increased productivity results in higher wages. Protection shifts workers out of industries that have a comparative advantage, which are the industries in which workers are most productive, and moves them into industries that do not have a comparative advantage, reducing the overall level of worker productivity. This is one of the most destructive aspects of protection. Most people understand this on a personal level. Would you make more money at a job that you are good at—that is, a job in which you have a comparative advantage—or at a job in which you are not very productive? The answer is clear. People tend to seek work in industries where they have a comparative advantage over others because they get paid more in these industries.[11] Protection, however, provides incentives to create jobs in less efficient industries, leading to lower wages.

Infant Industries

Economists who otherwise favor free trade often concede that tariffs are needed to protect infant industries. Industries, according to this argument, proceed through an infancy period, a period in which the industry loses money. Protection is needed during this time to allow the industry to reach maturity. Once the industry has matured, the industry will be competitive in world markets and we can remove the trade barriers and reap the benefits of free trade. One obvious problem with this argument is that protected industries rarely, if ever, seem to mature. Continuing the questionable biological analogy of this argument, consider a person that is protected from competition. He runs the 100-meter dash but is given a 30-meter head start over the other runners. If he loses, even with this advantage, he is given a larger head start. The race is rigged to the point that he always wins. We would

81

never expect to see this man become the fastest person in the world. In the same manner, protected industries never seem to claim that they are ready to face the foreign competition without a protective tariff.

There is an even stronger case against the infant-industry argument. Consider two industries, industry A and industry B. Both industries take losses of a hundred dollars, in present value terms, during their infancy periods. The present value of industry A's profits during its mature period is fifty dollars, while the value of industry B's profits is two hundred dollars. Given these costs and benefits, we should want to see only one of these industries mature. The net benefits of industry A are negative and the economy would be better off if this industry had never been born. Industry B represents the type of industry that provides net benefits to society. The infant-industry advocates should favor protecting industry B but not industry A. The problem here, however, is that private investors will be willing to fund industry B. It's common practice for businesses to take a loss on an investment if the investor believes that the future profits will more than make up for the earlier losses. Building factories, drilling oil wells, and constructing office buildings all require up-front losses. Entrepreneurs make these investments calculating that it's worth it in the long run. It's common for infant industries to mature without the aid of government assistance. The point is that private investors will fund the type of industries that we should want to mature. These industries do not need protection from international competition.[12]

One might argue that entrepreneurs may fail to see the long-term benefits of their investments and therefore fail to fund the appropriate industries. According to this view, government policymakers should recognize this entrepreneurial failure and protect industries such as industry B. This argument is wrong. The market rewards entrepreneurs for recognizing profit opportunities. Successful entrepreneurs profit from making the right choices, and entrepreneurs who invest in losing industries are punished with losses and tend to be driven from the market. Entrepreneurs may not spot every profit opportunity, but expecting government officials to do a better job of seeing the appropriate investments is absurd. Elected officials and their advisers have neither the incentive nor the ability to outperform private entrepreneurs in making these decisions.

Externalities

We now come to a more sophisticated protectionist argument. Whether the industry is an infant industry or not is irrelevant to this next point. Suppose that an industry generates what economists call positive externalities. A positive externality occurs when the production of a good generates benefits that are external to that particular market. People who have not paid for the good receive benefits from that good and the producers of that good are unable to capture those benefits in the form of revenues. An example of this possibility is research and development. In order to develop a new product, firms invest in research and development. This research generates new technologies that spill over to other industries, benefiting firms that did not pay for this research. These firms are able to employ these new technologies, increasing their efficiency, lowering their costs, and increasing their profits.

Since positive externalities are highly beneficial to other industries, the government should, according to one protectionist argument, try to protect positive-externality-generating industries from foreign competition in order to keep these industries located in our country and thus increase societal welfare. From this perspective, a free-trade policy would be less efficient than a strategic trade policy aimed at promoting the appropriate industries.[13]

There are several problems with the externality case for protection. Proponents of this argument commonly assume that the positive externalities either do not cross political borders or do so at a slow rate. If the external benefits of research and development spill over to other countries—and there is no reason to believe otherwise—then protection provides no net economic benefits. If a firm invests in research that results in positive gains for other industries, it makes little difference

83

where these firms are located. We should be happy to see firms in other countries engage in research that leads to new technologies that benefit domestic industries in the United States.

Another problem is that positive-externalities arguments focus on the external benefits of policies but not on the possible external costs. External costs occur when industries engage in actions that harm producers or consumers in other markets. If the United States is going to erect trade barriers to encourage positive externalities, it could also erect trade barriers to discourage negative externalities. A country could impose tariffs against oil imports, for example, to reduce pollution externalities.

Moreover, as trade barriers lead output in one industry to increase, resources are pulled away from other industries that may also be generating positive externalities. Policies aimed at increasing positive externalities may end up having a negative effect on them. These "costs" of intervention should also be taken into account when advocating protectionist policies. Some industries generate positive externalities and others create negative externalities. Changing the level of production in some industries affects the amount of production in other industries, and these other industries also produce positive and negative externalities. In order for trade policy to lead to net benefits, government officials would need to recognize the level of externalities in all of these industries. This is an impossible task. There is no reason to conclude that policymakers could do the calculations necessary to implement the appropriate policies.

The point here is that externalities are ubiquitous, and if countries begin to target them with trade barriers, when do they stop? The externality arguments are not trade arguments per se. As Leland B. Yeager and David G. Tuerck put it in their excellent book *Foreign Trade and U.S. Policy*, such arguments are just another case for "government meddling generally, and international trade is just one of many aspects of life that supposedly should not go uncontrolled."[14]

Job Exporting and Capital Flows

The most difficult issue to address regarding recent calls for protectionist policies is the effect of trade policy on capital flows.

Generally, when people hear the term *international trade*, they think of exports and imports. Another major category of trade is capital flows. Any manmade resource is capital. Every economy produces consumer goods and capital goods. Capital goods are the goods that are produced in order to be used to produce consumer goods. Factories, machinery, drilling rigs, heavy equipment, and the vehicles and computers that are purchased by firms are all examples of capital goods. An increasing capital stock increases productivity. It's more efficient to dig a hole in the ground using heavy equipment than it is using shovels, so heavy-equipment operators receive higher wages than do roustabouts with shovels.

When foreign investors invest in the U.S. economy, the United States experiences capital inflows; when U.S. investors invest capital in foreign countries, this represents a capital outflow from the U.S. point of view. One country's capital inflows are another country's capital outflows. In recent years, the United States has experienced trade deficits. The dollar value of our imports has exceeded the dollar value of our exports. Dollars have flowed out of the country because of this trade deficit, and the trade deficit has largely been offset by capital inflows. The dollars flow out when we purchase imports and they flow back into the country as foreign investors build factories and businesses in the United States, purchase real estate here, buy stock in U.S. firms, and loan money to the federal government by purchasing government securities.

What does this have to do with trade policy? Many protectionist advocates favor protection to reduce outsourcing. We hear that free trade leads to jobs being exported. Jobs are outsourced to other countries, say by hiring radiologists or computer engineers in India to read X-rays or develop computer software for U.S. consumers. If these exported jobs are not linked to capital outflows, then the case for free trade stands. The jobs are outsourced because the foreign workers have a comparative advantage over domestic workers in those industries. This type of outsourcing is clearly good for the U.S. consumer. Hiring cheap foreign labor allows the United States to garner gains from trade.

But if the outsourcing does involve capital outflows, such as when domestic firms build factories in other countries, that changes the discussion. This suggests a caveat to the classical argument for free trade. That argument is based on the premise that capital is immobile, that it does not easily flow across political borders. In many cases, however, it's relatively easy for domestic firms to invest in other countries. Multinational companies build factories and hire workers all over the world.

Consider a domestic industry that builds a factory or owns a subsidiary in a foreign country. This overseas investment increases the capital stock of the foreign country, leading to higher wages in that country. If the capital investment had occurred in the United States, our domestic economy would be reaping the benefits of having more capital. Here's where trade policy comes in. Since capital is mobile, protectionists argue that tariff policy could increase profits in domestic production, leading to capital formation in the United States and resulting in less capital flowing out of the country. The domestic economy would see the benefits of an increased capital stock. According to protectionists, appropriate trade policies would increase the prices of imports. This would make it less profitable to outsource the jobs, since the tariffs would eat up the profits of outsourcing, leading firms to invest domestically instead of overseas.

I take this to be one of the arguments advocated by protectionists such as Lou Dobbs, who objects to the "transfer of factors of production from developed nations to third world nations."[15] It is also the central point repeatedly stressed by Paul Craig Roberts.[16] This argument is not new, but it is a major point of contention in the current debate.

Roberts bases his arguments on the work of Ralph Gomory and William Baumol.[17] Gomory and Baumol's arguments are confused and their conclusions fallacious, as I have demonstrated in another essay.[18] While the economic analysis in Gomory and Baumol is poor, their fundamental point regarding capital flows needs to be discussed, for they attempt to analyze the distribution of capital among trading partners and conclude that free trade could lead to a dearth of capital in an economy.

As explained, trade deficits are linked to net capital inflows. Dollars that flow out of the country to purchase imports tend to flow back into the United States, either in the form of foreign investment or to purchase U.S. exports. If imports exceed exports, the difference tends to be made up with capital inflows. Generally speaking, in order to have a large amount of net capital inflows, the economy will need to run a large trade deficit.

Roberts maintains that current U.S. trade policies increase capital outflows and argues for protections to reduce those outflows. He and other protectionists see the immediate effects of trade barriers but fail to see the total impact of their proposals.

While it's true that imposing a tariff on one good may lead firms in that industry to produce the good domestically instead of moving their production offshore, we cannot conclude that this policy will necessarily lead to a large amount of net capital inflows. When firms move some of their production to the United States, the dollars that flowed into the country because of these capital inflows tend to be used to purchase additional imports. A net increase in capital inflows will be offset by a decrease in net exports (exports less imports). Imposing a tariff on a specific good has two conflicting effects: it gives the producers of that good an incentive to shift production to the United States, and it either increases the U.S. demand for imports or decreases the foreign demand for U.S. exports. The increased demand for imports gives U.S. investors an incentive to invest their capital overseas, and the lower demand for U.S. exports reduces the incentive to invest in capital projects in the United States. If the tariff protects an industry that is less capital intensive than the foreign industries that are aided by the tariff or the domestic industries that are harmed by the tariff, the trade barrier could conceivably have a negative effect on capital formation in the United States.

For example, the software industry is considered to be labor intensive, while oil production is capital intensive. Let's assume that a tariff that creates jobs in the domestic software industry also increases the demand for foreign oil. The jobs that the tariff creates in the software industry will generate little capital formation. The increased demand for oil imports will lead to U.S. investment in foreign oil production, and this investment is capital intensive. Protecting the software industry, in this example, would not be expected to have a significant positive effect on domestic capital formation.

Roberts provides examples of specific industries where domestic firms are moving their production offshore. Domestic software engineers and radiologists, according to Roberts's anecdotal evidence, are being replaced by their foreign counterparts.[19] The appropriate trade barriers would prevent these jobs from going overseas, since the barriers reduce the potential profits of foreign investments in these industries. For Roberts, however, the story ends there. The additional effects of the trade barrier are ignored.

There are two main points here. One, a theory that concludes that trade policy should be used to promote capital formation needs to take into account all of the effects of the proposed protectionist measures. Simply pointing to jobs that could be saved by protection should not lead us to conclude that the protection will increase the level of employment or the amount of capital in the economy. The second point is that considering all of the effects of protectionist policies leads to the conclusion that our trade policies have a relatively small effect on net capital flows.

This does not mean that capital outflows will not occur. They may. But we should conclude that the lack of trade barriers is not the primary cause of the loss of capital. Investors are seeking profits, and the general condition of the economy and governmental policies have more to do with capital outflows than do trade barriers. It's outside the scope of this essay to fully address this issue, but it must be mentioned. If the United States had an institutional structure that led investors to believe that they could make profits here, then we would see an increasing capital stock. Such a structure would involve a sound monetary policy that did not create the bubbles that lead to recessions like the current crisis, as well as responsible fiscal policies that included balanced budgets and lower tax burdens on labor, capital investments, and profits; reduced regulatory burdens, including eliminating the minimum wage; and forgoing bailouts that keep inefficient competitors in business. Domestic firms and entrepreneurs would take advantage of these opportunities, leading to increased investment and capital formation.

Protectionist Theories and Real-world Policies

A primary problem with economic theories concluding that protectionist policies increase societal welfare is that the theories generally cannot be applied to real-world policy prescriptions. The economic models used in the theories tend to overlook the complexities of policy decisions.

The fact that resources are scarce truly complicates any analysis of protectionist policies. Given that firms are competing for resources, any policy that changes the allocation of resources generates costs and benefits not only in the industry that the policy targets but in other related industries as well. These costs and benefits are difficult to predict and impossible for policymakers to estimate. Policymakers cannot claim that their interventions improve the consumers' standard of living, since the overall costs and benefits of the policy effects are unknown. Haberler calls this complication "the most serious difficulty of a successful strategic trade policy."[20] Gene Grossman, in his criticism of strategic trade policy, sums up this issue, concluding that "strategic export promotion could in principle be beneficial, but I will suggest instead that it is equally possible that it would be economically harmful and that the policymaker has no systematic basis for identifying instances where the former is true rather than the latter."[21] Popular advocates of protection generally fail even to recognize this problem.

Trade policies create other costs and benefits that need to be taken into account. The possibility of retaliation is of particular importance here. Retaliation and potential trade wars are one of the risks of imposing trade barriers. This risk is a cost associated with protectionist policies that advocates of protection tend to ignore. Also, many of the protectionist proposals that purportedly benefit the United States reduce the welfare of other countries, which often are relatively poorer. Should the negative effect on other countries be taken into account when implementing these policies? This beggar-thy-neighbor component of restricting trade also contributes to the possibility of retaliation.

Given the above complexities, is it possible for any government to have the information necessary to choose a policy that the protectionists can claim to be beneficial overall? In order to calculate the costs and benefits of intervention, government officials would need to know the demand and cost structures of all of the industries affected, both directly and indirectly; the true costs of raising any revenue needed in order to implement the policy; the effects of any externalities in the markets that are impacted by the policies; and the strategic response from firms and foreign governments. And they would need to make these assessments in a dynamic, ever-changing world. This is not remotely possible.[22] Yeager and Tuerck put it thusly: "The protectionist slogan that free trade may be right in theory but wrong in practice becomes more sensible when the word 'protectionism' replaces 'free trade.' . . . Free trade is a meaningful, specific, discussable policy proposal; ideal protectionism is not."[23]

Opposing Protectionism

Protectionists continue to make the case that imposing appropriate restrictions on international trade can increase wages, create jobs, encourage capital investments, and lead to better economic performance. Generally these arguments tend to be comprised of nationalistic emotion and erroneous reasoning. The primary deficiency of protectionist arguments tends to be the failure to see the full impact that trade barriers have on an economy. While some of the arguments contain grains of truth, the policy prescriptions will tend to be enacted in a manner that does more harm than good. Any potential gains of protection would be small, while the potential damage from harmful polices would be tremendous. Opposing protectionism is one of the actions we must take to halt society's march down the road to serfdom.

Entrepreneurship and Government

Dane Stangler

The importance of entrepreneurship to economic growth is beyond dispute. Ideas and innovations generated and commercialized by entrepreneurs have been at the core of the remarkable economic performance of the West for the past two hundred years and the rapid growth of other nations, principally those of east Asia, over the past thirty years.

In the United States, for example, entrepreneurs have brought some of the most groundbreaking innovations to market. From the airplane and the pacemaker to the automobile and the personal computer, entrepreneurs help transform entire economies. Along the way, they also generate the majority of new jobs—since 1977, firms less than five years old have accounted for nearly all net job creation in the United States.[1] Most of these jobs are created by startups—brand-new companies whose job creation record has proven more durable through recessions and expansions than that of established companies. As my colleague Tim Kane has pointed out, "Startups aren't everything, they're the only thing."[2] Jobs created by new and young firms, moreover, are not mere flares: while 50 percent of new companies fail to survive to age five, the surviving firms manage to retain 80 percent of the employment created at the moment of startup.[3] That is, job creation in surviving young firms proceeds more rapidly than job destruction in firms that fail.

The benefits brought by entrepreneurs and new firms, by propelling economic growth, have dramatically enhanced social welfare over the past century. Gustavus Swift's refrigerated train car, developed in the 1870s, made it possible for the first time for large quantities of meat to travel over long distances without spoilage. As a result, general nutrition levels across the United States improved. Likewise, the rise of mail-order companies such as Sears, Roebuck and Co. and Montgomery Ward offered millions of people access to previously unavailable consumer goods, raising the standard of living.[4] More recently, medical innovations such as new pharmaceuticals have been the leading source of improvements in life expectancy and quality of life.[5]

While the United States often stands out as a highly entrepreneurial country, it is not alone in the benefits it derives from entrepreneurs. The newly liberated countries of Eastern Europe have generally enjoyed strong economic growth, driven in part by entrepreneurs and high-growth companies.[6] Israel's persistent success and survival is often attributed to its being, on the whole, an entrepreneurial country.[7] Throughout human history, in fact, entrepreneurs have helped generate recurrent periods of prosperity.[8]

In a more fundamental sense, then, entrepreneurship can be seen as innate to human civilization.[9] But can this fundamental feature of human nature and essential source of prosperity be suppressed or snuffed out? This is not an idle question: just as entrepreneurs have contributed to periodic golden ages and generally rising human prosperity, so too have governments frequently brought golden ages to an end and, in modern times, cut off parts of the world from economic prosperity. The most famous examples of the former are the flourishing and subsequent stagnation of ancient Rome, imperial China, and medieval Islamic civilization, while the most notorious instances of the latter are North Korea, Cuba, and Zimbabwe. Clearly, the resilience and innateness of entrepreneurship can be overcome.

One might think that the twenty-first-century United States is exempt from such history. After all, entrepreneurship has been remarkably steady in this country, from Carter to Obama, from stagflation to stimulus.[10] How could this primary source of social and economic welfare be threatened in a society where it is so deeply ingrained?

But at a time when government is metastasizing—when the United States seems headed back on the road to serfdom—entrepreneurship is most certainly at risk. The concerns most often expressed about government intervention in the economy involve the most extreme aspects: central planning, outright expropriation, and so on. It is, however, the less-noticed dimensions of state encroachment that should concern us. Only by understanding how and why startups play a critical role not just in the economy but in the larger society can we grasp the full scope of the statist threat to entrepreneurship—and the temptations we must avoid if innovation and prosperity are to continue to be American hallmarks.[11]

Innovation

In 1988, anthropologist Joseph Tainter published a landmark book, *The Collapse of Complex Societies*, in which he attempted to tease out the lessons from the collapse of human civilizations over the past several millennia.[12] After dismissing most of the conventional explanations for collapse (e.g., resource depletion, invasions, loss of spiritual verve) as candidates for any sort of general explanation, Tainter laid out four concepts that not only served as the underpinning for his theory but also subsumed all prior theories. These were: human societies are problem-solving organizations; sociopolitical systems require energy for their maintenance; increased complexity carries with it increased costs per capita; and investment in sociopolitical complexity as a problem-solving response often reaches a point of declining marginal returns.[13]

As any society matures and grows, it invests in complexity, which Tainter defined as "the interlinked growth of the several subsystems that

THE MARGINAL PRODUCT OF INCREASING COMPLEXITY

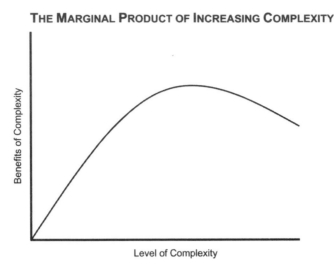

comprise a society."[14] This observation carries no subjective evaluation as to whether complexity is good or bad; it is merely a description of reality. A growing society becomes successful in large part because it enjoys increasing marginal returns to investments in complexity. For example, as ancient societies moved deeper into agricultural development, requiring irrigation systems, crop storage, and increasing administration and regulation, they reaped the benefits. Investments in productivity paid off in increasing returns, raising the overall standard of living.[15]

At some point, however, those investments in productivity and complexity will reach a point of stagnation and decline. A society will invest more and more in complexity, only to see a smaller and smaller payoff. Tainter wrote: "Growth in benefits relative to costs will [follow the above curve], which is to say that *at some point in the evolution of a society, continued investment in complexity as a problem-solving strategy yields a declining marginal return.*"[16] At that point, the level of complexity in society collapses. Such an outcome is not always catastrophic; the return to a lower level of complexity can "restore the marginal return on organizational investment to a more favorable level."[17]

In addition to collapse, Tainter also recognized the potential for a *renewal* of the productivity calculus, the complexity curve. Capital and technology can help spur a new round of economic development: "Among societies with the necessary capital, technological springboard, and economic and demographic incentives, obtaining a new energy subsidy . . . or *economic development,* can for a time either reverse a declining marginal curve, or at least provide the wealth to finance it."[18] (See chart below.)

It is now widely accepted that innovation explains the lion's share of productivity advancements and, thus, economic growth. The famous "Solow residual" in economics is meant to account for such innovation, but it is a giant black box. As the term "residual" implies, innovation— whether technological or organizational—is often treated as something that somehow just happens.

Innovation, however, does not magically visit itself upon the economy. It does not simply happen in the laboratories of universities and corporate research labs, or in garages, and it is not decreed into existence by government. Startups—new firms created for the purpose of commercializing or experimenting with innovations—are a primary source of renewal in the economy. Startups help explain why line B in the chart below turns upward while line A traces the conventional path sketched by Tainter.

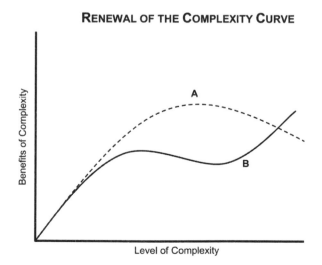

RENEWAL OF THE COMPLEXITY CURVE

Startups embody renewal. This is the real message of every single study that has looked at industry dynamics or economy-wide growth, from Clayton Christensen's to William Baumol's.[19] At some point, every subsystem of the economy—or the economy as a whole—reaches a point at which further investments in the prevailing model of complexity do not generate any more increasing returns. The curve turns positive again—or an entirely new curve appears—when new companies introduce new technologies and new ways of operating.

Consider transportation at the beginning of the twentieth century; consider retailing in the mid-twentieth century; consider mainframe computer hardware toward the end of the century. At each point, an entrepreneur, or cohort of entrepreneurs, came into existence and set the economy on a new trajectory of complexity and increasing returns. Henry Ford embodies the automobile revolution, but he was certainly not the only one: cadres of entrepreneurs completely reset transportation in this country. Sam Walton revolutionized retailing through his organizational innovations and helped drive enormous improvements in productivity. Bill Gates and Steve Jobs erased an entire future built around mainframe computers while a slew of other entrepreneurs renewed the complexity curves in industries such as disk storage (profiled by Christensen).

Or consider the great productivity slowdown of the American economy in the 1970s and 1980s. No amount of public- or private-sector investment appeared to do much to improve productivity until, seemingly all of a sudden in 1995, a number of factors came together in information technology to renew productivity across the entire economy. In the past few years, the rise of Web 2.0 companies has promised to renew the complexity curve of information technology that many thought was reaching its limit of increasing returns.

Startups are so essential to economic renewal not simply because they bring innovations into the market; just as important, they do so at lower levels of cost than existing firms can manage. In general, it doesn't cost that much money to start and begin to grow a company. The great majority of firms start off self-financed, with the founder(s) contributing capital and "sweat equity," and soliciting the proverbial trio of family, friends, and fools.[20] In his tour of startups across the United States, technology entrepreneur Robert Cringely has found that most of them are pioneering breakthrough technologies with low levels of financing.[21]

This perspective of startups and complexity also operates at the level of individual sectors and individual companies.[22] Large, established corporations have a difficult time innovating because they are locked into an inexorable curve on which further investments usually mean falling marginal returns. A new company frequently enjoys rapid growth in employment and revenues (and rising complexity), but at some point, every successful young firm becomes an older, established company and encounters tremendous difficulty trying to recapture its early days of increasing returns to investments in complexity.

This is why so many companies acquire younger, more innovative companies, or spin off organizations to commercialize new ideas, or create "skunk works"—operations quarantined from the rest of the company—intended to develop innovations. This is also why every year sees the publication of dozens of volumes devoted to enhancing innovation and productivity at large, established companies, and yet so few companies manage to find that spark of renewal. Apple is so celebrated because it is one of the rare firms that, after its initial period of entrepreneurial performance, managed to enjoy renewal twenty years later and find a new curve of growth.

The complexity curve applies, moreover, to nonprofit areas of the economy, which are not often thought to face issues of declining returns and renewal. Education, for example, appears to have reached a point, burdened by heavy regulation, intractable teachers unions, and poor performance, at which renewal is desperately needed. The proliferation of alternative models—from charter schools to KIPP programs—can be seen as various attempts to renew the complexity curve of education. Similar attempts at renewal occurred in higher education in the nineteenth century, when, under pressure from the demands of a rapidly industrializing economy and the appearance of new models in

Europe, a handful of entrepreneurs took it upon themselves to reshape American universities. Because of their efforts in creating new institutions and transforming old ones, the research university was born, and it contributed to economic growth in a way its predecessors could never have.[23] As a result, the complexity curve of higher education was reoriented on an upward path of increasing returns.

Of course, renewal is difficult to achieve because no one can foresee the point at which returns will begin to fall—or, more accurately, most people see it only when it is too late. Many large corporations attempt to restore a path of increasing returns only after returns have already begun falling, at which point the indicators within a firm are concrete and unavoidable. Across an economy or a sector, there will often be little internal impetus for renewal because of the heavy investments in increasing complexity and the chase for marginal returns. This is in part due to the very nature of innovation. No one called forth the automobile as the necessary next step in American economic evolution, particularly those already invested in the prevailing mode of transportation, railroads. Sam Walton did not respond to a national call for improvements in retailing productivity. Each innovation becomes invested along its own complexity curve and cannot break out of it. As economist Joseph Schumpeter put it: "Add as many mail-coaches as you please, you will never get a railroad by so doing."[24] The need for renewal frequently goes unnoticed—but once a new firm has entered the scene and pushed an innovation, the falling returns to complexity become obvious in retrospect.

Startups are thus an essential—and generally low-cost—driver in the economy. Yet most current proposals to reinvigorate innovation and entrepreneurship in the United States revolve around spending more money—especially federal dollars for research or for small business lending, but venture capital as well. As laudable as these efforts are, they run into diminishing returns because they fail to take account of how startups operate at their best and how innovation occurs.[25]

What's more, state intervention in the economy brings increased risks. It is quite conceivable that political and governmental involvement could reach a point that startups either do not start, experience a diminished power of renewal, or end up having perverse economic effects. That is, the state could overwhelm the power of startups and innovations to renew economic productivity.

Government Interference

There are four general routes by which the state might encroach on entrepreneurship and the private sector in general.[26]

The first, perhaps most obviously, involves a substantial degree of coercive economic control or intrusion, exemplified today by countries such as Venezuela and Zimbabwe.[27] The best contemporary indicator of a government's relationship to a country's private sector is the World Bank's *Doing Business* rankings, a relatively recent program that has helped to push countries to lower barriers for business formation. A simple comparison of a country's overall *Doing Business* ranking and any other indicator of economic health, such as per-capita income or corruption, illustrates a straightforward correlation: the harder it is to do business in a country, the worse off its economy and people. Here, too, we see the beneficial role the state might play in enhancing economic growth. Categories measured by the World Bank such as registering property, getting credit, protecting investors, and trading across borders make it clear that, while the problem in some countries is too much government, in others it is *not enough* government.

It's not clear, by the way, whether China should be included in this first general category. The popular image of China is of an overreaching national government that has nonetheless conjured up a historically unprecedented economic performance—hence the periodic calls for the United States to mimic the Chinese state's supposedly benign and enlightened economic policy. Yet recent scholarship has called into question the extent to which the Chinese government has really contributed to economic growth other than the conventional means of simply letting people go about their business. China, that is, might be enjoying extraordinary economic growth in spite, not because, of the state.[28]

In any case, it seems highly unlikely that the United States is in danger of going down this first path. The second route of state encroachment on the private sector is what we might call "soft planning," in which the national government takes an active role in guiding the economy. The United States has actually come reasonably close to soft planning on two occasions, in the 1930s and 1970s. Franklin Roosevelt's imperious actions, such as the creation of the National Recovery Administration, and his capriciousness regarding the gold standard are well known.[29] Perhaps less well known is that in the 1970s, there was serious discussion in the United States, under President Gerald Ford, of establishing national planning commissions. Inflation, sluggish growth, and rising foreign competition brought the country close to expanding the role of the state in the economy.

The third way in which the state can intrude upon entrepreneurship is through distorted incentives: either with misguided regulations or unintended consequences, the government could end up creating the wrong incentives for entrepreneurs. Will Baumol discussed such institutional incentives in a famous article in which he argued, "How the entrepreneur acts at a given time and place depends heavily on the rules of the game—the reward structure in the economy—that happen to prevail."[30] Problems arise when these rules of the game encourage "unproductive" entrepreneurial behavior. The principal example of such unproductive behavior is rent seeking, which occurs when companies pursue a bigger slice of economic activity by means other than market competition[31]—that is, when they graduate to seeking favors from Washington rather than seeking a competitive edge by means of innovation.[32] A company's entreaties to government for protective action often indicate a returns curve that has already turned negative.

The fourth and final general way by which the state encroaches on entrepreneurship is the least visible of all. Frequently it is mislabeled as simply the growth of big government, but it is much broader than that.[33] The growing power, scope, size, and impact of government represent increases in not only government heft but also complexity; indeed, a rise in government investments often occurs as we approach the point when declining marginal returns set in—or even after we have already passed that point. By definition, then, the rate of return on such government investments (the "public" or "social" rate of return, as it is often described) can't help but decline. This represents a potential threat to entrepreneurship because it could overburden entrepreneurs, crowd out entrepreneurs, distort incentives for entrepreneurs, and foster a climate of legal and regulatory uncertainty, the enemy of productive entrepreneurs

The biggest concern today involves the sheer scale of stimulus, both fiscal and monetary, that the U.S. federal government has poured into the economy since 2008. The point of this massive stimulus has been to prevent a descent into depression and to try to ignite a strong economic recovery. Unfortunately, the return on government investments has fallen precipitously. A JPMorgan analysis of government data in July 2010 indicated that, once you take account of the cost of trying to shake off the recession, the recovery was extraordinarily disappointing and weak.[34] By the middle of 2010, the increase in the ratio of federal debt to gross domestic product (GDP) stood at 18 percent, and was set to climb another several percentage points by the end of the year. This dwarfed any previous increase in federal money to fight recession; the previous high had been during the 1981–82 recession, when the debt-to-GDP ratio rose by 6 percent.

Has this unprecedented infusion of government money paid off commensurately? No. Consider such closely watched economic indicators as the surveys in manufacturing and services produced by the Institute for Supply Management (ISM). By the summer of 2010, the results of these surveys did indicate some recovery, but during six prior recessions since 1950, the ISM index recovered by higher levels—and with little to no increase in debt-to-GDP ratio.[35] Overall economic growth, too, has lagged well behind that of prior recoveries. Government stimulus in this recession has gotten precious little bang for the buck, at least by historical comparison.

Meanwhile, government regulation is escalating costs with no corresponding returns. The Dodd-Frank financial reform bill passed by Congress in July 2010 is only the most recent example of this—it is more than ten times as long as the Glass-Steagall Act of 1933, the seminal set of banking laws that the current legislation was meant to resurrect. The financial system is, obviously, far more complex today than in the 1930s, but the mounting regulations do not simply reflect a corresponding increase in complexity. Government adds more and more regulations and rarely pares back. Regulation feeds regulation.

The government's growing role in the economy can be seen from the fact that the national seat of political power is quickly becoming a seat of economic and geographic power. Much has been made in newspaper headlines of the transfer of national economic power from New York City (Wall Street) to Washington, D.C., but the undercurrents run much deeper. In the Milken Institute's 2009 report *Best Performing Cities*, the Washington metropolitan area ranked twenty-fifth out of the two hundred largest metro areas—an impressive gain of sixteen spots over its 2008 ranking of forty-first. On several indicators—job growth, salary growth, high-tech "location quotient"—Washington scored above the national average.[36] Additionally, when *Inc.* magazine published its 2009 list of the fastest-growing private companies in the United States, the Washington area had the most companies of any metro area in the entire country. More than half of those in the Washington area were in the Government Services sector. While some of this is a function of government outsourcing to private companies, much of it represents a perverse state of affairs: entrepreneurial behavior dependent on the increasing scope and geographic concentration of government.[37] (This concerns not only the federal government; the same phenomenon may play itself out at the state level. My own research on American metropolitan areas has noticed rising economic performance of some state capitals.)

On top of all this, of course, is the growing power of the federal government, particularly the executive branch. Constitutional law scholar Jack Balkin has observed that President Obama entered office as perhaps the most powerful president in history.[38] Balkin was referring

104

specifically to the inheritance of President George W. Bush's aggrandized national security power, but the economic and financial events since 2008 have conferred upon the executive an increasing degree of economic power. The combination of these is, historically speaking, quite startling. As anachronistic as it may sound today, there is a very intimate relationship built into our Constitution between the distribution of political power in government and the operation of the economy. James Madison, under the influence of David Hume, perceived an indelible link between economic and political freedom: commerce provided the underpinning for political freedom while the competition of economic "factions" would help guarantee it.[39]

The growing co-location of political and economic power should be disquieting; it conveys an impression of courtiers rather than entrepreneurs, as Lewis Lapham pointed out long ago.[40] One cannot visit the House and Senate office buildings in Washington without having an uneasy sense of what Louis XIV's court at Versailles must have felt like—courtiers seeking favor, the powerful doling out graces, some of the brightest young minds in the country lured by the specter of power.

A National Innovation Strategy?

The Great Recession has spooked a great many people in its apparent realignment of geopolitical power, with China, India, and Brazil seen to be rising at the expense of the United States. These worries have led to a push for some type of national innovation or competitiveness strategy, to be led by the federal government.

Based on what we know of the complexity curve, the essential role that startups play, and the difficulty government has in avoiding a fall in marginal returns, we should greet such plans with a skeptical eye. In a derivative of Goodhart's Law, we may have more to fear from the proposals to "save" the U.S. economy than from the purported threats they identify. Goodhart's Law posits that, once policymakers choose to target a certain behavior or activity for promotion, the target tends to diminish in malleability and thus value. In this case, explicit attempts to use government to promote entrepreneurship may have the perverse effect of undermining entrepreneurship.

The push for a national competitiveness strategy is not necessarily a result of the recession—calls began to come forth a few years ago—but it has gained steam since 2008. The best-known report in this vein is "Rising Above the Gathering Storm," released in 2007 by the National Academies' Committee on Prospering in the Global Economy of the Twenty-first Century.[41] The report contains an exhaustive amount of data and raises serious concerns about the economic future of the United States. That same year, the Alliance for Science and Technology Research in America (ASTRA) released a similar report, and, two years earlier, the Council on Competitiveness published "Innovate America."[42] Also in 2007, management consultant John Kao published a book, *Innovation Nation*.[43] All of these publications call for some form of government action, typically in the form of "national" guidance on investment and technology and innovation. They justify this tilt by suggesting that we are in the early stages of a transformation in human affairs, a historical inflection point that requires large-scale government action. Only government, these authors argue, can take a long-term view and set the country on the right course, pushing and pulling it into the as-yet-unimagined future of political economy.

For example, "Rising Above the Gathering Storm" reports that current trends "indicate that the United States may not fare as well in the future without government intervention."[44] The Council on Competitiveness recommends that the federal government "create at least ten innovation Hot Spots" around the country.[45] Nearly every one of the fourteen items on ASTRA's "action agenda" contains the phrase "the Federal government should." This culminates in the final item, calling for "a Federal innovation policy and investment agenda commensurate with new economic realities and 21st century competitiveness challenges."[46] Kao, in his book, proposes a National Innovation Council: "This would be a 'guiding coalition,' setting direction and overseeing the innovation transformation process for our country. . . . As the steward of the national innovation vision, the council would select and apply a well-chosen set of metrics to assess the country's progress."[47]

The steady lament over the prevalence of short-term thinking at the expense of long-term thinking should strike the reader as somewhat misplaced; it is basically a complaint about human nature. It appears that some of these proposals wish for the government to assume super- (or supra-) human powers.

But the fundamental shortcoming of the continuing calls for a national innovation strategy (understandably given great urgency in the context of recession) is that, by focusing almost exclusively on established institutions, they contradict the very essence of innovation and entrepreneurship. Who will give out the increased federal R&D funding? The same agencies as before. Who will receive the funding? The same universities and institutes as before. Whom will the government consult as it designs a national innovation "architecture"? Established firms and organizations. As economist Carl J. Schramm has argued, "It is those ideas on the margins, challenging the status quo, that lift the trajectory of an economy's performance."[48] Greater government involvement—whether through more research funding, more money for education, stronger laws, new or different regulations—will also call into play colliding interests and power politics. There can be no dispassionate economic policy making for the simple reason that policy always involves politics.

By aggrandizing existing institutional structures in the American economy, many of the competitiveness recommendations could actually slow America's capacity to innovate faster. Harold Evans, in his book *They Made America*, relates the story of gas turbines that made jet propulsion possible. Frank Whittle invented the jet engine in England in 1930, but production was delayed by the "inertia of the British Air Ministry." The United States eventually gained possession of the turbine design and within short order became the world leader in jet engines and thus commercial aviation. Evans ascribes this to "American openness and enthusiasm for innovation," as compared to the "inertia" and "skepticism" of the British establishment.[49]

This is a common historical pattern on scales large and small. In the early twentieth century, Los Angeles became the international epicenter of film in part because established entertainment organizations in New York sought to control and limit the emerging film industry, driving away studios and individuals, including William Fox and Carl Laemmle (creator of Universal Studios). In the mid-twentieth century, the Radio Corporation of America (RCA) saw the electronic future in terms of AM radio, while Western Electric saw it in terms of vacuum tubes. These assumptions were completely reasonable at the time given the commercial dominance (and certainty) of AM radio and the uncertainty surrounding transistors. Western Electric licensed the patent to transistor radios to the Japanese company Sony, at the time a symbol of almost comically inferior products.

This messy reality of innovation has no place in the neat strategies set forth by the champions of national competitiveness. Solace and justification are found in comparisons to the Manhattan Project, the Marshall Plan, and the space race in the 1960s. Such analogies, however, are wholly inapposite. Those were discrete projects with identifiable objectives that could be managed: build the atomic bomb, help Europe rebuild, land a man on the moon. Setting the U.S. economy on a new course of innovation and growth cannot be done this way. How much growth is optimal? What if it produces inequality? Is there a defined endpoint? A major deficiency with any government program so large is the difficulty of ending it. Innovation is not a discrete project; economic growth does not have a defined endpoint.

This was the distinction Joseph Schumpeter drew between what he called the "adaptive response" and the "creative response."[50] The New York entertainment establishment, RCA, Western Electric, and the British Air Ministry embodied the adaptive response—action that is relatively predictable and done within the framework of "existing practice."[51] This can obviously be a mark of progress, and can be completely reasonable, but we rarely derive leaps of innovation from the adaptive response.

It is the creative response, "something that is outside of the range of existing practice,"[52] that really pushes and pulls economic and social progress. The entrepreneurs who turned the jet turbine into something commercially successful; the men who created a new industry and a new metropolis around movies; the innovators who saw the enormous potential of transistors and FM radios—these are examples of the creative response: "Creative response changes social and economic situations for good, or, to put it differently, it creates situations from which there is no bridge to those situations that might have emerged in its absence."[53] In other words, the creative response—embodied in entrepreneurs—resets the complexity curve of the economy, generating a renewed boost of productivity growth.

Clearly, those who promote a national competitiveness agenda see the American economic future as dependent on creativity. This is obvious in their exhortations for more innovation and for education geared toward an "innovation-based economy." But by seeking to design an "architecture" for innovation and creativity, they miss the fundamental point. As Schumpeter expressed it: "From the standpoint of the observer who is in full possession of all relevant facts, [the creative response] can always be understood *ex post*; but it can practically never be understood *ex ante*; that is to say, it cannot be predicted by applying the ordinary rules of inference from the pre-existing facts."[54]

Startups represent such important sources of renewal because they can engage more readily, and more cheaply, in experimentation. There is no Platonic future out there that can be foreseen or is merely waiting to be discovered, whether by government or any other institution. It can only be created bit by bit, carved out of the unknown. This is what entrepreneurs do.[55]

Unintended Consequences

None of this is to say that the state should play *no* role in supporting entrepreneurship and assisting new companies. One of the cornerstones of entrepreneurship, after all, is the right to property, a right that would lose much of its meaning in the absence of state action. Likewise, the government is important for entrepreneurship in areas such as intellectual property—many new companies, especially in technology-related fields, depend on patents or licenses—as well as contract enforcement and antitrust law. Large, established companies frequently seek protection from new competitors, but government can help keep barriers to entry low.

Since the onset of this most recent recession in late 2007, the federal government has taken steps to try to promote firm formation, most notably by expanding loan guarantees and exhorting banks to begin lending again. The government has also tried to thaw credit markets to help companies.

The key question, then, often is not between more or less government; rather, it concerns the type or orientation of government action. Whenever the government intervenes in the economy, we must ask what that means for the operation of markets and also for the ability of new firms to come into existence and compete. It is not the most obvious or extreme manifestations of government intervention that should worry us, but rather the less visible—and thus potentially more insidious—dimensions of state encroachment. The rising complexity of government—whether gauged as size, scope, geographic concentration, or sheer power—inevitably approaches a point of diminishing returns and threatens entrepreneurship.

Ironically, the most recent manifestation of this is the growing clamor for a national industrial policy to *promote* entrepreneurship and innovation. The fact that entrepreneurship is on the national public policy radar is an unqualifiedly positive step. But if we're not careful, we could end up suppressing the very thing we want to encourage.

The Cultural Costs of Corporatism: How Government-Business Collusion Denigrates the Entrepreneur and Rewards the Sycophant

Timothy P. Carney

One of the many vicious customs of our media is to fit every story into an evenly matched, two-sided debate, set in a familiar template.

Regarding government intervention, the standard frame is this: On one side are the "public interest" groups fighting to protect the consumer, or worker, or environment by calling on the government to enact new regulations. On the other side is industry, fighting to be left alone.

But this simplistic template rarely reflects the truth. The business lobby is far from uniform, and it is even farther from advocating laissez-faire. Often, regulation debates pit one big business against another—or one industry versus another. On other occasions, it's less evenly matched: on the pro-regulation side are big business, big labor, and the "public interest" groups; on the anti-regulation side is small business. You can guess who wins.

Despite the widespread assumption that a free market is the ideal economy for big business, and that regulation checks the power of big business, more often the opposite is true. Regulation, by adding to the cost of doing business, disproportionately hurts smaller business and acts as a barrier to entry, keeping out new competitors. Likewise, government subsidies can be far more valuable, or at least more reliable, than income from consumers, for which businesses must continually fight with competitors. The dynamics of the lobbying game are crucial here. Bigger companies enjoy a greater advantage in Washington than they do in the market. Not only can bigger companies hire the better lobbyists—former lawmakers or top administration aides—and hand out more in campaign contributions, but they also *matter* more to lawmakers. The more workers you employ and the more taxes you pay, the more lawmakers care about your well-being, desires, and wishes.

In short, big business has a strong motivation to support big government: profit. To use the terminology of economist Joseph Schumpeter, big government enables *political* entrepreneurs—those who influence government to grant subsidies or harm competitors through regulation—to succeed over *market* entrepreneurs.

Thus we frequently see big business–big government collusion, which goes by many names: rent-seeking, corporatism, corporate socialism, corporate welfare, regulatory robbery, and subsidy-suckling, to name a few. Indeed, throughout our country's history, some of the greatest enemies of the free market have come from the big-business lobby.

When Theodore Roosevelt proposed federal inspection of meat and meatpacking, the biggest meatpackers applauded.[1] During FDR's New Deal, big business almost universally supported the National Recovery Act, which was a legalized system of cartels.[2] Richard Nixon's firmest backers for his 1971 wage and price controls were from big business, led by the National Association of Manufacturers.[3] Bill Clinton's new regulations on genetically modified foods, requiring expansive testing before such foods could be sold, had an ally in Monsanto, the world leader in such food.[4]

In the twenty-first century, it seems, such corporate-government collusion has accelerated. Consider the two biggest big-government programs of George W. Bush (besides his wars): creating a prescription drug subsidy under Medicare, and ramming through Congress the Troubled Asset Relief Program (TARP), which bailed out Wall Street and Detroit. The Medicare drug bill was the creature of drug companies, which got to pocket the subsidies, and insurers, which were legislated in as middlemen. The TARP bailouts were the pinnacle of corporate welfare—government transferring wealth from taxpayers to the largest corporations in America.

While Barack Obama pledged to drive lobbyists out of Washington and has portrayed himself as the scourge of special interests, corporatism has flourished under the Obama administration. This is evident in Obama's signature achievement, his overhaul of the health-care system—a package of mandates, regulations, taxes, and subsidies. Supporting the White House all along was the drug industry, which spent more on lobbying (by a huge margin) in 2009 than any other industry.[5] Leading the drugmakers' charge was the Pharmaceutical Researchers and Manufacturers of America (PhRMA),[6] the largest single-industry lobby group in the country.[7]

The climate-change debate is typically portrayed as a battle between industry and environmentalists, with the latter leading the charge for government constraints on greenhouse-gas emissions, and the former desperately lobbying to be left alone. In fact, the only climate proposals to see the light of legislative day were crafted by industry— energy companies seeking subsidies, dealers in dubious greenhouse-gas "offsets," agrichemical companies jockeying for handouts, and others of the same stripe. Supporters included BP, General Electric, Duke Energy, and Nike.[8]

Clearly, a rapidly growing government is insinuating itself in practically every corner of the market and of the broader culture. What is less obvious is that the road to serfdom is not being paved by government alone; in many cases the business community supports and enables the growth of government power. The reason is that big government brings ample benefits to big business. Unfortunately, it exacts many costs from the rest of society.

The Roots of Corporatism

Economists explain that government intervention reduces society's wealth by reallocating it away from where the money will be most useful (where consumer demand is high or where investors see profits) to politically favored corners of the economy. This insight points us toward the cultural ramifications of growing corporatism.

Favoring big business over small business promotes uniformity over diversity and localism. It can weaken towns, cities, neighborhoods, and even families. It can destroy downtowns and replace them with strip malls. This is the opposite of the standard account, which blames Wal-Mart for crushing Mom and Pop. Wal-Mart dominates through government as much as through capitalism. An unbridled free market isn't killing Mom and Pop; an untethered state is. Big-government efforts at building infrastructure and subsidizing all forms of travel and shipping undermine a local economy and prop up a global economy. Localism's enemy is not capitalism but corporatism.

Beyond harming communities, business-government collusion denigrates the entrepreneur and elevates the lobbyist. Whenever government gains greater control over the economy, economic actors will depend more on government. Activist government makes political connections more valuable. This drives up the value of a lobbyist.

And the lobbyist's gain has costs. Every new subsidy takes power away from consumers, because business goes where the money is. With Uncle Sam handing out cash, producers and investors become more interested in what the government wants than in what regular people want. Every mandate or regulation similarly disenfranchises consumers, but it also hurts entrepreneurs. Regulations, taxes, and mandates narrow the playing field, and by doing so, they narrow the opportunities for innovation. Most importantly, government intervention hurts anyone who is not politically connected. If you haven't invested time and money befriending politicians and bureaucrats, you're at a disadvantage. If you don't have a lobbyist, you're behind the eight ball.

As a result, entrepreneurs either (a) spend more time and resources greasing the political skids and thus less time and resources developing a better product, or (b) go out of business because they can't compete with the politically connected. The more regulated and subsidized an economy is, the less sense it makes to work for yourself, and the more sense it makes to work for a well-established business.

Killing the Small Guys

It's easy to find stories of government regulation of an industry helping the biggest businesses by killing the smallest ones—thus hurting consumers, promoting uniformity, killing local economies, and stifling entrepreneurship.

When President Obama signed a bill in 2009 heightening federal regulation of tobacco, he held a Rose Garden ceremony at which he claimed that the bill had passed "despite decades of lobbying and advertising by the tobacco industry."[9] But Philip Morris, the country's largest tobacco company, had supported the bill for a decade—during which period it spent more on lobbying than every other tobacco company combined.[10]

The bill was officially named the Family Smoking Prevention and Tobacco Control Act (FSPTCA), suggesting that the regulation was intended to protect consumers, and especially children. But smaller cigarette companies called the bill the "Marlboro Monopoly Act," referring to Philip Morris's leading brand, which sells more cigarettes a year than every brand sold by the number-two cigarette company, R. J. Reynolds. In fact, Philip Morris typically sells half the cigarettes bought in America every year.[11]

The new tobacco legislation enacted strict regulations on manufacturing, testing, and disclosure. Such regulations impose new overhead costs. Why would Philip Morris support that? Because its massive economies of scale make it easier for the company to handle the added costs. The bill also restricted advertising and marketing, which helps lock out new companies and lock in place Philip Morris's market share.

The tobacco giant made sure it had a seat at the table as the Food and Drug Administration (FDA) began implementing the regulations. Altria, Philip Morris's parent company, hired lawyer/lobbyist Coleen Klasmeier to work with the FDA on the proposed rules. Klasmeier had worked at the FDA until 2005, when she joined the lobbying firm Sidley Austin as head of its FDA regulatory practice. She contributed the maximum legal contribution to Obama's 2008 campaign.[12]

Smaller tobacco companies weren't so well connected or so positive about the new law in their comments to the FDA. Smokin Joes, a cigarette maker owned by a Native American tribe, expressed its concerns about the proposed ban on free samples, asking the FDA whether "manufacturers cannot give free samples of their cigarettes to wholesalers so the wholesalers can determine if it is a brand they are interested in carrying?"[13] Smokin Joes, unlike Philip Morris, needed to hustle for distribution. Constraining publicity would cement Philip Morris's market share. But Smokin Joes didn't have a prominent law firm or lobbyist firm working on regulations. Company attorney Karen Delaney submitted these queries.

Philip Morris, realizing that it couldn't avoid government, decided to partner with it. When forced to, the company abandoned market entrepreneurship for political entrepreneurship—and it worked.

Beaten into Submission

Although many businesses have learned the importance of lobbying government, sometimes it takes coaxing by politicians to bring big business to Washington. For all the talk from politicians about the corrupting influence of lobbyists, Washington officials make it very clear to business: lobby or else.

Apple, the successful maker of the Macintosh, iPod, and iPhone, got the treatment in 2010. *Politico*, something of a trade journal for the industry of politics and government, reported, "While Apple's success has earned rock-star status in Silicon Valley, its low-wattage approach in Washington is becoming more glaring to policymakers."[14]

Translated: politicians were getting upset that a successful company wasn't lobbying very much or giving very much to politicians.

The article drew out the details: "It is one of the few major technology companies not to have a political action committee. . . . Compared with other tech giants, Apple's lobbying expenditures are small. In 2009, Apple spent only $1.5 million to lobby the federal government, less than Amazon, Yahoo and IBM."

One D.C. insider offered Apple some unsolicited advice. *Politico* quoted Jonathan Zuck, president of the Association for Competitive Technology, as saying: "They've been very focused on their own innovation, and they don't have a history of coming to town to get their competitors regulated. But they're expanding into so many areas that they're going to find themselves in other companies' cross hairs, so they probably should be ready to play defense."

Apple, of course, was not the first company politicians threatened into lobbying more. The most famous case might have been Microsoft in the late 1990s.

Microsoft's smaller competitors, led by Sun Microsystems and Oracle, financed the campaigns of Republican and Democratic state attorneys general who pursued an antitrust case against Microsoft. In 1998 Senate Judiciary Committee chairman Orrin Hatch called a hearing, ostensibly to discuss the competitiveness of the software industry, but really to give senators a televised opportunity to beat up Microsoft founder Bill Gates. Many people on Capitol Hill were outraged by Microsoft's refusal to grovel in Washington. *BusinessWeek* captured that ire with this quote from a March 1998 article: "'The industry had an attitude that government should do what it needs to do, but leave us alone,' complains one Hill technology staffer. 'Their hands-off approach to Washington will come back to haunt them.'"[15]

At the hearing, Gates was not appropriately deferential. At one point, he spoke about how the United States would continue to be the technological leader only "if innovation is not restricted by government." That line received a firm rebuke from fellow tech mogul Regis McKenna, who had already acclimated to Washington, and would become a leading Democratic donor: "Bill Gates perfectly represents the techno-elitist view. He came out and said the government was full of B.S."[16]

In official Washington, a belief in one's product—and a desire to be left alone to improve the product and sell it to willing consumers— is arrogant and elitist. The *BusinessWeek* article summed up the matter: "Veterans of the Beltway predict that even the most arrogant and libertarian software execs will quickly learn to play the Washington game. They can't afford not to, considering the multitude of issues on the horizon."

Even Gates admitted that he would start playing the Washington game, writing, "It's been a year since the last time I was in D.C. I think I'm going to be making the trip a lot more frequently from now on." A decade later, Microsoft was playing the game expertly. By 2010, the company was averaging more than $8 million per year in lobbying, had seventeen lobbyists working in-house, and had hired about twenty-five outside lobbying firms. Lobbying issues included health care, financial regulation, cyber security, the stimulus bill, immigration, education, taxes, trade, climate change, and dozens more.[17]

Bill Gates's desire that innovation not be "restricted by government"? That evaporated. By 2006, Microsoft had become a leading advocate for "net neutrality" regulations to prevent telecom networks from changing their business models for carrying digital data.[18] In short, Microsoft went native.

Any company branded as a capitalist titan—or free-market evangelist—is likely to feel the pinch just as Apple and Microsoft did.

Wal-Mart underwent this process—from freewheeling capitalist to rent-seeking lobbyist—in the first decade of the twentieth-first century. Vilified as the epitome of greed, and attacked for the wages and benefits the company paid, Wal-Mart took a beating for years. While happy to receive handouts and subsidies from county and city politicians, the company wasn't sticking its hands too deep into Washington's pockets.

Then, in October 2005, new CEO Lee Scott changed that. "While it is unusual for us to take a public position on a public policy issue of this kind," he said that month, "we simply believe it is time for Congress to take a responsible look at the minimum wage and other legislation that may help working families."[19] Scott declared the $5.15 minimum wage "out of date with the times." He supported a bill to increase the minimum wage to $7.25 an hour—less than Wal-Mart paid its workers, but more than Mom and Pop paid their part-time help.

A year later, Wal-Mart hired longtime Democratic operative and lobbyist Leslie Dach as a strategist.[20] Around the same time, Wal-Mart announced support for a policy that would be central to Barack Obama's health-care overhaul: a federal mandate that employers provide health insurance for their workers. Again, Wal-Mart could afford this overhead more than smaller employers could.

Big business learned that if you stopped fighting big government, you could profit from it by killing your smaller competitors.

Lawmakers Need Lobbyists

Lawmakers benefit from a surge in lobbyists. It means more power, more fundraisers, and more opportunities to be feted.

The travel industry provides one telling story. In 2005 Congressman Bill Delahunt, who represents Cape Cod, addressed the Washington Summit of the Travel Business Roundtable, an organization made up of hotels, airlines, cruise lines, amusement parks, and other travel-related companies. *Fed News* reported of the speech, "The Congressman called on the industry to wage a more aggressive, bipartisan campaign."[21] In other words, Delahunt told his audience to lobby more.

The Travel Business Roundtable obliged with enthusiasm, registering as a lobbying organization in 2006. It soon renamed itself the Discover America Partnership and hired a K Street lobbyist—Steven Schwadron, Delahunt's longtime chief of staff.

The next year, Delahunt introduced HR 2935, the Travel Promotion Act, which would put the U.S. government in the business of encouraging foreigners to visit the United States.

Hedge funds had a more interesting ride into Washington. Just after Democrats took control of Congress in 2007, Senator Chuck Schumer of New York (also head of the Democratic Senatorial Campaign Committee, and thus the chief fundraiser for Senate Democrats) called leading hedge-fund managers to a dinner. The *New York Times* reported that Schumer "had some simple advice for the billionaires in his midst: If you want Washington to work with you, you had better work better with one another."[22]

Sure enough, they did. Hedge funds revved up their previously dormant lobbying and fundraising arms. The Managed Funds Association, the industry's leading lobbyist, hired Richard Baker away from Congress to be its CEO.

Hedge-fund lobbying jumped from $870,000 in 2006 to $6.7 million in 2007. The industry's campaign contributions grew from $5.4 million in the 2006 election to $18 million in the 2008 election.[23]

In 2007 Schumer's banking staffer, Carmencita Whonder, left Capitol Hill for K Street, becoming a lobbyist at the firm Brownstein, Hyatt, Farber, Schrek. Within weeks of her joining, the firm signed up seven new hedge-fund and private-equity clients. By the time the financial-regulation bill came up, the Managed Funds Association also had Whonder as a lobbyist.

Whonder, meanwhile, became a top volunteer fundraiser for Schumer, bundling hedge-fund money and delivering it to her former boss, who had spurred the industry's lobbying boom.

Hedge funds, previously happy to game the market, now were gaming government.

Government Electric

The best case study in political entrepreneurship may be General Electric. CEO Jeffrey Immelt pretty clearly laid out his approach in a letter to stockholders in the depths of the 2008–9 recession, and just days after the inauguration of Barack Obama, who promised to "remake America."

Immelt wrote:

The global economy, and capitalism, will be "reset" in several ways. The interaction between government and business will change forever. In a reset economy, the government will be a regulator; and also an industry policy champion, a financier, and a key partner. . . . Successful companies won't just "hunker down"; they will seek out the new opportunities in a reset world.

Later in the letter, Immelt stated more directly that GE saw the government as its best potential customer:

GE's broad technical portfolio positions us as a natural partner as the role of government increases in the current crisis. Over the past decade, we have positioned GE to lead in the "big themes." These include emerging market growth, clean energy, and sustainable healthcare. . . .

Governments will invest to stimulate their economies, solve societal problems, and create jobs. GE's broad portfolio and expertise position us as a natural partner. Tackling important problems together will require teamwork and respect between business, government, and society. We know how to do this and intend to play an important part in solving these essential challenges.

The message was clear: the government is getting bigger, and so we're hopping on the subsidy bandwagon.

It's important here to dispel two myths about how business and government relate, and what role lobbyists play. The two myths are mirror images of each other.

First, the story told by politicians and most in the media: *Business, desperate to block important regulations or win special favors, hires lobbyists. These lobbyists corrupt the legislative process with special-interest pleading.*

The opposite story isn't aired in the mainstream media much, but it's one you'll encounter if you run in Republican, free-market, or conservative circles: *Government sets up perverse incentives, and politicians shake down business. Businesses have no choice but to march to the tune the politicians are playing.*

Both stories are untrue, but both capture some of the actual dynamic. Big business and big government feed off of each other. When government gets bigger, companies reposition themselves to profit more from government. Also, big companies are more able to craft policies to fit their businesses. In other words, neither big business nor big government is bossing the other around—they're both playing off of each other.

General Electric, then, is doing two things that it is uniquely experienced in doing: adapting its business to whatever the government favors and shaping government policy so that it benefits GE.

GE's flexibility is famous. The company deals in—or has dealt in—a startling array of businesses: medical devices, finances, jet engines, light bulbs, refrigerators, locomotives, electronics. If some business starts to look less promising, it's dropped. If another looks more promising, it's acquired. Market conditions are often the impetus for change. But increasingly, it's government policy that seems to be steering GE.

President Obama in early 2009 authorized subsidies for embryo-destroying stem-cell research, and soon GE partnered with Geron, a leading stem-cell company.[24] As policies advanced to restrict greenhouse-gas emissions and begin a credit-trading scheme, GE launched a joint venture dealing in carbon credits.[25] These were new businesses to GE, and ones the company would never have undertaken without the prospect of government intervention creating value in them.

Lobbying is also a GE strongpoint. From 1998 through 2009—the entire period for which lobbying expenses have been reported—GE spent more on lobbying the federal government than any other company: $204.7 million. That's 33 percent more than the second-place company, AT&T.[26] In early 2010 the company retained thirty-four different K Street lobby firms, with lobbyists including three former senators plus the wife of another, a former House majority leader, and prominent former staffers from Capitol Hill and the Bush and Clinton administrations.[27]

Providing air support for this influence effort is a barrage of campaign contributions to powerful politicians. The General Electric Political Action Committee (GEPAC) spent $2.4 million in each of the 2006 and 2008 election cycles.[28]

GE's executives made very clear that political giving was about getting favorable legislation. In a 2009 letter soliciting PAC contributions from other GE executives, vice chairman John Rice wrote, "The intersection between GE's interests and government action is clearer than ever." For instance, he wrote, "On climate change, we were able to work closely with key authors of the Waxman-Markey climate and energy bill, recently passed by the House of Representatives. If this bill is enacted into law it would benefit many GE businesses."

But what purpose does a corporate PAC serve? Once again, there are two competing narratives, and once again, neither is really true. The media tend to tell a sensationalist story: that PAC contributions are bribes—that lawmakers effectively are auctioning off their vote to whatever company or industry gives the most. But PAC giving is disclosed publicly, which would make it a poor avenue for bribery.

Politicians and companies, meanwhile, give a perfectly innocent account: PACs are there to help elect politicians who already share the company's views. GE's Rice put this forward in his fundraising memo to colleagues, saying that the PAC would "make sure that candidates who share GE's values and goals get elected to office."

The facts belie this explanation, too. Just using GE as an example, the company's PAC gave $30,000 each (the legal maximum) to both the National Republican Senatorial Committee and its counterpart, the Democratic Senatorial Campaign Committee—and the same with the House campaign committees. GEPAC giving also favored powerful incumbents facing safe reelections. If this was an effort to affect election outcomes, it was about as inefficient an effort as one could dream up.

Instead, what GEPAC—like other big-business PACs—is doing is gaining access. It's not that a lawmaker is likely to be bought off by a

GEPAC gift, but that he's likely to make time to hear the arguments of GE's lobbyists. Smaller businesses, without a $2.4-million-per-election PAC and without three former senators as lobbyists, are less likely to get the ear of a committee chairman.

So GE's size provides some market advantages—economies of scale and cheaper financing, for example—but the political advantages that come with size may be even greater. For that reason, it's not surprising that the company has decided to embrace bigger government. The two arms of this embrace are the political (lobbying for more government) and the business (adapting the company's business so as to profit from bigger government).

GE is a good example of a company rationally responding to the incentives created by bigger government. And the results are disheartening.

A Tale of Four Factories

The fates of four General Electric manufacturing plants tell an instructive tale.

In April 2009 President Obama and Vice President Joe Biden announced a big federal push to expand the use of rail in America, including the development of advanced technologies for trains. Obama's talk had a nationalistic bent: "There's no reason why we can't do this. This is America. There's no reason why the future of travel should lie somewhere else beyond our borders."[29]

But this wasn't just a pep talk to rally the industry—it was a justification for spending $13 billion in taxpayer money on high-speed and freight rail. This is a new incarnation of economic nationalism. The old government means of boosting domestic industrial activities—tariffs and other import restrictions—are derided by the elites of both parties as "protectionism." But generously subsidizing U.S. companies in order to "create jobs" is avant-garde.

The month after Obama's call to arms, GE gave three responses. "GE has the know-how and the manufacturing base to develop the next generation of high-speed passenger locomotives," the CEO of GE Transportation told a crowd of employees and government officials. "We are ready to partner with the federal government and Amtrak to make high-speed rail a reality."[30]

Second, GE Transportation hired lobbyist Linda Daschle to work on rail issues. Linda's husband, Tom Daschle, was the former majority leader of the U.S. Senate and a close confidant of Obama.

At about the same time, GE also announced that it was building a $100 million battery factory in upstate New York to help power hybrid locomotives. Big government formed the backdrop for the factory groundbreaking. New York governor David Patterson was at the press conference, where he portrayed the state as a partner with GE, saying, "We have a tremendous capacity to beat anybody else to this," and "We are betting big on batteries." Sure enough, the New York State government provided a $15 million grant to the GE factory, while the local Albany Metroplex Development Authority kicked in another $5 million. So taxpayers paid for 20 percent of GE's up-front costs.

In addition to state and local government, GE had two other potential sources of major funding for its battery plant. According to the *New York Times*'s account: "The battery industry, despite its high costs, has become a favorite of the venture capital industry. G.E. also hopes that the federal government, with its green-energy push, will help with the financing."[31]

Even the venture-capital industry's interest was driven by government. The *Times* had recently covered the increased venture-capital attention to batteries, with some telling details:

The stimulus package has likely helped to keep the cash flowing. While the bill, enacted in February, includes provisions for a broad swath of clean technologies, government agencies are still working out how to allocate most of the money. The batteries—and electric vehicles—sector has been one of the few that already has received government solicitations, and venture capitalists seem to be anteing-up in response.

The $2 billion set aside for batteries in the stimulus comes on top of up to $25 billion in direct loans that became available last year for advanced vehicles, including related energy-storage technologies.[32]

As the factory was being built, GE called on the Department of Energy for subsidies through the stimulus bill. The department said no, but that didn't mean the factory was getting no federal help. Indeed, the factory's product was worth making only because of government subsidies from recent stimulus and energy legislation.

GE's battery factory was part of its "ecomagination" initiative—making money off of products purportedly good for the environment. Ecomagination's chief, GE executive Steve Fludder, touted his business's improved prospects in the light of Obama's elections and the bailouts. "I'd prefer not to think of words like 'subsidies' and that type of a construct," Fludder said. "I think it is more supporting the creation of scale."[33]

Vice President Biden, famously inartful in his speech, used blunter language in celebrating another GE factory success. The vice president was in Louisville, Kentucky, to announce that federal subsidies had saved four hundred jobs at the plant by spurring GE to make electric-hybrid water heaters there. "So those who talk about 'this is big government,'" Biden said, "this is big government giving a little bit of help to jump-start America to lead the world in the twenty-first century." He called it part of a "new foundation for a new economy."

But a few weeks later, seventy-five miles east of that Louisville plant, workers at GE's Kentucky Glass Plant saw the other side of big government and the "new economy." These workers made the glass that went into GE's flagship product—the traditional incandescent bulb invented by the company's founder, Thomas Edison. GE, however, decided to close the Winchester Lamp Plant (Virginia), where Kentucky Glass shipped its product. Left with no customers, the Kentucky Glass Plant also had to be shuttered. Similarly, GE closed down a glass plant in Niles, Ohio, in early 2010.

GE explained these plant closures in a 2009 press release: "A variety of energy regulations that establish lighting efficiency standards are being implemented in the U.S. and other countries, in some cases this year, and will soon make the familiar lighting products produced at the Winchester Plant obsolete." Specifically, regulations in the 2007 energy bill set a minimum legal energy efficiency standard for light bulbs. Any bulb that couldn't meet those standards would be illegal to manufacture for sale in the United States by 2012. Traditional incandescent—like the ones made in Winchester—didn't make the cut.

So was GE, in this case, a victim of big government? Not exactly. GE's prolific lobbying team had supported the light-bulb regulations. The company makes more profit off of compact fluorescent bulbs, which meet the federal efficiency standards. These are more profitable because the company can charge more, and also because it makes those bulbs in China, with cheaper labor costs and fewer environmental regulations.

The real key for GE may not be compact fluorescents but light-emitting diode (LED) bulbs. They could cost more than twenty dollars a bulb, and would not be made in Winchester. The day the light-bulb law passed, GE stock jumped 8 percent.[34]

About five hundred workers lost their jobs between the Lexington, Winchester, and Niles factories. But even for those workers, big government had an answer. The Labor Department in 2010 declared the Ohio plant an "adversely affected employer" under the 1974 Trade Act, thus entitling these workers to federal aid, such as subsidized job training.

It's true that imports are killing these jobs, but they're GE imports.

Replacing Unsubsidized Work with Subsidized Work

Big government helped kill some GE manufacturing jobs (the light-bulb jobs), and it helped save some other GE manufacturing jobs (battery and water-heater jobs). Depending on how one counts, government might be creating more GE jobs than it's killing, or may be killing more than it's making.

But, as celebrated nineteenth-century economist Frédéric Bastiat would put it, there are the *unseen* victims of the government's interactions with GE.

First are light-bulb consumers—which means every business and family—who no longer can choose the low-cost traditional incandescent. Government nannies will say that these consumers are better off because of the long-term savings in efficiency, but those savings are unproven. And the compact fluorescents would be available to them even without a law effectively banning traditional incandescent.

Then there are the entrepreneurs who lost out. Think about those venture capitalists who followed the government's lead into batteries. Absent government battery subsidies, some of them would have invested their money elsewhere. The result: some entrepreneur who would have gotten a capital injection in a freer market is left in the cold thanks to big government.

The same is true for consumer dollars—subsidies to make hybrid water heaters or high-tech batteries cheaper will have an effect on consumer spending. For most consumers, buying a hybrid water heater means not buying something else (or at least not buying a traditional water heater). Their would-be suppliers are also losers.

Finally, there are the victims of government spending and future deficits. Taxpayers, present and future, suffer from subsidies. Direct outlays, like the $20 million to GE's battery plant, come out of the pockets of taxpayers. Special targeted tax credits increase the deficit, thus leading either to future tax increases or to other negative effects of long-term deficits, such as inflation or higher interest rates.

Aside from these direct economic effects, there are the cultural-economic effects. Think about what big government is doing within GE: It is replacing unsubsidized jobs with subsidized jobs. It is forbidding the sale of safe products for which there is real consumer demand, and promoting the sale of products for which consumers wouldn't pay without a government subsidy.

Incentives

What incentives does this set within GE and for other entrepreneurs who are watching? No longer does it make sense for an inventor to ask himself, "Can I make a better mousetrap?" because the threat is greater that the government might ban his mousetrap, however safe and efficient it is.

Nobody can predict what standards or rules government will establish in the future. In the early 1990s, the *Washington Post* celebrated the catalytic converter for turning pollution into "harmless carbon dioxide."[35] By 2010, reducing CO_2 emissions had become the prime objective of government environmental policy.

The result is that "regulatory certainty" is a myth. "Regulatory certainty" is one excuse big business gives for supporting more government. Business can adjust to new rules; it simply wants to know what the rules are. This argument appears to put big-business interests in line with small-business interests. But it's a bit of a farce, since a change in party control of Congress, a change in president, a new committee chairman, or even a shift in political winds can be the difference between a product's being subsidized and its being slapped with a special tax. Fuel additive MTBE, for example, was effectively mandated shortly before it was banned on the state level.

Government, then, is just as fickle and unpredictable as the market, with two important differences: Government's fits and alternations are bigger and more sudden than the market's. And gaming the government's oscillations is easier than gaming the market's—as long as you're plugged in to people in power.

And so reading the market is no longer as valuable as reading the polls. Research and development is not as good an investment as political connections. A good lobbyist is now worth more than a good idea.

Through corporatism, ironically, government creates an economy that looks just like the socialist's caricature of capitalism. The big get bigger while the small guys are frozen out. People with money make sure to buy off the powerful. It is a zero-sum game, and the game is rigged, with the rules constantly changing. And the incentives are all bad.

In a free market, commerce fosters virtue. A free economic exchange involves two parties voluntarily trading for their mutual benefit. Commerce doesn't simply enrich a society; it also fosters community and trust. Diligence, reliability, friendliness, and honesty are all rewarded in the long run in a free market.

Under corporatism, commerce erodes virtue. Sycophancy is rewarded instead of insight. Cleverness is more valuable than innovation. Businessmen get the message: stay small, or be prepared to play ball with politicians. Everyone becomes a welfare recipient or sharecropper for government or big business.

There are ripple effects, too. Onerous regulation and the need for political connections both act as huge barriers to entry. This heightens incentives to work for a big company instead of going out on your own. Over the generations, the spirit of entrepreneurship vanishes.

Thanks to government, the pursuit of profit becomes a corrupting process rather than an ennobling one.

It's Not the Markets, It's the Morals: How Excessively Blaming Markets Undermines Civil Society

John Larrivee

The extreme ideologies of the twentieth century—Communism, fascism, and National Socialism—produced totalitarian disaster wherever they were implemented. Crucially, a main reason that so many countries experimented with those horrific systems is that they wanted to stop the evils supposedly spawned by capitalism. The fact that these experiments failed (while causing far more destruction than markets ever did) suggests that the ideologies fundamentally misunderstood the source of society's problems by placing far too much emphasis on economic factors. This overweighting of economic factors was one of the major errors of the twentieth century.

Although those totalitarian regimes are no longer with us, the overemphasis on market problems persists. In many intellectual circles there is a strong tendency to exaggerate potential problems in markets, which overemphasizes the extent to which economic factors shape individuals and society. Such a perspective subtly reinforces an ethos of materialism and economic determinism. If economic factors completely explained social outcomes, there would be little room for individual choice. But the failures of twentieth-century antimarket ideologies show that market forces are not the only significant factor in society. Those regimes failed in large part because they underestimated the extent to which other factors—family, religion, civic organizations, and the other institutions of civil society—matter. These are the institutions that shape values and the underlying vision of the human person.

Today, a danger to these institutions, and free society generally, arises from an additional, but surprising, source: well-intentioned people concerned with religion and civil society who believe they are defending them from the onslaught of markets. Alas, in their attacks on moral dimensions of capitalism, they turn for conceptual weapons to theoretical systems that have been *directly* hostile to faith and civil society or that now foster a materialist philosophy that corrodes the respect for religion and justifies expanding the state and displacing civil society.

They do this because we have not learned well what the failures of the economic experiments imply about their underlying theories. We've seen that Communism is inefficient, and that the excessive nationalism of fascism too easily decays into hatred of others. But there remain critical lessons to be learned about the economic theories they held in common with each other (and with much of the intellectual Left today): the destructiveness of markets and its implied weakness of civil society. As result, such theories persist, and the suspicion they foster toward civil society remains dominant.

I do not mean to suggest that markets have no bad effects. I believe markets should be criticized appropriately for bad effects, to the degree that they are in fact culpable. The problem is that disproportionate blame translates into excessive negativity toward markets.

And excessive criticism of markets does not just harm the economy. It adds to the social forces that undermine the role of values, faith, and civil society, and exaggerates the case for government involvement to solve the problems of markets, which opens the door for expansion of the state.

The way out of this quandary is truth—an accurate understanding of the existence and magnitude of potential problems, and of the interdependent roles of the market, the state, religion, and civil society.

Recognizing the truth about markets and morals is especially important now. For we face a future in which aggressive secularism threatens to undermine the religious and philosophical foundations needed for society, and in which markets themselves will offer new technologies that challenge us with what it means even to be human. Consequently, the values and ideals fostered by religion and civil society will be more crucial than ever. Making the case for their role will require dispelling the materialist bias against them.

Thinking about Markets

Most moral critiques of capitalism can be divided into two broad categories. The first involves claims about economic or material justice— that is, supposed injustices either in individual exchanges or, more broadly, in the distribution of resources across society. The familiar lament that "the rich get richer and the poor get poorer" falls into this category. At base, assessing such criticisms is straightforward: Does capitalism fairly provide improvements in material well-being or not? Is it a system in which only the rich get richer or one in which most people who make reasonable effort advance materially? Such questions can be answered using hard data.

The second category is less concrete, but no less a cause of concern for many. This set of critiques revolves around the personal, moral, spiritual, or social impact of capitalism. While some market defenders argue that markets actually foster virtues, or at least depend on virtues and are not uniquely corrosive of them, by far the most common view is negative: that economic exchange specifically and the market system generally induce materialism, selfishness, and greed; undermine communities, society, and concern for truth; weaken social relationships; and erode religious zeal.

In order to assess this properly, moving beyond mere speculation about the market's effects on people, one cannot simply look at capitalist economies but rather must examine both market and non-

133

market systems. For example, many people claim that greed in the United States is the result of capitalism, but noncapitalist regimes have experienced similar problems with greed and self-interest. In the Soviet Union, Communist Party officials lived well, receiving good pay and other perks—summer homes, faster access to goods, special stores, and more—while the rest of society toiled for little.[1] This fact implies that something other than just economic factors must be involved.

Nobel Prize–winning economic historian Robert Fogel makes precisely this argument. As we will see, Fogel, perhaps the world's leading expert in measuring material well-being across time, has answered the first category of critiques of capitalism by showing the many ways in which average people have gained materially. But he also raises important questions about the second category of criticisms. His research demonstrates that many social indicators have gotten worse as material conditions improved, meaning that material deprivation or inequities cannot be the cause. Fogel argues for the importance of what he terms "spiritual resources," a combination of worldview and virtues.

For instance, many attribute high divorce rates and out-of-wedlock birth rates to decreasing earnings options for low-skilled men. But this cannot be enough of an explanation. Humankind has faced many eras of low pay and harsh employment prospects (such as the Great Depression and the early Industrial Revolution) without either problem hitting the levels we have now.[2] Moreover, the rate of such problems is not as high among new immigrants who face the same economic circumstances as those who've been here longer. Changes in values must play a part, and attributing the problem to decreased opportunities in the labor market at the very least overstates the importance of economic factors.

Civil Society

While it's fairly clear how beliefs about the answers to moral questions feed into perceptions of capitalism, less well understood is how views about faith became linked to views about markets. Figure 1 provides insights

Attitudes toward Religion, Civil Society, and the Market			
		Religion and Civil Society	
		Bad/Impotent/Unnecessary	Good/Necessary
Markets	Good	**1. Nonreligious libertarians:** The Invisible Hand is good enough for society.	**3. Religious conservatives:** Religion and markets are both good but serve different purposes.
	Bad	**2. Fascists, Communists, National Socialists, intellectual leftists:** Markets are bad, causing injustice and undermining society. Problems are too big for civil society.	**4. Religious liberals and some traditionalists:** Religion is good, but markets are bad, leading to injustice and immorality.

into this by examining four different intellectual schools based upon these two factors: attitudes toward markets and the role of religion in society.

Quadrant 1 includes people who are skeptical of religion but think markets are good. This would include the eighteenth-century political economist Bernard de Mandeville, who asserted that vice, particularly greed, is actually good for society, as well as modern writers like Ayn Rand. For these people, religion is unnecessary because an invisible hand-like dynamic will be adequate to hold people together: since people get paid only if they provide something others value, they have an incentive to serve others. Self-interest is all you need. Markets are good because they allow maximum freedom for people to do what they want.

Quadrant 2 includes those hostile to both religion and markets. They see markets as destructive to society, causing social injustice and undermining social relations and commitment to the common good. At best, religion is too weak against these market forces. Others in this quadrant, such as Marxists, view religion as more deleterious— the product or even the tool of those in power. This thinking formed the dominant theoretical foundation for Communism, fascism, and National Socialism. All of these ideologies were hostile to markets and rejected civil society, including religion, as outdated, or as something to be controlled by the state. Although modern liberalism doesn't follow the extremes of these three, it shares with them the key assumptions that markets cause economic and social problems, that civil society is too weak, and that a stronger state is needed to address the shortcomings.

Quadrant 3 includes those who view both markets and religion as positive social forces. They tend to see markets as good in their own way, but not as the primary means by which people are formed and develop their relationships. Instead, this group stresses the importance of a strong civil society, particularly religion and family. Like quadrant 1 types, people in this group emphasize freedom, but this is circumscribed by religious/cultural forces that inform people of what matters in life.

Quadrant 4 includes those who are hostile to markets but believe that religion is important for society. In general, liberal members of this group tend to worry more about social justice, while more conservative members often focus on the potential personal, spiritual, or social problems of markets. They encourage government roles to rein in these problems, but see religion as the primary social force for encouraging virtue.

Quadrants 1 and 2 share important similarities. Though they disagree about the role of markets, they assume that market forces are powerful and thus consider civil society to be relatively unimportant. Therefore, both assume that the right economic/political mix is all that society needs. For quadrant 1 types, this is a strong market and weak state, with the market serving as the primary formative institution with maximum freedom. On the other hand, quadrant 2 types want a strong state to constrain market forces, institutions, and structures, and to encourage social harmony.

Many religious people in categories 3 and 4 worry about the justice or personal/social impact of markets. Quadrant 1 people often have the capacity to explain to quadrant 3 and 4 types why markets are good, or at least not bad. But justifications relying on appeals to simple self-interest are repulsive to people worried that markets foster selfishness. Sadly, extreme views from this group, such as those of Ayn Rand and Mandeville, define the pro-market position for many in quadrant 4, reinforcing the notion that capitalism is all about selfishness and personal consumption.

Lacking good answers to the moral questions about markets, many religious people have fallen from quadrant 3 to 4, either turned off by the antireligious libertarianism of many in quadrant 1 or lured away by the siren songs of quadrant 2. Alas, few realize the dangers in this response. An excessively worrisome view of markets implies that civil society, and faith itself, is too weak. Thus religious people unintentionally contribute to a materialist ethos and undermine the belief that faith matters for society. In addition, fear of the market can lead people to turn to the state and ultimately accept policies likely to crowd out religion and civil society.

The challenge is to provide adequate assurance to those worried about the impact of markets—taking their concerns seriously because they are asking the right questions, but explaining the limits of blame that can be assigned to markets and the importance of faith and civil society more broadly.

"Spiritual Resources"

Take the case of markets and material well-being. "Some proponents of egalitarianism," Robert Fogel writes, "insist on characterizing the *material* level of the poor today as being harsh."[3] But Fogel demonstrates that by almost any measure, material well-being has risen enormously for everyone in the West over the past century—including, or perhaps especially, the poor.

In income, everyone saw such massive gains in the United States that the poverty rate fell from about 95 percent of the population in the 1890s to about 12–14 percent today. The real income of the bottom 20 percent rose an astounding nineteen times, far greater than the percentage gains of the middle and upper classes. In fact, the income of the average household *below* the poverty line today would place them in the richest 5–10 percent of households a century ago.[4] As a result, income inequality fell enormously.[5]

Efficiency increases both raised earnings and decreased the costs of goods. The result was a vast broadening of consumption as well. While rich people always got goods and services first, poor people now

137

obtain the benefits of technology sooner than ever before. Consider the goods and services available to the poor that were never available to the richest people in history: refrigeration, microwaves, phones, electricity, cars, airplane transport, indoor heating and cooling, and much more. By the end of the twentieth century, essentially every poor family in the United States had indoor plumbing, something even the Hapsburgs didn't have in their summer palace on the eve of World War I.[6] New medicines like aspirin and penicillin provided relief and cures that Louis XIV never envisioned at Versailles. Electric lighting meant that the poor could stop wasting time cleaning the kerosene lamps every day. Cheap clothing meant that the poor no longer had to scavenge from dumps and the dead to get clothes. And it wasn't just consumption: leisure increased for all as people worked fewer hours per day and days per year and retired ever earlier.

Biomedical measures, which provide a fuller picture of well-being than income because they summarize the cumulative impact of material events on people, also show unprecedented gains for the poor and reductions in inequality. For example, in England in the late 1800s there was a five-inch difference in height and a seventeen-year difference in life expectancy between rich and poor; by the twenty-first century the gaps stood at under one inch and about two years, respectively. The increase in life expectancy of the poor in Western countries from slightly more than forty years of age to nearly eighty today was the greatest increase in longevity in the history of humanity.[7]

Income inequality has risen in recent decades, but this results from a much more complex set of causes than in the past, not merely concentration of ownership of the means of production. Some inequality does arise from external circumstances beyond people's control that are worrisome developments in the economy, such as rising returns to education and competition from globalization and immigration at the low-skill end of the labor market. But some causes are actually good. For instance, greater numbers of elderly people who are healthy enough to live longer on their own increase the pool of "low-income" households. The increasing importance of human capital means that middle-aged people get paid much more than when they were in their twenties; this difference drives up measured annual inequality across households, but it is hardly discouraging that the young who are poor in the current sample will be the well-off in the samples twenty years from now. And much inequality results from individual choices about family, work, leisure, and education that have little to do with an oppressive economic system. On the positive side, some people will retire early or take jobs with less pay and less stress. On the worrisome side, family breakdown from divorce and out-of-wedlock births produces single-parent families with far less earnings than couples in which both spouses work, and with reduced time to serve their children.

Fogel, a Communist Party member in his youth, doesn't recite such statistics to celebrate markets and disregard the poor today. Instead, he worries that ignoring such gains prevents us from recognizing that addressing the remaining poverty will require not solving an economic problem but providing "spiritual resources" that affect people's willingness and ability to work productively and cooperatively, such as a sense of purpose, discipline, perseverance, a sense of family, and a sense of community. As he argues, "Failure to recognize the enormous material gains over the last century, even for the poor, impedes rather than advances the struggle in rich nations against chronic poverty, whose principle characteristic is the *spiritual estrangement* from the mainstream society of those so afflicted" (emphasis in original).[8]

Ignoring these gains—in other words, excessively criticizing markets—impedes progress against chronic poverty because it perpetuates the materialist view that economic factors are the only problems. As Fogel writes, "The theory projected by the Social Gospelers, and embraced by modernism generally, held that cultural crises could be resolved by raising incomes. That theory has been given a long trial and has turned out to be incorrect. Despite the sharp rise in incomes, especially at the low end of the income distribution, the moral crisis of the cities remains unresolved."[9]

In a sense, we engaged in a massive social experiment to test the hypothesis underlying fascism, Communism, and much of the intellectual Left that social breakdown is caused by harsh economic conditions and thus can be eliminated by increasing material well-being. Material conditions improved beyond the wildest imaginations of the social reformers of the late 1800s. But social problems generally got worse in the 1960s and 1970s, after those enormous gains. These facts contradict their theories and point to the role of spiritual resources fostered by religion and civil society. But excessive criticism of markets that denies or ignores these massive gains misses those lessons and an opportunity to make the case for civil society.

Fogel's arguments are critical, because they address the mistake—adopted by governments and religious groups alike—that places too much weight on material factors. Ignorant or skeptical of the role of these spiritual resources, neither policymakers nor academics nor the poor themselves focus on acquiring them. His analysis validates the importance of institutions, such as churches and civic organizations, that are effective at building up these virtues—and could be more effective if the modernist materialist argument did not hold such sway.

Are Markets the Problem?

But what if markets themselves are to blame for the erosion of those spiritual values?

The best way to address this question is to consider what has happened across all economic systems. Alas, that analysis has not been done effectively. This has arisen partly from intellectual sloppiness—concluding that problems one sees in the United States are uniquely attributable to capitalism and ignoring their existence elsewhere—and partly from intellectuals' deliberate use of double standards to absolve Communism.[10]

When different types of economic systems are examined honestly, it becomes clear that capitalism is not solely to blame for eroding spiritual resources. For example, it's common to assume that the material success of the United States thanks to capitalism undermines religious practice.

More likely is that economic and religious freedom support each other. Religious practice is far stronger in the more capitalist United States than in Europe. Moreover, the Communist countries assailed religion, rotting demand for faith with their materialist philosophy and ideological attacks, and assaulting churches directly through government infiltration and outright oppression.[11] Stalin arrested 165,200 clergy and killed 106,800 of them between 1937 and 1938 alone.[12] Ultimately, concentrated state power and antagonistic ideologies were far more destructive to faith than material success or market mechanisms.

Similarly, many workers hate their jobs and find them meaningless. It's easy to ascribe it to market incentives: the profit motive will press employers into further specialization until every job is monotonous, naturally leaving workers feeling like cogs in a giant machine. It sounds plausible, and enough real cases exist to verify people's suspicions.

Except that the same problem occurred in Communist regimes far more. In 1983 Tatyana Zaslavskaya, who rose to become perhaps the most prominent Soviet sociologist, reported the identical phenomenon in the Soviet Union, the country established with common ownership and without the profit motive to save workers from exploitation and alienation. She later wrote:

> The primary reasons for the need for *perestroika* were not the sluggish economy and the rate of technical development but an underlying mass alienation of working people from significant social goals and values. This social alienation is rooted in the economic system formed in the 1930s, which made state property, run by a vast bureaucratic apparatus, the dominant form of ownership. . . . For 50 years it was said that this was public property and belonged to everyone, but no way was ever found to make workers feel they were the co-owners and masters of the factories, farms, and enterprises. They felt themselves to be cogs in a gigantic machine.[13]

Ultimately, economic freedom in the market improved working conditions to allow many to move out of grinding, monotonous jobs and channel their creative efforts into an ever-widening array of directions.

Much the same lesson can be learned from a careful examination of other failings frequently attributed to capitalism: the problems turned out to be worse in the nonmarket systems established to solve these very problems. Consider several examples.

Oppression and exploitation: Many critics of capitalism argue that a market system will inherently lead to exploitation, just as Marx predicted. Such critics point not only to income inequality but also to such obvious problems as the existence of sweatshops. Sweatshops undeniably exist, many of them supplying large multinational companies. These deserve condemnation, and such exploitation should be ended.

Of course, the existence of sweatshops is not enough to confirm the perception that capitalism exploits and oppresses people. For starters, one must be careful to distinguish between harsh working conditions that workers in economically inefficient countries actually seek in order to maximize their meager pay from the true exploitation of those who have such conditions imposed upon them by firms capable of paying and providing their workers better. In addition, the view that capitalism is inherently exploitative ignores how many people have escaped oppressive conditions thanks to capitalism. Even more important, it ignores how much suffering has occurred in nonmarket systems, where real oppression and persecution vastly outdid anything occurring in capitalist countries. Communist regimes engaged in far more persecution and for a far longer time, killing about 100 million people and imprisoning scores of millions more in the most extensive systems of reeducation/work camps in human history.[14] Regimes dedicated to eliminating the feared bogeyman of capitalist exploitation created a new ruling class worse than what they replaced. How could this have happened?

Few recognize the inherent contradiction of Communism: its goal of equality is impossible to achieve without creating the conditions ripe for exploitation, because attempts to get equality of *outcomes* require inequality of *power*—that is, massive power concentrated in the hands of the state.[15]

But couldn't such power be used for good? Theoretically, yes. Realistically, no. As Friedrich Hayek argued in *The Road to Serfdom*, government planning by its nature involves going against what people want to do on their own (otherwise the force of government wouldn't be needed).[16] Thus rulers must appoint people who can get things done—individuals who have the least qualms about forcing others to do what the state wants. Access to power attracts people, since that becomes the only means to get ahead—and it attracts the worst types of people, those with the least concern for others. This is what happened in regimes whose ideological foundation cut them off from the past and left the morality of actions by revolutionaries uncertain.[17] However bad capitalism might be in theory, too few have applied the same critical lens to what nonmarket systems became in reality: all-powerful states dominated by moral monsters.

Distorted human relationships: Another common complaint is that the inherent nature of capitalism, being based on impersonal exchange, weakens relationships.[18] In a market, people can make decisions according to their own exchange value of the good or service, not any interpersonal relationship between producer and consumer. The likely result is that neither party cares about others: firms put profits before customers, and customers don't care about producers. By extension, over time, that repeated process of economic calculation fosters excessive preoccupation with people's own goals and interests, cheapening other dimensions of human relationships and atomizing society.

In the brand-new Communist world, Marxists hoped that human relations would flourish, uncontaminated by capitalism. Without profits to corrupt things, producers would genuinely care about customers. Free of market incentives and exploitation, people could develop honest relationships with one another, even between owners and workers, producers and consumers.

The error of these naive assumptions could be seen by a visit to any store in Communist countries. Store clerks and managers were notoriously unconcerned about customers and what they wanted. Profits may be selfish, but at least they provide an incentive to consider one's customers. In Communism, there wasn't even that, just the "promise" that things should be different since it was Communist. The replacement of the "cash nexus" of naked self-interest with intentional exchange under planning did nothing to improve human relationships.

Instead, as John Clark and Aaron Wildavsky show in their study of Polish society, Communism made things worse. People were plagued with constant scarcity. Even when goods existed, planning made coordination so slow that much of the supply remained undistributed at factories (or held back by dishonest managers for black-market distribution). Often goods were to be had only if one had the right friends and connections. Over time friendships and family relations were corrupted, as everyone used one another to obtain access to some good by illegal means. People began to look upon others, to evaluate their relationships, as means of access to the scarce items.[19]

Moreover, driven by its ideology that civil society was irrelevant, or the product of capitalist relations that had to be ended, the state increasingly crowded out or repressed civil society. Soon everything was dominated by the omnipresent party. Since the party was corrupt too, civil society, where people form their most important and enduring relationships, could not serve as the refuge and defense for the identities of the people. When these problems combined with ideologies that emphasized the collective over the individual and rejected individual dignity, there was little left to defend people from the material, political, and ideological onslaught of the state. They were more isolated than ever. Trust eroded. Individualism rose. State power and an ideology that claimed to be concerned about people's alienation from the community in capitalism caused far more alienation than capitalism ever did.

Consumerism and materialism: Consumerism is a problem. It's dangerous when people see the primary goal in life to be the increase of consumption and define themselves by that consumption rather than something deeper or truer. It is natural to imagine that capitalism breeds consumerism, since a market system grows only when people consume more, and firms have an incentive to encourage more consumption of their products.

But the problem isn't *consumerism* specifically; it's *materialism* generally, the belief that the material world is all that there is. Consumerism is just one form. And it arises more easily when people already have the materialist bug. If the material world is all there is, if there are no transcendent values or beings, why not live for consumption?

This problem arises not from capitalism itself but from modern materialist philosophical trends. In fact, it is disconcerting when religious people assume that materialism is inherent to and uniquely bad in capitalism, ignoring the fact that materialism was the foundation of antimarket ideologies that further undermined spiritual values.

Alexander Yakovlev provides an interesting insight into this matter. Yakovlev worked for many years on the committee on propaganda for the Communist Party in the Soviet Union. Years later, after ultimately rejecting Marxist theory, he was appointed to head the propaganda committee and served as Mikhail Gorbachev's intellectual adviser on the transition from Marxism. Yakovlev writes:

The very idea of taking the individual out of the aggregate of social relations, trying to reduce all contradictions of human existence to the contradictions of the economy, eclipsed the human factors of existence. It pushed aside the fact that the individual suffers not only from economic inequality but also from spiritual and bodily vulnerability, from fear of death, from the inherent solitude of human beings. The world and life create a multitude of problems that have their own meaning and that cannot be fixed by achieving an equal relationship to the means of production.

Thus Marxism proclaims the primacy of material over spiritual values. Consequently, it transforms the whole hierarchy of values, which can be expressed as antispirituality.[20]

The perversion of the meaning of the word *materialism* into just its consumerist form prevents people from recognizing how materialism is a common problem of modernity, whatever the system. Whether the issue is consumerism or a kind of statolatry in which people effectively live for the wishes of the corrupt state, the problem is still the same: seeing the material world as all there is.

The materialist philosophy undermines the importance of personal virtue and absolute values and enables oppression. As Yakovlev argues:

> Materialism inevitably leads to fetishism, . . . enabling the problem of spiritual choice to be removed and thus eliminating personal responsibility, sin, and repentance. Materialism disarms a person spiritually, making him vulnerable to ideological manipulation. From the perspective of materialism, the human being is a functional phenomenon, merely a particle of nature, one of the ways material systems function. Materialism is therefore ideologically related to authoritarianism.[21]

When Communist regimes collapsed, no ground of meaning was left for those who had traded in traditional sources of meaning for the fashionable new ideological ones. Years of antireligious governments had corroded the perception of the transcendent, leaving behind populations who were extremely materialistic even in the consumerist sense, even if they had little material goods to be "materialistic" about. Ultimately, Communist regimes fostered far more materialism (properly understood) than did capitalism.

Dishonesty: Yes, the financial crisis in the United States exposed massive dishonesty—from banks, to rating agencies, to average people lying on their mortgage forms. Enron and Arthur Andersen epitomize corporate dishonesty. Since examples exist, and a plausible explanation is available—that some people will go along with bad deals if they have a chance of making a buck—many conclude that markets themselves undermine respect for truth.

But how does that explain the recent fiscal problems of Greece, which misrepresented its fiscal fitness to obtain entry to the European Union? False financial reporting to avoid taxes and stay afloat is bad for an American firm, but okay for a country trying to fool its citizens and bilk the responsible Germans of hundreds of billions of Euros?

And it doesn't come close to explaining the rampant dishonesty that pervaded the centrally planned economies, from outright lies to massive propaganda divisions. Perhaps surprisingly, there is strong evidence to suggest not that *capitalism* is uniquely threatening to truth but the reverse: that collectivist systems are more likely to undermine the idea of truth.

Just as there are incentives to lie, there are incentives to tell the truth. Few understand how the move from capitalism undermines those incentives for truth. With government ownership of all the means of production, customers have no way to punish producers for dishonest representation of products. No investors exist to move funds from dishonest firms.

For example, as Clark and Wildavsky report, since central planning targets were wildly unrealistic, the choice was to attempt to meet an impossible goal, or lie. Many chose to lie.[22] This was true for individuals as well. Communist policy outlawed even simple exchanges between people as "market activity." But with living standards low due to the overall inefficiency of the planned economy, virtually everyone engaged in such illegal behavior just to get by. The system thus created incentives for dishonesty and disrespect for law.[23] Historian Richard Pipes writes:

> Restrictions on public expression resulted in descriptions that bore little resemblance to reality. This not only made it difficult to survive psychologically, it also left a psychic legacy that outlasted Communism. Lying became a means of survival, and from lying to cheating was but a small step. Social ethics, which make possible a civil society, were shattered, and a regime that wanted everyone to sacrifice his private advantage to the com-

mon good ended up with a situation where everyone looked out only for himself because he could count on no one else.[24]

Again, Hayek was closer to the truth than the market critics. The more centralized the command, the more state domination of people's lives is required. The state must either coerce people or get them to make the effort voluntarily. Since coercion is hard, states prefer voluntary effort if they can get it. To secure this cooperation, the state must indoctrinate people into accepting the theories on which the state's goals are based. It also must not admit when it is failing or when goals and theories are wrong; nor can it allow discussion of such occurrences. This explains why centralized states adopted the most extensive propaganda machines in human history. Across fascist, Nazi, and Communist systems, even universities were enrolled in this process of distorting truth and stifling alternative (accurate) views.

Moral decay: Does capitalism corrode character? Plausible theories have been offered to support the view that it does, such as sociologist Daniel Bell's assertion that markets can succeed only if they encourage indulgence. Likewise, capitalism's critics can point to real experiences of selfish businesspeople or rising individualism. But once again, the mere presence of moral decay in market systems is not proof that capitalism is the cause or that it is uniquely problematic.

Only in the past century have we had the experience of entire noncapitalist societies from which to draw conclusions about how various systems affect people. For many, one of the most shocking results in Communist and fascist regimes was the decline of morality. What produced that? Soviet economists Nikolai Shmelev and Vladimir Popov argued that the very nature of the command economy itself caused a degeneration in mores and ideals. Absent a profit motive, and with no private property to ensure that one retained the fruit of one's work, there was little incentive to be industrious or explore the needs of others. The direction of everything from the top decreased people's sense of initiative and responsibility. The result wasn't merely low production but a destruction of virtue itself. In 1989 Shmelev and Popov wrote:

Economic inefficiency and "leveled distribution" have brought about profound shifts in human psychology. These changes have perverted human values and priorities.

A purely administrative view of economic problems took root. Officials developed an almost religious belief in the "organization." . . . The public became apathetic and indifferent, acquired a parasitic belief in guaranteed jobs and social security, and considered that it was useless and even humiliating to put their shoulders to the wheel and work unsparingly ("we pretend to work, and you pretend to pay us"). A significant part of the nation degenerated physically and spiritually as a result of drink and idleness; ethics and morality declined; massive theft of public property and disregard for honest labor was accompanied by bitter envy of others who were able to increase their incomes.[25]

Bourgeois Virtues and Charitable Activity

Shmelev and Popov's statement points to another possibility: perhaps markets actually contribute more to the development of virtues in society than they undermine them. This is not to suggest that capitalist economics will produce societies full of moral heroes, but rather that, as economist Deirdre McCloskey argues, the case against markets has been so one-sided as to prevent us from learning the appropriate lessons.[26]

Take personal virtue. Work provides an opportunity for growth in personal and interpersonal skills. When people own their own property and get the returns from it, they have two critical things: responsibility and authority. They have an incentive to care for what they own and use it in ways others value. And this is coupled with authority to do so. When property is owned in common, incentives for responsibility are lacking and authority is not clear.

Similarly, producers must be industrious, constantly alert to what people like and how to improve production, prudent in their decisions, courageous in proceeding. Markets provide incentives for people to set aside their differences and get along, and to cultivate that agreeable disposition.

But couldn't much of this "virtue" be simply to get along for a buck, a shallow cooperation out of self-interest with little genuine concern for others?

One way to assess this is in volunteer and charity activities. These are interesting to examine because neither government nor business is directly involved. People have no commercial incentive to assist people who have no connection to them, and they get little monetary gain from doing so. If capitalism is so destructive of social relations, we would expect less volunteer work in a market society than in a socialist system. So what do we get?

Studies find the exact reverse: charitable donations, of both time and money, are far greater in the more capitalist United States. Arthur Brooks, an economist who has specialized in this area, compares the United States and Europe:

> There is so little private charity in Europe that it is difficult to find information on the subject—so irrelevant is it that few researchers have even bothered to investigate it recently. Specifically, no Western European population comes remotely close to the United States in per capita private charity. . . . Even accounting for differences in standard of living, Americans give more than twice as high a percentage of their incomes to charity as the Dutch, almost three times as much as the French, more than five times as much as the Germans, and more than ten times as much as the Italians.
>
> What about gifts of time? . . . No European country reaches American volunteering levels—indeed, most don't even come remotely close.[27]

The theory arguing that capitalism undermines relationships either is wrong or greatly exaggerates the effects. A likely explanation is that civil society is the primary place in which people form relationships, more so than via government or market ties. When government takes over too many functions in civil society, it weakens the institutions that form relationships, leaving market and state relationships that are too thin.

The Road Ahead

Communism failed. But what does that mean? While nearly everyone seems to have realized that centrally directed economies were inefficient, many other important lessons have gone unlearned.

One frequently overlooked issue is that central direction was never the point of the extreme ideologies of the twentieth century; rather, it was only a means to solve problems attributed to markets. Communism, fascism, and National Socialism all agreed on many ways that market systems were bad, and they sought to save society from the expected ravages. They differed, however, on the means to do so. Communists argued that the problems would disappear when private property and markets were eliminated. Fascists and National Socialists believed that market forces could be overcome if the state—or race— were held up as the national goal, and if *everything* was made subservient to the state, including the economy and civil society. From this perspective, national interest trumped class interest.[28]

Moreover, all three systems could justify their rejection of the Western heritage of faith and reason, grounded in a Judeo-Christian understanding of the human person, by decrying that heritage as not only backwards but also inadequate to solve the problems ascribed to capitalism. Thus supposed problems of markets became part of the ideologies that sought to eliminate faith.

The fact that these experiments failed—and failed to solve the social problems attributed to capitalism that they were intended to solve—should call into question the entire edifice of these systems' theories, including their views on religion and civil society. At a minimum, the theories placed far too much weight on economic factors.

Alas, the stunning failures of such theories, from the disasters of the totalitarian states to increases in social problems here in the United States *after* increases in well-being, are still not widely acknowledged. The same underlying assumptions that drove the twentieth century's ideological regimes—that market forces are powerful and destructive, and, by implication, that religion and civil society are unimportant—infused much social theory in the United States in the past century and continue to do so today. The modernist emphasis on economic factors as the source of so many problems remains, complete with the implications that governments must solve them because civil society is too weak. Clearly, we haven't learned the lessons or won the intellectual battle.

In some ways the current crisis has exacerbated the problem. From the millions undeniably hurt by the downturn to the myriad intellectuals ever eager to seize upon such events to vent their antimarket views, the crisis contributes to the general perception of markets as a uniquely pernicious social force, needing constant correction by the state. And the correction is rarely temporary or neutral. Spending-based stimulus of the type used in this crisis, and the massive expansions in regulation and oversight initiated as well, create far too many opportunities to politicize sectors of society, and augment the power of the state generally. As Hayek, Milton Friedman, and so many others pointed out, a state with power, means, and inclination to intervene so heavily in economic affairs is unlikely to stop there. In the process of all this, religion and civil society are crowded out, appreciation for their role languishes, and the groundwork is laid for more restrictions on them in the future.

Unfortunately, this is just when their contributions are needed more than ever. Culturally, in the West, we are rapidly abandoning the religious heritage that gave birth to our democratic institutions. As for markets, while I have argued that the problems attributed to capitalism are vastly overstated, that does not mean capitalism will be a force only for good. In the past, markets moved to provide what people wanted, and that mix of such basics as food, clothing, and shelter was generally good. In the future, however, markets will increasingly offer goods and services that challenge our very nature, such as performance-enhancing drugs and some forms of genetic engineering.

Consequently, while markets have not been as bad as people claim them to be, they will offer dangers in the future. What will rein in these dangers? Not the state. In fact, government incentives will probably support many of these measures. Rather, the key to addressing these threats is a vibrant civil society that helps people develop an understanding of humanity rich enough to temper demands for what the market might offer. This will require a society sure of the values it holds, understanding when the goods and services offered are more poison than solution. But today we are more unsure of those values and hostile to their contributions than ever before. How do we deal with that hostility and defend their role?

A crucial first step is to learn the lessons we should have gleaned from failed economic experiments. We need to recognize that we have already tested the belief that material factors were the source of so many problems, and that government is needed to solve the problems because religion and civil society are too weak.

That's why it is so critical to be cautious about the ways in which we argue for the importance of material/economic factors. The values and virtues nurtured by faith and civil society will be even more important for dealing with problems in the future than they have been in the past. A proper understanding of the magnitude of problems, and of the sources of those problems, is essential to preserving and protecting the vital resources that religion and civil society provide us.

Religion, the Market, and the State

Gerard Casey

"What has Athens to do with Jerusalem?" asked Tertullian, expressing his skepticism about the value of philosophy and pagan learning for Christian believers. This sentiment might be echoed in another mode by the question "What has religion to do with the market?" One thinks of Jesus driving the merchants and money changers from the temple (Matthew 21:12–13): "And Jesus went into the temple of God, and cast out all them that sold and bought in the temple, and overthrew the tables of the moneychangers, and the seats of them that sold doves, and said unto them, 'It is written, My house shall be called the house of prayer; but ye have made it a den of thieves.'" The precise theological significance of this stirring scriptural event is a matter of much debate. Are we to understand Jesus to be saying that buying and selling and money-changing, just as such, is a form of thievery? Or, somewhat less expansively, that such activities are not appropriate within the precincts of the temple? Or is he saying something else entirely? Whatever else it may mean, on the face of it, this passage doesn't seem to be sympathetic to the idea that Christianity and the market should occupy the same space.

Of course, the question of the relationship of religion to the market is likely to be answered differently depending on *which* religion we are dealing with. To be sure, the ethical systems of the different religions display a general consensus in basic ethical matters. While they differ in particulars and in degree of emphasis, most religions agree in prohibiting behavior that destroys human life and property. Moreover, all religions recognize that market activity is part—and only part—of a complete human life. But beyond those basics, key differences emerge. Religion covers a wide spectrum of possible options—from the theistic religions with which people in the West are most familiar (Judaism, Christianity, and Islam), to quasi-transcendent religions (such as Buddhism and Hinduism), to immanent and this-worldly religions (such as Confucianism). Understood broadly, religions provide the overarching schemas of meaning and significance within which we locate our own particular and limited experiences. Indeed, since the twentieth century there have emerged popular forms of *secular* religion, including fascism, Communism, Freudianism, dogmatic Darwinism, economism, and, most recently ascendant, environmentalism. As Robert Nelson writes in *The New Holy Wars*, "Secular religion became the most powerful religious force in western Europe and the United States in the twentieth century. The nation-states of the West had their state religions, turning the apparatus of the nation-state into a secular state church."[1]

Secularism became so powerful, in fact, that supposedly right-thinking (that is, secularist) people came to agree that traditional religion (by which they meant primarily Christianity) was dying as a dominant intellectual and social force—and a good thing, too. What a shock, then, to find that the infamous beast hasn't died but is, on the contrary, alive and well. And matters are going to get even worse for the devout secularist in the future. In his provocatively titled book *Shall the Religious Inherit the Earth?* Eric Kaufmann presents convincing demographic evidence that followers of religions, in particular religions of the more fundamentalist variety, are on the increase and that the trend of secularism will be reversed before 2050.[2]

Thus, contrary to the beliefs (and hopes) of secularists, the Judeo-Christian tradition that shaped the West remains the dominant tradition in the developed world. In this discussion I will focus on this still-central tradition as a way to explore the relationship between religion and the market today.[3]

Such a discussion would be incomplete if it did not also take account of religion's relationship to the *state*. Religion and politics have long been intertwined, but in an age of growing government authority, the connection between religion and the state is particularly important to consider. Some argue that the Judeo-Christian ethical tradition calls adherents to support the welfare state as the best provider of justice. But in fact, as we will see, the Judeo-Christian tradition claims that the state, apart from its dubiously ethical status, is both ineffectual and unprincipled in its role of welfare provider. This tradition values the market: it honors production and exchange, demands respect for private property, and requires believers to be generous to others with their possessions.

Work: Man as Procreator

For Jews and Christians alike, God is the creator of the world. Characteristic of both religions is a belief in the radical nonidentity of God and the universe He freely creates. God is not to be identified with any aspect of creation—the sun, the moon, the stars, or even the universe as a whole. Man, like everything else in the universe, is God's creature, but, unlike everything else in the universe, man is made in God's image and likeness, thus mirroring, in a finite and limited way, God's will and intellect. Because of this imaging, man, without compromising God's radical creativity, cooperates with God in a kind of subcreation. It might be said that if God is the creator *of* the world, then man is a creator *in* the world; if God creates *ex nihilo*, man procreates and transforms. Just as God rested at the end of his creative endeavors and saw that what he had done was good, so, too, is man's work, and the result of that work, good. Rabbi Jonathan Sacks notes that "Judaism did not share either the aristocratic disdain for work found in classical

Greece or the occasional tendency to other-worldliness found in early Christianity. It saw this-worldly prosperity as a sign of God's blessing, and work as man's 'partnership with God in the work of creation.'"[4] Man's work in the world is, in a limited way, an image of God's creative activity and as such cannot but be regarded positively by Jewish and Christian believers. The same holds for man's production and exchange of goods and services in the market, that complex, dynamic, ever-changing assemblage of free and uncoerced exchanges between individual human beings or between particular groups of human beings acting through individuals.

Property

What does the Judeo-Christian tradition have to say about private property, the protection of which is essential to a properly functioning market? Two of the Ten Commandments common to both Judaism and Christianity concern themselves with respect for property.[5] The first of the two commandments—*Thou shalt not steal* (Exodus 20:15)—flatly prohibits the misappropriation of another's property. Rabbi Sacks notes:

> Individual property rights were therefore as important to the Hebrew Bible as they later were to John Locke. One of the great biblical dramas is Elijah's challenge to King Ahab, who seizes Naboth's vineyard (1 Kings 21). Kings did not have the right to appropriate private property. The prophet Micah dreamed of a day in which 'every man will sit under his own vine and under his own fig tree and none will make him afraid' (Mic. 4:4).[6]

The second property-related commandment—*Thou shalt not covet thy neighbor's house; thou shalt not covet thy neighbor's wife, or male or female slave, or ox, or donkey, or anything that belongs to thy neighbor* (Exodus 20:17)—goes much further than the first. It prohibits not just the actual misappropriation of another's property but the very desire to have another's property for oneself. No policeman is going to arrest you or a court convict you for this coveting, at least not yet, but the commandment recognizes covetousness as a disordered moral disposition and as a serious source of social and spiritual disorder.

Many contemporary public discussions of equality and inequality appear to be grounded not so much in a desire that those who have little should have more as in a desire that those who have should be deprived of their possessions, if necessary, by force. Apart from the economically unsound presuppositions of this attitude (which seem to regard the creation and distribution of wealth as a zero-sum matter), the attitude is also ethically unsound, being grounded in covetousness and its sister vice, envy, which Jewish and Christian believers, if they take their religion seriously, must regard as sins—indeed, as deadly sins.

In addition to prohibitions contained in the commandments, additional aspects of the Christian attitude towards property can be gleaned from the Parable of the Talents (Matthew 25:14–30) and the Parable of the Workers in the Vineyard (Matthew 20:1–16).

In the Parable of the Talents, a man prepares to go on a journey. Before leaving, he summons three of his employees. He entrusts the first with a substantial amount of money, the second with a smaller but still large amount of money, and the third with somewhat less. The first employee trades with what he has received and makes as much again as he has been given. The second employee does likewise. But the third just squirrels away what he has been given and does nothing with it. When the employer returns, he is pleased with the productive employees but reprimands the third, saying, "You ought to have invested my money with the bankers, and at my coming I should have received what was my own with interest."

If the activities of trading and banking were morally problematic, they could have no place in the parable and the actions of the productive employees could not be commended. Luke's account of the parable (Luke 19:12–27) makes the point even more clearly: when giving money to his employees, the departing employer explicitly instructs them to trade with the money he has given them.

So trading and banking are ethically in order. Are there any restrictions on what one may do with one's money? The answer to this question comes in the Parable of the Workers in the Vineyard. In this parable, a man agrees to a wage rate with some workers for a day's labor. A little later, he hires some more workers, not agreeing to a wage rate with them but saying he will give them whatever is right. He does this three more times during the day, the last time being very near the end of the workday. The workers who were hired last are paid first and receive the amount agreed between the employer and the workers he first hired. When these come to be paid, they expect more than they originally bargained for and they complain when they don't get it. Their employer responds: "Friend, I am doing you no wrong; did you not agree with me for a denarius? Take what belongs to you, and go; I choose to give to this last as I give to you. Am I not allowed to do what I choose with what belongs to me? Or do you begrudge my generosity?" Although it may not be its most theologically significant aspect, the parable makes it quite clear that the disposition of one's wealth is not a matter for others to decide, whether those others be one's neighbors, friends, employees, or the state.

That brings us to neatly to the next topic.

Charity: Caring for Others

As believers, we are obliged to love God and to love our neighbors. How we satisfy that commandment is up to us. It is not the place of anyone else or any organization to do our loving for us; coerced charity is not charity. Nor does the end of alleviating poverty, desirable though that end may be, justify another in confiscating my resources from me for that end, even assuming that those resources would in fact be devoted to that purpose and not, as is often the case, simply wasted.

If you and I are walking down the Champs-Élysées and we come upon a chap with a sign around his neck saying he is homeless and requesting donations, you are perfectly at liberty to slip him five dollars; after all, you may do as you wish with your own money. Suppose, on the other hand, that I refuse to make a donation. If you think I should make a contribution, you can attempt to persuade me, plead with me, condemn me for my hard-heartedness; all these actions, though perhaps ineffectual, are permissible. What is impermissible is for you to put your hand in my pocket, take my money, and give it to another. That's theft. As the Parable of the Workers in the Vineyard makes abundantly clear, what I have is mine to do with what I will, just as what you have is yours to do with what you will. Likewise, the first of the property-respecting commandment says, "Thou shalt not steal," not, "Thou shalt not steal—unless you do it for the purpose of giving the proceeds to a deserving third party."

If we have the right to dispose of our property as we see fit, we also have the responsibility to answer for the choices we make. The key Christian text on our obligations to others is, of course, the Parable of the Good Samaritan, at the end of which the lawyer who puts the question "Who is my neighbor?" to Jesus is pointedly told, "Go, and do likewise." Provided that we are willing to act on the obligations we have towards others in need and that we do so when appropriate, our accumulation of wealth cannot be a vice. How indeed is one to be charitable unless one has the wherewithal to be charitable? The Samaritan could not have helped the man set upon by robbers unless he had the money to pay the innkeeper. In a Jewish context, Rabbi Sacks notes the double aspect of property when he remarks: "Wealth is seen as both a blessing and as a responsibility. The wealthy are expected to share their blessings with others and to be personal role models of social and communal responsibility: *Richesse oblige.*"[7]

There is evidence that some in the early Christian community displayed a somewhat cavalier attitude towards material possessions. In the Acts of the Apostles (Acts 2:44; 4:32–37) we seem to have a form of proto-Communism, with believers being encouraged to sell all they have and give it to others according to their needs. (One needs to ask: where did they sell what they had and to whom? Clearly, only to other people in a market.) This curious behavior is understandable when one realizes that the early Christians appear to have expected an imminent Second Coming of Christ and, consequently, the end of the world. In light of that, their time preference schedules differed dramatically from those of their non-Christian neighbors, as would yours if you believed the world was going to end soon. Once the expectation of a more or less immediate return of Christ faded, Christians had to come to terms with living in the same world occupied by everyone else. At that point their early quasi-socialistic practices ceased.

One's charitable obligations, then, are personal and cannot be satisfied by indirect proxy, certainly not by the interventionist state. According to a standard account, *the* central and ineliminable function of the state is to provide the conditions of peace, security, and justice that are necessary for individuals freely to relate to one another to their mutual advantage—which is to say, to make possible the operation of a market, broadly construed. It is not the function of such a state, even a state of a historically religious character, to take upon itself the specifically religious tasks of sharing goods, providing welfare. There are two reasons for this: the first, consequential; the second, principled.

As consequences indicate, the state is profligate and inefficient in attempting to provide welfare. Ask yourself: if you had some extra cash lying around that you were willing to give for the relief of poverty, would you (a) give it to a state agency or (b) either give it to a private charity or disburse it yourself? To ask this question is to answer it.

Even if, in the face of overwhelming evidence, one could show that the state were not profligate and inefficient in its attempts at welfare provision, there remains the principled problem that the state has no resources of its own to devote to welfare. As with any other organization, if people are willing freely to donate to it, then it may disburse this money according to its articles of association. The state, however, obtains its resources by forcibly extracting them from its captive taxpaying citizenry; it is difficult to see any significant moral distinction between this and common acts of theft. In acting as it does, the welfare state, however well-intentioned, bears a striking resemblance to your soon-to-be ex-friend on the Champs-Élysées who helped himself to your money.

Supporting a coercive state apparatus cannot possibly be the only way you can satisfy your religious obligations to feed the hungry, give drink to the thirsty, clothe the naked, and shelter the homeless. It would be difficult to find any passage in the Jewish or Christian scriptures which suggests that our love for our neighbor should be demonstrated in a practical way by setting up a government agency. Significantly, in the Parable of the Good Samaritan, those who pass by without helping the wounded man—the priest and the Levite—are the representatives of officialdom.[8]

The State

It is fair to say that, on balance, both the Jewish and Christian scriptures exhibit a somewhat less than enthusiastic attitude towards those who aspire to rule us.[9] Most relevant scriptural passages are deeply skeptical of the value of secular political rule. Perhaps the best-known example is the passage in the Book of Samuel (1 Samuel 8:4–22) in which the elders of Israel ask Samuel to give them a king, saying to him: "Behold, thou art old, and thy sons walk not in thy ways. Now make us a king to judge us, like all the nations." Samuel isn't happy about this demand and consults God, who tells him that this request indicates that the people of Israel have rejected God's reign over them. He instructs Samuel to listen to what the people have said but to point out to them what their request involves. So Samuel tells the people what to expect if they get a king. The king, he says, will take their sons and daughters and put them to work in his service as soldiers and servants, and will confiscate their fields and vineyards and olive groves. In short, they will find that having a king is expensive and unpleasant business. This good advice is accorded the reception generally given to good advice—it is ignored. (The subsequent history of the kings of Israel, from Saul, through David, Solomon, and Rehoboam, followed by the division of the kingdom, is distinctly unedifying and can be seen as a partial fulfillment of Samuel's warning.)

Only a few scriptural passages appear to run against this general current. The best-known and most often cited passage is Romans 13:1–7.[10] This passage is worth quoting in full:

> Let every person be subject to the governing authorities. For there is no authority except from God, and those that exist have been instituted by God. Therefore he who resists the authorities resists what God has appointed, and those who resist will incur judgment. For rulers are not a terror to good conduct but to bad. Would you have no fear of him who is in authority? Then do what is good and you will receive his approval, for he is God's servant for your good. But if you do wrong, be afraid, for he does not bear the sword in vain; he is the servant of God to execute his wrath on the wrongdoer. Therefore, one must be subject, not only to avoid God's wrath but also for the sake of conscience. For the same reason you also pay taxes, for the authorities are ministers of God, attending to this very thing. Pay all of them their dues, taxes to whom taxes are due, revenue to whom revenue is due, respect to whom respect is due, honor to whom honor is due.

Many, indeed most, commentators assume that in this passage St. Paul refers to the secular authorities and enjoins obedience to them. But why should we make this assumption? Let's place this passage in context. In the previous chapter (Romans 12:2), St. Paul has just written, "Do not be conformed to the world . . ."; why should we think that he would almost immediately contradict himself and counsel conformity to the world? The bulk of chapter 12, and the verses of chapter 13 that occur immediately after the passage just cited, concern themselves with what is required of the *Christian* in living a *Christian* life, of the mutual duties and responsibilities *among Christians*. Nothing explicit in these two chapters supports the claim that St. Paul has switched his focus in the early verses of chapter 13 to discuss the Christian's relationship to *civil* government.

In fact, the context seems to support the contrary: St. Paul is dealing with spiritual authority within the Church, the Body of Christ, and the individual member's relationship to that authority. The apostle tells us to submit to the higher powers and then quotes the law of the higher powers, of which the particular commandments are only particular exemplifications. What St. Paul is talking about here is the law of God; what has this to do with the dictates of the secular authorities? Why would St. Paul suddenly switch to a completely different topic, only to switch back again just as quickly to what he was speaking of in chapter 12? It would be much less arbitrary to conclude that St. Paul is exhorting those to whom he is writing this letter to be obedient to *their* authorities.

Let us recall, too, how the secular authorities persecuted the Church: killing all the male children in Bethlehem under two (Matthew 2:16); beheading John the Baptist (Matthew 14:10); slaughtering the Galileans whose blood Pilate mingled with their sacrifices (Luke 13:1); arresting the apostles for preaching the gospel (Acts 4:3 and 5:40); executing James and arresting Peter (Acts 12:2–3); beating Paul and Silas with rods and imprisoning them (Acts 16:19–24). Moreover, tradition holds that St. Peter and St. Paul were judicially executed, and there is no reason to doubt that the tradition is valid. And last, but by no means least, we have the arraignment of Jesus by the Jewish authorities, and his judicial torture and execution by the Roman procurator Pontius Pilate, despite Pilate's not being able to find any case against him. After all this, are we seriously to believe that St. Paul is demanding that Roman Christians obey the secular authorities in any matter in which those authorities care to command them?[11]

Religion and Politics

From the earliest recorded times, religion and politics have been inter-twined, either mutually supportive or, in some cases, considered as two different aspects of the same thing. In many countries, the supreme political leader was also the chief priest of the state religion. One of the chief functions of the Chinese emperor was to act as an intermediary between the earthly and heavenly realms. The position of the Egyptian pharaohs was similarly sacerdotal, and even the practical Romans couldn't resist the temptation to divinize their emperors.

For the first three hundred years of its institutional life, Christianity was a nonestablishment, oftentimes persecuted religion. Its adherents were believed to be atheists—that is to say, *they did not worship the gods of the state*—and therefore politically subversive. The Constantinian settlement resulting from the Edict of Milan in A.D. 313 was undertaken as much to see what support Christianity could bring to the Roman state as to see what support the Roman state could bring to Christianity.

The settlement was not an unmixed blessing for Christianity, as the emperors showed a strong disposition to assume a leadership role in the Church. "Caesaropapism," the effective union of political and religious power, quickly became the norm of Church governance—with secular government playing the major role in the partnership. This norm prevailed in the Eastern Empire until its fall in A.D. 1453.

In the post-Roman West, the story was somewhat different. After the collapse of the Western Roman Empire, the rulers of the various barbarian tribes retained their original sacral functions even when Christianized—a kind of caesaropapism in miniature. All this changed with the Papal Revolution inaugurated by Gregory VII in 1075. Over the next four hundred years, the Catholic Church tried, and to a large extent succeeded, in establishing its independence from the various political orders, whether local, regional, or imperial. This welcome development came to a shuddering halt with the onset of the Reformation.

Leaving to one side its purely religious dimensions and its complicated theological debates, one of the Reformation's most significant and deleterious consequences was the reemergence of regional forms of caesaropapism in the newly emerging autonomous, and more often than not absolutist, states. These regional caesaropapisms were to be found primarily in the areas under the sway of the Reformed traditions, Lutheran or Calvinist, but were also witnessed in areas that remained Catholic. To an extent that had not been seen since the eleventh century, the Church, or rather Churches, now came under pressure to become departments in the various sovereign and independent states, a pressure to which they largely yielded.

The history of the West since the sixteenth and seventeenth centuries has been a sad and tangled tale of the intermixture of religion and politics that, whatever benefits it may have brought to political authorities, has done significant damage to religion.

Religion in the Marketplace

As a human activity, the practice of religion is itself subject to the laws of the market. When religion is monopolized by the state, we shouldn't be surprised to find that the outcome is the same as that of any other artificially created monopoly: the service becomes expensive and inefficient; the "business" is run more for the welfare of the employees than for the benefit of its "owners" and "customers"; and the employees are often merely quasi–state functionaries, uncommitted to the original ends of the enterprise.

The benefit to a religion of its exercising a state-backed monopoly is primarily financial. It is supported financially not through the voluntary donations of its members but by a tax levied on all citizens of the state, believers and unbelievers alike. The downside of state establishment is that state functionaries frequently interfere in the control, management, and even the doctrine of the church, while evangelical fervor usually diminishes among the mass of erstwhile believers. Adam Smith remarks on this in his *Wealth of Nations*: "The teachers of new religions have always had a considerable advantage in attacking those antient and established systems of which the clergy, reposing themselves upon their benefices, had neglected to keep up the fervour of faith and devotion in the great body of the people."[12] Similarly, the leading contemporary commentator in this area, Laurence Iannaccone, remarks that as religious provision in a state approaches monopoly, "Church attendance rates, frequency of prayer, belief in God, and virtually every other measure of piety decline as religious market concentration increases."[13] On the other hand, when the state ceases to maintain an established church and religion is deregulated, the rate of participation in religious practice increases.

Finally, religion and markets exhibit similar structural features. Religion teaches self-restraint, deferred gratification of desires, and the construction of social capital; the market requires savings, deferred spending, and the accumulation of capital. Religion demands the service of others, which produces both social and spiritual order; the market requires the service of others if either psychic or material profit is to be produced. Religion requires at least a minimal basic morality, oriented towards the elements of justice, and actively encourages much more than this; the market cannot function without a basic morality, and its flourishing requires more than this.

Conclusion

It can be difficult to separate religion and the market from the state in the modern era, in which the welfare state has spread throughout the West and government has made ever greater inroads into individual and community life. If the eighteenth century saw a need to separate church and state for the sake of the state, surely we now need to separate the state from the many areas into which its tentacles have reached during what can only be described as the state-intoxicated twentieth century. We need to separate the provision of health care from the inefficient and clumsy state bureaucracies; we need to separate the provision of real education from the indoctrination supplied by state schools; we need to separate genuine welfare provision, respectful of human dignity, from the expensive yet paradoxically poverty-inducing state programs.

We are told that our current economic troubles have resulted from "market failure," and this of course has led to calls for the markets to be regulated—regulated by the very state which has contributed most to those troubles through its cavalier disregard for economic reality. Our current economic troubles are not the product of the operation of a free market, about which we might say, as Gandhi is supposed to have said about Western civilization, that it would be a good idea. And the solution to our problems will not be found by deficit spending or quantitative easing or any other ingenious but fundamentally unsound scheme. Rather, it will be found by allowing the market to do what it does best when not shackled—that is, to create wealth, wealth that improves the lot of all in society, the poor as well as the rich.

Just like markets, religion suffers from too much government intrusion and flourishes when freed from such restraints. Equally important, we cannot simply accept that the common functioning of the welfare state—with government increasing its role in our lives and its control of the economy—represents a proper understanding of what the dominant religious tradition in the West has to say about the role of the market and the state. In fact, the Judeo-Christian tradition values work and wealth, supports free markets and free enterprise, demands respect for private property, encourages generosity towards those who are poor, and is deeply skeptical about the value of government action in most spheres, particularly in its self-appointed role of welfare provider. Genuine religious followers of the Judeo-Christian tradition should be uncomfortable with any form of state sponsorship of religion, not least because of its destructive effect on religious belief and practice and the stifling effect it has on the religious obligation to care for the poor.

The Road to Cultural Serfdom: America's First Television Czar

Paul A. Cantor

Have you ever wondered why the "tiny ship" famously tossed in the opening credits of *Gilligan's Island* was named the SS *Minnow?* The creator of the show, Sherwood Schwartz, has revealed that he intended the name as a swipe at Newton Minow, the chairman of the Federal Communications Commission (FCC) appointed by President John F. Kennedy at the beginning of his administration. Minow created a sensation by attacking the whole television industry in a speech before the National Association of Broadcasters (NAB) in Washington, D.C., on May 9, 1961. Describing television as a "vast wasteland," Minow called upon the networks to clean up their houses and improve their programming. Schwartz regarded the results of Minow's speech as "disastrous." As he explains:

> Until his speech, the networks were conduits and they had no control of programming. Sponsors had more power, and the creative people who created the shows had more authority. Minow gave networks authority and placed the power of programming in the hands of three network heads, who, for a long time, controlled everything coming into your living

room. They eventually became the de facto producers of all prime-time programs by having creative control over writing, casting, and directing.[1]

If Schwartz is correct, then Minow's campaign to improve television programming is a typical story of ill-advised government intervention in the marketplace. His charge to the television industry was clear: "You must provide a wider range of choices, more diversity, more alternatives."[2] Yet Schwartz claims that Minow's speech resulted in centralizing power in the television industry and thus actually reducing the range of choices in programs. In the terms of Friedrich Hayek's analysis of government intervention, Minow's crusade was a classic case of government regulation having unintended consequences, and it illustrates perfectly the folly of top-down models of social order.

In a pattern that has become all-too-familiar in subsequent decades, Minow adopted the role of a "culture czar."[3] He assumed that he was in a position to oversee the whole realm of television and dictate the new directions it should take. He claimed to know exactly what was best for the American public (curiously, it coincided with his own taste in television). Moreover, he was confident that, under his wise leadership, all that network executives had to do was to order up more creative programming and it would automatically be forthcoming, as if a higher level of culture could be produced on command.

Minow was typical of the cockiness of the Kennedy administration; his speech is full of the rhetoric of the New Frontier. In true Camelot fashion, he thought of himself as a knight in shining armor, riding to the rescue of a television industry in distress, ready to lead the network executives out of the darkness of commerce into the light of the public interest. And yet, according to Schwartz—a producer with years of experience in the media—Minow succeeded only in making American television worse. If this turns out to be the case, then the story of Minow's intervention in the television industry provides a cautionary tale, a warning against the federal government's persistent efforts to control not just the modern media but culture itself.

As Hayek knew, the arrogance of government power extends even to the cultural realm. In an era when government "czars" and other bureaucrats intrude in practically all aspects of our lives, we would do well to examine the federal government's early interventions in mass media. We must understand that it is not only in economics that central planning is a mistake. As Hayek warned throughout his writings, there are always dangers associated with such top-down attempts to remake society.

Newt's Nuclear Option

Schwartz undoubtedly overstated Minow's role when he claimed that the FCC chairman "gave networks authority and placed the power of programming in the hands of three network heads." Minow did not have the statutory authority to intervene this directly in the television industry. But the historical record shows that Minow's speech and his follow-up actions indirectly had just the effects Schwartz describes. Throughout his speech Minow walked a thin line. He insisted that he had faith in the free-enterprise system in general and the broadcasting industry in particular, and denied that he had any intention of imposing his will on it. But his words contained clear threats that if the television industry did not voluntarily do what he wanted, the FCC would make sure that it did.

His impudence surfaced early in the speech when he addressed "an editorialist in the trade press" who "wrote 'that the FCC of the New Frontier is going to be one of the toughest FCC's in the history of broadcast regulation'":

> If he meant that we intend to enforce the law in the public interest, let me make it perfectly clear that he is right: We do. If he meant that we intend to muzzle or censor broadcasting, he is dead wrong. It wouldn't surprise me if some of you expected me to come here today and say to you in effect, "Clean up your

own house or the government will do it for you." Well, in a limited sense, you would be right because I've just said it.

Here we see how Minow tried to have it both ways: he manages to make his threat in the very act of denying that he is making it.

The trump card Minow knew he was holding was the FCC's power to deny renewal of the networks' broadcasting licenses, without which they could not operate on the airways. In common parlance, this would be known as the nuclear option. It did not take Minow long to make it explicit that under his leadership the FCC might choose to exercise this option: "I understand that many people feel that in the past licenses were often renewed *pro forma*. I say to you now: renewal will not be *pro forma* in the future. There is nothing permanent or sacred about a broadcast license." Minow could not dictate directly to the networks how to run their business, but he could put them out of business if they failed to respond to his demands.

As the legal scholar Robert Corn-Revere observes, Minow's speech "was an exercise in public interest piracy—a naked effort to coerce broadcasters indirectly into doing what the government could not compel directly. It is the kind of speech that puts the bully in the bully pulpit."[4] After raising a possibility intimidating enough in itself—holding public hearings on the networks' performance—Minow taunted his audience with the prospect of annihilation: "Now some of you may say, 'Yes, but I still do not know where the line is between a grant of a renewal and the hearing you just spoke of.' My answer is: Why should you want to know how close you can come to the edge of the cliff?" Minow deliberately left vague when and how he might intervene in the affairs of the networks, thus leaving the executives in his audience uncertain about their future, and then professed mock astonishment that they might be concerned about the very survival of their business.

It is hardly surprising, then, that the television networks took Minow's demands very seriously.[5] And his demands were extensive, including more public-affairs and educational programming, shows more suitable for children, more local programming, less violence, fewer commercials, and, last but not least, higher-quality shows. It is typical of a government bureaucrat's mentality that Minow evidently believed that the network executives were in a position to effect all these changes—and to do so immediately. Government departments are arranged hierarchically; those at the top are used to issuing orders and expect them to be carried out by their subordinates right down the line. Minow assumed that a cultural institution like television has a similar hierarchical structure, as if television executives could requisition more creative programming the way a bureaucrat orders new pencils or department stationery.

In fact, Minow's speech shows that he misunderstood the structure of the industry he was supposed to be regulating. That was almost inevitable, given the fact that he did not have the slightest experience with the television industry when Kennedy appointed him chairman of the FCC. Minow was a lawyer by profession, a partner in the law firm of two-time Democratic presidential candidate Adlai Stevenson. His chief "qualification" for the FCC job was the fact that he was a personal friend of the president's brother Robert Kennedy.[6] Minow epitomized the would-be managerial revolution of the Kennedy administration, the idea that "the best and the brightest" could be entrusted with remaking any American institution on the basis of their general expertise, rather than on any particular experience with the institution. In his NAB address, Minow clearly conceived of himself as one member of the managerial elite speaking to others, and he thought of television as just one more problem of administration that the Kennedy whiz kids were going to solve.

As Sherwood Schwartz explained, however, Minow overestimated the degree to which television executives in 1961 controlled the programming on their networks. To be sure, CBS, NBC, and ABC produced their news and public-affairs programs in-house, as well as their morning and late-night shows. But for their prime-time programming, the TV networks generally still followed a pattern they had inherited from radio, in which they sold airtime to sponsors, who developed shows largely independently, often in concert with their advertising agencies. A television producer might approach a potential sponsor with an idea for a show, or a sponsor might try to interest a TV or movie star in a new show format. The networks might get involved in such negotiations, but basically they were not responsible for the content of most of the programs they aired in prime time.

In his inaugural speech as FCC chairman, Minow announced that he was unilaterally changing the rules of the game. With the threat of denying license renewal to the networks, he forced CBS, NBC, and ABC to become more directly involved in developing their prime-time programming, and indeed to assume control over its content. This is what Schwartz really meant when he said that Minow "placed the power of programming in the hands of three network heads." The networks suddenly took it upon themselves to initiate programming possibilities and to supervise all aspects of program development and production. In effect, Minow imposed upon the television industry the top-down structure that he, as a bureaucrat, had assumed was characteristic of it in the first place. Bureaucrats always prefer dealing with other bureaucrats.

Of course, Minow was not solely responsible for these developments. The television industry had already been trending toward a more hierarchical structure, as the broadcasting companies, with their concern for ratings and profits, were seeking greater command over programming. Even without Minow and the FCC, the three networks undoubtedly would have become more involved in producing programs in the 1960s. But there can be no question that Minow's actions greatly accelerated this process, and profoundly influenced the precise form the networks' intervention took.

"Wildly Galloping New Frontiersmen"

We can now see what Schwartz was complaining about in Minow's actions as FCC chairman. When sponsors were largely responsible for developing prime-time shows, the television industry had a more freewheeling, bottom-up structure. Just about any business was a potential sponsor, and anyone with an idea for a TV show could shop his proposal to a wide variety of prospects. He might still be turned down by everybody, but at least he had many options to explore. Under the new post–Minow regime in television, if a producer could not sell his idea for a program to one of the three networks, he was out of luck.[7] By drastically reducing the number and variety of people involved in deciding which shows made it onto the air, Minow substantially decreased the diversity of television programming—exactly the opposite of what he was calling for to improve the medium.

But Minow's effect on the television industry went deeper than merely concentrating programming power in the hands of CBS, NBC, and ABC. Once the networks assumed this power, they inevitably used it to try to placate Minow and thereby to fend off hostile FCC actions against them. Minow swore in his NAB address: "I am unalterably opposed to governmental censorship. There will be no suppression of programming which does not meet bureaucratic taste." In fact, he never intervened personally to censor any television program. Instead, he let frightened network executives do his dirty work for him. By the spring of 1962, a trade journal summed up what had happened in the industry in familiar Kennedy imagery: "With a posse of wildly galloping New Frontiersmen breathing down their necks, and the shadow of the hanging tree lengthening over the land, the television industry's own sheriffs are intensifying their efforts to bring law and order to some of the wilder domains of the medium."[8]

The result of all these efforts was precisely to impose "bureaucratic taste" on American television. Lacking any magic formula that would instantaneously conjure up quality programs, the networks could not be sure of pleasing Minow. Thus they settled for not offending him. A number of prominent industry voices from the time testify to the chilling effect Minow had on television creativity. ABC producer Roy Huggins said: "Now for the first time in [television's] brief history, a decline in quality and spirit is underway, and the abrupt reversal is largely the result of Newton Minow's policies as Chairman of the Fed-

Back on the Road to Serfdom

eral Communications Commission. . . . Imagination does not flourish in a climate of coercion."[9] When Minow expressed support for having "questionable" shows prescreened by the NAB for its approval, CBS president Frank Stanton condemned the idea at the annual meeting of the network's affiliated stations in the spring of 1962:

> I am persuaded that this is a bad deal for the broadcasters because it is a bad deal for the public. With the programming veto power centralized, you can't help but get a drastic watering down of programming content. You end up with nothing but a great big bowl of Junket. . . . Creative television would die a slow and agonizing death. The tendency to produce what would "get by" would be irresistible. . . . Experimentation, innovation, all chance-taking would cease as a group of timid, well-meaning men took over the responsibility of deciding what was to be shown on 50 million receivers.[10]

Media historian Mary Ann Watson writes: "Ultimately, the pre-screening provision was never enacted, but nonetheless, a distinct chill continued to run through the creative community."[11]

A detailed analysis of the damage Minow did to American television was offered by Mark Goodson, of Goodson-Todman Productions, one of the most influential forces in shaping television in its early days. In a speech to the 1962 convention of the American Women in Radio and Television, Goodson explained:

> When a presentation of a new show lands on my desk, I . . . let my eye move down the page to scan the contents. . . . My attention is flagged somewhere down the page by a name. That name is Minow. . . . I have even developed a pet name for this usage. With no disrespect intended, I call it the "Minow Paragraph."
>
> A crude translation might be "You may not like this show. The public may not like it—but *he will*." . . . The program mate-

rial of these shows is generally antiseptic, somewhat didactic, slightly dull, offensive to no one and above all else "justifiable." The words "entertainment" or "pleasure" are seldom, if ever, mentioned. Like Latin and spinach, these shows are supposed to be good for you.[12]

Goodson offers a perfect description of "bureaucratic taste," and explains how Minow succeeded in imposing it on the television industry. To improve programming would have required the network executives to take risks with new formulas, but that was the last thing they wanted to do when facing the threat of losing their licenses—and their jobs.

Instead, the executives fell back upon tried-and-true formulas that were proven not to offend anybody. As Watson recounts:

As the first Minow Season evolved during the spring and summer of 1962, the innovation in programming the industry had promised after the Wasteland speech failed to materialize. Old stars and old formats appeared on tentative prime-time schedules. Television critic Hal Humphrey believed fear of the unknown precluded breaking new ground. "It's as if the program vice-presidents had decided to find safety by re-living their past," the critic said. Big doses of crime and sex had to go. And, Humphrey pointed out, "nobody ever beefed about Jack Gleason or Lucy Ball, did they?"[13]

Watson and Humphrey are describing bureaucratic behavior at its most bureaucratic. Network executives became obsessed with protecting their jobs by doing as little as possible to rock the boat. As a result, the 1960s became arguably the blandest decade of American television. Situation comedies of the most formulaic and innocuous kind came to dominate the three networks' prime-time schedules. As Watson writes: "When the 1962–63 season finally aired, comedy shows stole the limelight from westerns and action series. Seven of the top ten

179

programs were comedies, with *The Beverly Hillbillies*, a surprise ratings blockbuster, as number one. Most critics were appalled."[14] So much for Minow's revolution in the quality of television programming.

Top-down versus Bottom-up Culture

With his New Frontier faith in the power of government to solve any problem, Minow failed to grasp how complex culture is and how elusive artistic creativity can be. One cannot simply command better television programs, especially not original and innovative shows. Government bureaucrats and network executives are not themselves creative people. On their own, they cannot foresee what better programming will look like or how it can be produced. At best, they can recognize creative programming when real talent produces it. That is why the television business is, to put it bluntly, a crapshoot. It works best by a process of trial and error, what one might call cultural selection on the analogy of Darwin's natural selection. In the ideal situation, a large variety of television producers will be in competition, with the freedom to experiment, trying out all sorts of possibilities, to see what will click with both critics and the public.[15]

As in all circumstances, in cultural production a market economy is more likely than a command economy to achieve higher quality, simply because markets multiply the forces participating in the creative process and thus draw upon a greater range of knowledge, skill, experience, and talent. What looks like chaos to a government bureaucrat is in fact the lifeblood of culture. By concentrating the power of programming in fewer hands and thereby significantly reducing the range of experimentation, Minow's project was doomed from the start. The government cannot force people to be creative.

From the beginning, Minow acted like the typical government bureaucrat. He identified what he regarded as a problem—a preponderance of low-quality shows on television, what he called the "vast wasteland." He never considered that this situation might be inherent

180

to the medium of television—that with so many thousands of television hours to program every year, there is just not enough talent to ensure that the average show is of high artistic quality.[16] Instead of recognizing this inescapable fact of television as a mass medium, Minow looked around for a villain and blamed the commercial nature of television for what he regarded as its failings. Here he betrayed his antimarket prejudices: greedy businessmen must be responsible for the low quality of television.[17] Having made the problem into one of private versus public interest, Minow naturally thought that the federal government could come to the rescue of television.

We are confronted here with two radically opposed models of how culture operates, a top-down versus a bottom-up view. For Minow, the way for culture to prosper is to have the government, from its superior vantage point, instruct television executives to plan better programming. That is to say, he was certain that central planning would significantly improve television. But given the unpredictability of artistic success, a culture flourishes when no one is in a position to try to impose order on it, but its energies are free to bubble up, as it were, from below. Having thoroughly misconceived the nature of the problem, Minow not surprisingly came up with a cure that turned out to be worse than the disease.

A good example of how Minow's intervention affected television programming involves *The Untouchables*, the popular series Desilu Studios produced for ABC, in which the straight-arrow lawman Eliot Ness made war on Chicago gangsters. This show quickly became as notorious as the criminals whose stories it chronicled. Taking violence on television to new levels of frequency and brutality, it was often the focus of Minow's complaints. As a result of all the attacks from Congress and the FCC, ABC felt compelled to do something about the series. The Desilu executive producer was forced to concede for the 1962–63 season: "The pressure is on us because it's a marked series. . . . There will be less violence in the series. . . . We have stories in which no killings occur."[18] The new, eviscerated version of the show failed to please the public, and its ratings plummeted, leading to its swift cancellation.[19] But Minow was happy, commenting with approval: "The blood on the living room floor isn't as deep as it was a year ago."[20]

The case of *The Untouchables* helps to reveal the nature of government intervention in television programming. Although I remember the show with some fondness, I would not claim that it was an artistic masterpiece. Nevertheless, in its own way, the show was well done, highly stylized, with attention to period details and, generally speaking, exciting plots that centered on the age-old conflict between good and evil. The casting was strong; in fact, the performances of Nehemiah Persoff as Jake "Greasy Thumb" Guzik and Bruce Gordon as Frank "The Enforcer" Nitti were exceptional, arguably among the most effective portrayals of villains in the history of television. But that was the problem—critics of the show complained about gangsters being presented as such memorable characters. That means that the objections to the show were moral, not artistic. *The Untouchables* was condemned for being not aesthetically deficient but politically incorrect. This impression is confirmed by one of the other major criticisms of the show—that it consistently presented Italian-Americans in an unfavorable light. (The fact that Al Capone's mob did consist chiefly of Italian-Americans was not regarded as a legitimate defense.) Organizations representing Italian-Americans put pressure on Desilu and ABC to stop what they regarded as ethnic stereotyping, and in its final season *The Untouchables* was forced to become an equal-opportunity employer of gangsters. After all these years, I am a little hazy on the details, but I believe that in one of the final episodes the dramatic tension was somewhat reduced when Ness was confronted with a ring of WASP gangsters who were spiking the iced tea at church picnics and rigging the bingo games. He chastised them severely.

Politics Trumps Aesthetics

The Untouchables was one of the early victims of political correctness on television, and Minow's obsession with the series shows that artistic considerations were never foremost in his mind as his emphasis on "higher quality" in programming implied. Not surprisingly, when the government regulates culture, political and not artistic criteria will in the end become primary. For one thing, Minow was in no position to make expert aesthetic judgments about anything. Born in Milwaukee, he was a perfect representative of Middle American, middlebrow cultural taste, as became evident in his NAB speech. Attempting to offer examples of television at its best, he knew that he should mention *Playhouse 90* and *Studio One*, as well as a dramatization of Joseph Conrad's novel *Victory*. But I suspect that Minow's own taste emerged when he added *The Bing Crosby Special* to the mix, and later listed *Peter Pan* as one of the great moments in TV history.[21]

Minow was of course entitled to his personal taste in American television. The problem was that he was trying to impose it on the whole country. What business did he have mentioning specific shows he approved of in a speech in which he was threatening the networks with the loss of their licenses if they did not come up with what he regarded as better programming? Even his supporter Watson has her doubts about his speech:

> The most controversial aspect of Minow's address that afternoon . . . was his direct commentary, both favorable and critical, on television programming. Minow's specific references to programs he felt were "eminently worthwhile," such as *The Twilight Zone*, *CBS Reports*, and *The Fred Astaire Show*, would provide some ammunition for his critics who charged the Number One regulator was attempting to impose his idea of good taste on millions of American viewers.[22]

As we have seen, "What would Newt like?" quickly became the question on the minds of all the network executives.[23] No single person should have such power over any aspect of American culture, especially someone who had no claim whatsoever to being especially cultured himself.

Minow's interference in television illustrates one of Hayek's principal objections to government intervention in society. Like any central planner, Minow acted largely out of ignorance, unfamiliar with the domain he was governing, and above all he lacked the local knowledge and experience that was actually needed to improve television. He stepped in as a complete outsider and effectively remade the structure of the industry in ways that many experts in the field claim led to a new era of bland uniformity in programming.

Lacking any grasp of aesthetic criteria, Minow had to employ political criteria in his evaluation of television, and the industry responded accordingly. As Watson documents, the changes in television content in the 1960s chiefly followed a political agenda—greater representation of minorities on shows, especially African-Americans; more dramas devoted to controversial political issues, displaying a deepened social conscience; in particular a number of shows dealing with the issue of civil rights, which not coincidentally was being promoted at the same time by the Kennedy and Johnson administrations.[24] Watson wholeheartedly approves of all this, but does not note the interesting fact that television in the 1960s increasingly fell in line with the program of the Democratic Party. This is exactly what one might have predicted under the leadership of an activist FCC chairman appointed by a Democratic president. As is evident in the NAB speech, Minow's interest in television was fundamentally political to begin with. One just has to look at his laundry list for improving television. He wanted television to increase Americans' participation in the political process; to make better citizens; to project a more positive image of America abroad; and to contribute to the cause of world peace. In sum, he wanted television to become an arm of the Kennedy regime. The fact that he viewed all these goals as noncontroversial shows how truly partisan he was; he could not think outside of the New Frontier box. Inevitably, the NAB speech builds up to a ringing Kennedy climax: "I say to you ladies and gentleman: Ask not what broadcasting can do for you; ask what you can do for broadcasting. And ask what broadcasting can do for America."

As with everything else on the New Frontier, Minow's agenda for television was closely bound up with the Cold War. When he stressed the need for more educational programming, he did so in the context of competition with the Communist world, as Watson reports:

> In October 1961, when Minow gave the keynote address to the annual meeting of the National Association of Educational Broadcasters, he reminded his audience that communist countries were developing educational television programming with alacrity. Soviet children, for instance, had been learning English through televised lessons since 1959. And with the aid of technicians and equipment from Russia, Red China, and East Germany, even the tiny country of Albania was airing three and one-half hours of educational television each day.[25]

As a rule, I tend to distrust people who speak well of Albania and especially those who speak well of Albanian television. Minow's impulse to offer it as a model for America suggests that he thought of himself not as a culture czar but as a culture commissar. Indeed, this speech embodies all that was most questionable in the Cold War fixation of the Kennedy administration—above all, the tendency to remake the United States on the pattern of the very enemies it was fighting.

In sum, in the spirit of the Kennedy administration, Minow wanted to enlist television in a national crusade, to make America and the whole world a better place. Reading the NAB speech, one finds all the standard themes of Wilsonian progressivism. Minow wanted television to do no less than bring peace and understanding to the world, and to make it safe for democracy (or at least for the Democratic Party). Fortunately the fact that the television industry in the United States is largely in private hands limited the impact Minow could have on it and the damage he could do to it. Still, he did leave television worse than he found it, and his brief tenure as FCC chairman illustrates the basic principle of Hayek's critique of government intervention.

Utopianism and the Road to Serfdom

Ultimately Minow's hopes for television were utopian. The NAB speech is almost religious in tone at times (it certainly is preachy), with flashes of apocalyptic fears and millennial hopes:

> In today's world, with chaos in Laos and the Congo aflame, with Communist tyranny on our Caribbean doorstep, relentless pressures on our Atlantic alliance, with social and economic problems at home of the gravest nature, yes, and with the technological knowledge that makes it possible, as our President has said, not only to destroy our world but to destroy poverty around the world—in a time of peril and opportunity, the old complacent, unbalanced fare of action-adventure and situation comedies is simply not good enough.

Faced with all these global problems, one might well ask: why was a federal official worrying about *Leave It to Beaver?*

The answer is: when a government develops a grandiose vision of remaking the world (the New Frontier), no aspect of society is too trivial to escape its intervention. Minow refused to accept the fact that by the 1960s, television—like every other mass medium before it—had become woven into the fabric of ordinary life in America, developed and run by ordinary people to satisfy ordinary human desires and needs. He wanted television to be a world-transforming force, and when it failed to live up to that role, he could only regard it as a force for evil. His view of television can best be described as Manichean, an all-or-nothing attitude, according to which the medium could function as an agent of either salvation or damnation but nothing in between. Consider the lines in his NAB speech that lead up to the "vast wasteland" phrase: "When television is good, nothing—not the theater, not the magazines or newspapers—nothing is better. But when television is bad, nothing is worse."

In Minow's utopian vision, everything becomes cast in absolute terms. Television must be either the best medium or the worst. It cannot be in the middle, where in fact all the mass media lie. Dedicated to serving average Americans, the mass media tend to gravitate toward an average level of accomplishment—that is a fact of democratic life. Minow's quarrel with television was the petulant reaction of a disillusioned idealist. If television could not help in bringing about Minow's vision of a perfect world (a world without poverty), then it must be complicit in all the evil forces that make the world imperfect. He could not abide the fact that the American people were simply enjoying television, when he thought that in this new medium, humanity had finally found the instrument to bring about the perfect society.

Throughout his writings Friedrich Hayek warned against the dangers of trying to remake society on the basis of an abstract image of social perfection. He argued that such social engineering would always backfire, producing a world inferior to the one we live in. As we have seen, Minow's idealistic crusade to improve television largely resulted in making it worse. He hoped that under his leadership television would lead us to the island of utopia; instead what he ended up giving us was *Gilligan's Island*. Sherwood Schwartz really did know what he was doing when he named the Skipper's boat after Minow. And as we think about the career of America's first programmer-in-chief, we should view with alarm the persistence and proliferation of would-be culture czars in our world today. Indeed, if we are wondering whether we are truly back on the road to serfdom in the United States, we need only look at all the czars now trying to run our lives.

Notes

Economic Policy and the Road to Serfdom:
The Watershed of 1913
Brian Domitrovic

1. P. A. Samuelson, "For Senator Kennedy: Notes on the Economic Problem of Growth," Box 1, F "Growth Work 1960 [2 of 2]," 7, James M. Tobin papers, John F. Kennedy Presidential Library, Boston, MA.

2. The CIA National Intelligence estimates of Soviet output proved one of the great black eyes the agency ever endured, and its representatives fought back hard. But in contentious responses to charges made in the 1990s about the low quality of its official estimates, the CIA did not back off the fact that its sizing of Soviet GDP fell between "60 percent" and "two-fifths" of U.S. output. Douglas J. MacEachin, "CIA Assessments of the Soviet Union: The Record Versus the Charges," subheading "The Tyrannical Numbers," available at https://www.cia.gov/library/center-for-the-study-of-intelligence/csi-publications/books-and-monographs/cia-assessments-of-the-soviet-union-the-record-versus-the-charges/3496toc.html. See also James Noren, "CIA's Analysis of the Soviet Economy," in "CIA's Analysis of the Soviet Union, 1947–1991," available at https://www.cia.gov/library/center-for-the-study-of-intelligence/csi-publications/books-and-monographs/watching-the-bear-essays-on-cias-analysis-of-the-soviet-

union/intro.htm; and Noel E. Firth and James H. Noren, *Soviet Defense Spending: A History of CIA Estimates, 1950–1990* (College Station, TX: Texas A&M University Press, 1998).

3. Yuri Maltsev, "Too Big to Fail? Lessons in Economics from the Demise of the Soviet Union," paper, Gulf Coast Economics Association Conference, Savannah, GA, November 9, 2009; William Easterly and Stanley Fischer, "The Soviet Economic Decline," *World Bank Economic Review* 9, no. 3, 341–71.

4. F. A. Hayek, *The Road to Serfdom* (Chicago: University of Chicago Press, 1994), 234.

5. Ibid., 233.

6. Germany's growth from the trough of the Depression in 1932 until 1940 was nearly twice that of Britain's: 71 percent to 39 percent. See the Angus Maddison database, "Statistics on World Population, GDP, and Per Capita GDP, 1–2008 AD" (which is the foundation of the OECD database), at http://www.ggdc.net/maddison/.

7. Christina Duckworth Romer, "The Instability of the Prewar Economy Reconsidered: A Critical Reexamination of Historical Macroeconomic Data," Ph.D. dissertation, MIT, Cambridge, MA, 1985.

8. Jeffrey Miron and Christina Romer, "A New Monthly Index of Industrial Production, 1884–1940," *Journal of Economic History* 50, no. 2 (June 1990), 327; Ron Chernow, *The House of Morgan: An American Banking Dynasty and the Rise of Modern Finance* (New York: Grove Press, 1990), 158–59.

9. Inflation statistics are derived from "Table Containing History of CPI-U.S.: All Items Indexes and Annual Percent Changes from 1913 to Present," Bureau of Labor Statistics, at bls.gov; growth statistics come from measuringworth.com and bea.gov (Bureau of Economic Analysis); and tax statistics come from the Tax Foundation, http://www.taxfoundation.org/files/federalindividualratehistory-20080107.pdf.

Hamiltonianism: The Origins of the Modern State
Carey Roberts

1. Thomas Jefferson, Jefferson's Account of the Bargain on the Assumption and Residence Bills, *The Papers of Thomas Jefferson*, vol. 17, Julian Boyd, et al., eds. (Princeton, NJ: Princeton University Press, 1955–), 206.

2. For a comprehensive treatment of the "Hamilton image" in American public life, see Stephen F. Knott, *Alexander Hamilton and the Persistence of Myth* (Lawrence, KS: University of Kansas Press, 2005).

3. Edwin Perkins, *American Public Finance and Financial Service, 1700–1815* (Columbus, OH: Ohio State University Press, 1994), 103.

4. Ibid., 209–11.

5. The best succinct but comprehensive treatment of public debt and its legacy within the Anglo-American inheritance remains Richard Vernier, "The Fortunes of Orthodoxy: The Political Economy of Public Debt in England and America during the 1780s," in Rebecca Starr, ed., *Articulating America: Fashioning a National Political Culture in Early America* (Lanham, MD: Rowman and Littlefield, 2000), 93–130. Much of the argument here is derived from Vernier's scholarship. Three important book-length treatments include E. James Ferguson, *The Power of the Purse* (Chapel Hill, NC: University of North Carolina Press for the Institute of Early American History and Culture, 1961); Curtis Nettles, *The Emergence of a National Economy* (New York: Holt, Rinehart and Winston, 1962); and Perkins, *American Public Finance and Financial Service, 1700–1815*.

6. To be sure, the policies Hamilton advocated carried certain continuities with British forms of public finance. Most obviously, he modeled his national bank on the Bank of England. This proved to be a publicity problem. Hamilton's detractors, such as Thomas Jefferson and George Mason (who had witnessed Hamilton defend British monarchism before the Constitutional Convention at Philadelphia), seized on these similarities to a government recently at war with the United States and to policies some argued had led to that war. Hamilton was too British, they said. For the connection between Hamilton's plans and its European antecedents, see Donald F. Swanson and Andrew P. Trout, "Alexander Hamilton, 'the Celebrated Mr. Neckar,' and Public Credit," *William and Mary Quarterly*, third series, 47, no. 3 (July 1990), 422–30; and Donald F. Swanson and Andrew P. Trout, "Alexander Hamilton's Report on the Public Credit (1790) in a European Perspective," *Journal of European Economic History* 19 (1990), 623–33. The principal biography of Hamilton remains Forrest McDonald, *Alexander Hamilton: A Biography* (New York: W. W. Norton, 1982). The fullest and most accessible treatment of Federalist financial policies in light of the general tenor of early national politics is Stanley Elkins and Eric McKitrick, *The Age of Federalism: The Early American Republic,*

1788–1800 (New York: Oxford University Press, 1993). A considerable number of new biographies of Hamilton emerged in the early 2000s, most notably Ron Chernow, *Alexander Hamilton* (New York: Penguin Press, 2004). Sympathetic treatments of Hamiltonian finance can be found in John Steele Gordon, *Hamilton's Blessing: The Extraordinary Life and Times of Our National Debt* (New York: Penguin, 1998), and to some degree in Robert E. Wright, *One Nation Under Debt: Hamilton, Jefferson, and the History of What We Owe* (New York: McGraw-Hill, 2008). An extended survey of scholarly opinion of Hamilton can be found in Robert W. T. Martin and Douglas Ambrose, eds., *The Many Faces of Alexander Hamilton* (New York: NYU Press, 2006).

7. Scholars heatedly dispute whether Hamiltonian finance was indeed "mercantilistic," and solid arguments are offered on both sides. Nonetheless, Hamilton's basic assumptions followed those of most British financiers at the time, not the emerging arguments made by classical liberals such as Adam Smith and David Hume. Most scholars agree that Hamilton was no advocate of laissez-faire capitalism.

8. The best succinct treatment of Hamilton's restructuring of the country's debt is Donald F. Swanson and Andrew P. Trout, "Alexander Hamilton, Conversion, and Debt Reduction," *Explorations in Economic History* 29, no. 4 (October 1992), 417–29.

9. Key Jeffersonian criticisms of Federalist financial measures include: Albert Gallatin, *A Sketch of the Finances of the United States* (New York: William A. Davis, 1796); George Logan, *Excise, the Favorite System of Aristocrats* (Philadelphia, 1797); James Monroe, *View of the Conduct of the Executive* (Philadelphia: Bache, 1797); and three critical pamphlets by John Taylor, *An Examination of the Late Proceedings in Congress Respecting the Official Conduct of the Secretary of the Treasury* (Richmond, 1793), *A Definition of Parties, or the Political Effects of the Paper System* (Philadelphia: Francis Bailey, 1794), and *An Enquiry into the Principles and Tendencies of Certain Public Measures* (Philadelphia: Thomas Dobson, 1794). See also Lance Banning, *The Jeffersonian Persuasion: Evolution of Party Ideology* (Ithaca, NY: Cornell University Press, 1978); and Joyce Appleby, *Capitalism and a New Social Order: The Republican Vision of the 1790s* (New York: NYU Press, 1984).

10. For an introduction to this aspect of Jeffersonian thought, see Clyde N. Wilson, "The Jeffersonian Conservative Tradition," reprinted in *From*

Union to Empire: Essays in the Jeffersonian Tradition (Columbia, SC: The Foundation for American Education, 2003), 1–15.

11. Taylor, *Enquiry*, 7–11, 30, and 41–42.

12. See John Francis Mercer, Speech on Public Debt, March 29, 1792, *Annals of Congress*, 2nd Cong., 1st Sess., 499–500; Thomas Jefferson, "Proposition Submitted by Richard Gem," ca. September 1–6, 1798, *Papers*, vol. 15, 391; Jefferson to John Wayles Eppes, June 24, September 11, and November 6, 1813, *The Writings of Thomas Jefferson*, vol. 9, Paul L. Ford, ed. (New York: G. P. Putnam's and Sons, 1895), 390–91, 395–96, and 411–12; and Jefferson to George Washington, May 23, 1792, *Papers*, vol. 23, 536–39.

13. William Stephens Smith to Jefferson, December 3, 1787, *Papers*, vol. 12, 391; Jefferson, "Notes on Washington's Second Inauguration and Republicanism," February 28, 1793, *Papers*, vol. 25, 301; and Jefferson to James Madison, August 3, 1797, *Writings*, vol. 7, 165.

14. See G. Alan Tarr, *Understanding State Constitutions* (Princeton, NJ: Princeton University Press, 2000), 94–135; and John J. Wallis, "Constitutions, Corporations, and Corruption: American States and Constitutional Change, 1842 to 1852," *Journal of Economic History* 65, no. 1 (March 2005), 211–56.

15. A detailed examination of one state's role in the development of this tradition can be found in Kevin R. C. Gutzman, *Virginia's American Revolution: From Dominion to Republic, 1776–1840* (Lanham, MD: Lexington Books, 2007). See also Adam Tate, *Conservatism and Southern Intellectuals, 1789–1861: Liberty, Tradition, and the Good Society* (Columbia, MO: University of Missouri Press, 2005); Sean R. Busick, *A Sober Desire for History: William Gilmore Simms as Historian* (Columbia, SC: University of South Carolina Press, 2005); and Richard C. Lounsbury, ed., *Louisa S. McCord: Selected Writings* (Charlottesville, VA: University of Virginia Press, 1997).

16. Clay actually used the term "American policy" in his subsequent speech in reply to Barbour. Henry Clay, Speech on the Tariff Bill, March 31, 1824, *Annals of Congress*, 18th Cong., 1st Sess., 1970.

17. Philip P. Barbour, Speech on the Tariff Bill, March 26, 1824, *Annals of Congress*, 18th Cong., 1st Sess., 1920, 1924, and 1925.

18. James M. Garnett, Speech on the Tariff Bill, April 2, 1924, *Annals of Congress*, 18th Cong., 1st Sess., 2096.

19. Washington Irving, "The Creole Village," reprinted in *The Complete*

Tales of Washington Irving, Charles Neider, ed. (New York: Da Capo Press, 1998), 654–60.

The Modern Welfare State:
Leading the Way on the Road to Serfdom
Per Bylund

1. While the precise shape of a welfare state depends on the particularities of the society it attempts to change, we can identify three primary kinds: the Anglo-Saxon welfare state, the conservative welfare state (existing primarily in continental Europe), and the "universal" welfare state. The Anglo-Saxon welfare state is generally smaller in scope than the other types. This is perhaps because it fundamentally relies on the common-law legal framework, and also because individuals in these countries often are granted specific rights against the state, which serves as a limit to taxation and therefore slows down state growth. The conservative welfare state is characterized by a relatively high tax burden on individuals and businesses, which finances welfare programs specifically designed to aid groups or individuals in particularly difficult circumstances. The universal or Scandinavian welfare state is known for its world-record tax rates, the relatively high level of achieved equality, and the (mostly) unlimited and universal nature of its welfare benefits. See Peter Santesson-Wilson and Gissur Ó. Erlingsson, "Förändring Och Tröghet I Välfärdsstaterna," in Peter Santesson-Wilson and Gissur Ó. Erlingsson, eds., *Reform—Förändring Och Tröghet I Välfärdsstaterna* (Stockholm: Norstedts, 2009), 8–17.

2. The universality of welfare benefits is what distinguishes the Scandinavian welfare states. "Universality" here means that welfare benefits are available without requirement of filing an application or the conducting of an investigation of eligibility, and that the availability of benefits is not limited. For example, the Swedish child grant is a fixed amount made available to all parents regardless of income, social class, etc. It should be noted that the so-called universal welfare state is universal only to a limited degree: The philosophy guiding the structuring of welfare programs is universal, but in reality, many if not most programs are restricted in one way or another.

3. Lei Delsen and Tom van Veen, "The Swedish Model: Relevant for Other European Countries?" *British Journal of Industrial Relations* 30(1), 1992,

83–105; Erik Lundberg, "The Rise and Fall of the Swedish Model," *Journal of Economic Literature* 23, no. 1 (1985); and Miriam Nordfors, "Vad Är Den Svenska Modellen?" *The Swedish Model* (Stockholm: Ratio, 2006).

4. Paul Krugman, *The Great Unraveling: Losing Our Way in the New Century* (New York: W. W. Norton, 2004), 401.

5. This point was stressed by a leader of the Swedish Social Democratic Party in a personal conversation with the author.

6. Eugen von Böhm-Bawerk, *Control or Economic Law* (Auburn, AL: Ludwig von Mises Institute, [1914] 2010).

7. Between 1850 and 1930 more than 1.2 million Swedes emigrated to the United States, of whom approximately 200,000 returned. More than 1 percent of the population emigrated each year at the height of this wave during the 1880s. For the sake of reference, the Swedish population increased from approximately 4.5 million in 1880 to 5.5 million in 1910, which means 20 percent of the population emigrated to the United States. See Andreas Bergh, *Den Kapitalistiska Välfärdsstaten* (Falun: Nordstedts akademiska förlag, 2009); Eric S. Einhorn and John Logue, *Modern Welfare States: Politics and Policies in Social Democratic Scandinavia* (Westport, CT: Praeger Publishers, 1989); and Joel E. Cohen, "Population Forecasts and Confidence Intervals for Sweden: A Comparison of Model-Based and Empirical Approaches," *Demography* 23, no. 1 (1986), 105–26.

8. Eric S. Einhorn and John Logue describe Sweden as backwards and "terribly poor" before the 1870s. See Einhorn and Logue, 9.

9. Bergh, 30.

10. Examples of inventions that were capitalized in corporations that are still among the biggest and most influential are the centrifugal separator developed and sold by Alfa Laval (founded in 1883); lighthouse gas lighting (especially the flashing beacon, the sun valve, and the Dalén mixer) in AGA (founded in 1904); the ball bearing developed by and sold through SKF (founded in 1907); and the refrigerator and inventions used in vacuum cleaners successfully sold and distributed globally by Electrolux (founded in 1910). Many state of the art, highly industrialized corporations were established during the same time period and still make up the bulk of Sweden's large corporations, for example: Sandvik, producer of industrial steel products, founded in 1862; Atlas Copco, producer of construction materials and heavy machinery, founded in 1873; L. M. Ericsson, producer of telegraphs, telephones, and communications infrastructure, founded in

1876; ASEA, producer of electric lights and generators, founded in 1883 (now part of ABB); LKAB, iron ore mining, founded in 1890; Scania, developer and producer of trucks, founded in 1891.

11. Lennart Schön, *En Modern Svensk Ekonomisk Historia: Tillväxt Och Omvandling under Två Sekel* (Stockholm: SNS Förlag, 2000).

12. Johan Norberg, *Den Svenska Liberalismens Historia* (Stockholm: Timbro, 1998).

13. Olle Gasslander, *J. A. Gripenstedt: Statsman Och Företagare* (Lund: CWK Gleerup, 1949); Per T. Ohlsson, *100 År Av Tillväxt: Johan August Gripenstedt Och Den Liberala Revolutionen* (Stockholm: Bromberg, 1994); Harald Wieselgren, *Lars Johan Hierta. Biografisk Studie* (Stockholm: P. A. Norstedt & Söner, 1880); Leif Kihlberg, *Lars Hierta I Helfigur* (Stockholm: Bonnier, 1968); Ami Lönnroth and Per Eric Mattsson, *Tidningskungen Lars Johan Hierta: Den Förste Moderne Svensken* (Stockholm: Wahlström & Widstrand, 1996).

14. Bergh, 13–22. Erik Lundberg describes the Swedish model in terms of effects: full employment, low inflation, cyclical stability, no balance of payment troubles, rapid public sector growth, absence of structural imbalances, and satisfactory economic growth rate. See Lundberg, 3.

15. Lundberg, 1.

16. The Social Democrats have been in the Swedish government 1917–20, 1920, 1921–23, 1924–25, 1925–26, 1932–76, 1982–91, and 1994–2006. See Torsten Svensson, *Socialdemokratins Dominans: En Studie Av Den Svenska Socialdemokratins Partistrategi* (Uppsala: Almqvist & Wiksell, 1994).

17. Only recently have the Social Democrats been successfully challenged. The conservative party Moderaterna (the Moderates), which under the name of Nya Moderaterna (New Moderates), adopted a new image and accepted much of the socialist agenda in order to gain influence, is arguably a reason the so-called nonsocialist parties successfully formed a four-party coalition government in 2006. The coalition seems, at the time of writing, to remain in government after the general elections held on September 19 2010, but with only minority support in parliament, dependent on support from either the Environmentalist Party or the extreme right Sweden Democrats. The Social Democrats remain the largest party in Swedish politics, however with very slight (and decreasing) margin.

18. Depending on how overall tax rates are calculated, Sweden generally has the highest or second-highest (after Denmark) rates. The standard

value-added tax rate in Sweden is 25 percent. Total tax is progressive, and according to the 2009 Swedish Taxpayers' Association fact sheet, rates start around 59.8 percent on very low annual incomes (SEK 100,000 or $13,000).

19. The Swedish tax rate on business firms' earnings is 28 percent, which is very low considering that firms in Sweden often have several ways of adjusting their effective tax rates through deductions and exemptions. As a result, large corporations tend to pay close to or zero taxes on earnings. For example, Volvo Personvagnar reported zero taxable income in 1996 and 1997 despite reported profits of almost $1 billion. See "Volvo Personvagnar Fortsätter Nolltaxera," *Aftonbladet,* July 15, 1998, available at http://dcliveryc.aftonbladet.se/nyheter/9807/15/telegram/inrikes63.html.

20. Bergh, 21.

21. Lundberg, 7.

22. Bergh mentions in passing that Swedish policies were on the whole Keynesian and supposed to counteract fluctuations in the market to create stable economic growth, price stability, and full employment. See also Assar Lindbeck, *Swedish Economic Policy* (Berkeley and Los Angeles: University of California Press, 1974); and Assar Lindbeck, "Consequences of the Advanced Welfare State," *World Economy* 11, no. 1 (1988), 19–38.

23. Lundberg, 7.

24. Bergh, 39–40.

25. See, for example, Hunter Lewis, *Where Keynes Went Wrong: And Why World Governments Keep Creating Inflation, Bubbles, and Busts* (Mount Jackson, VA: Axios Press, 2009).

26. See John Maynard Keynes, *The General Theory of Employment, Interest, and Money* (New Delhi, India: Atlantic Publishers & Distributors, [1936] 2008), and Lewis, *Where Keynes Went Wrong.*

27. For a discussion of destruction and economic growth, see, for example, Frédéric Bastiat, *That Which Is Seen, and That Which Is Not Seen: An Economic Essay* (World Library Classics, [1850] 2010).

28. Bergh, 21.

29. Early retirement and disability pension programs were recently regulated, but before that, government agencies used them extensively to force down the official statistics for the rate of long-term unemployment or sick leaves in the labor force.

30. Fredrik Bergström and Robert Gidehag, *Sverige versus USA: En Analys*

Av Tillväxtens Betydelse (Stockholm: Timbro, 2004), 29.

31. Assar Lindbeck, *Det Svenska Experimentet* (Kristianstad: SNS Förlag, 1998); Bergh, 54–57.

32. See the "Austrian" analyses of the structure of production and the origins and effects of malinvestments in, for example, Ludwig von Mises, *Human Action: A Treatise on Economics* (New Haven, CT: Yale University Press, 1949) and Thomas E. Woods Jr., *Meltdown: A Free-Market Look at Why the Stock Market Collapsed, the Economy Tanked, and Government Bailouts Will Make Things Worse* (Washington, DC: Regnery, 2009). Compare Murray Rothbard's statement that "government investment or subsidized investment is either malinvestment or not investment at all, but simply waste assets or 'consumption' of waste for the prestige of government officials." See Murray N. Rothbard, *Man, Economy, and State with Power and Market: Scholar's Edition* (Auburn, AL: Ludwig von Mises Institute, [1962] 2004), 969.

33. Fredrik Bergström and Robert Gidehag, "Tänk Om Sverige Varit En Amerikansk Delstat: En Diskussion Och Analys Av Hushållsinkomster I Sverige Och USA Och Betydelsen Av Ekonomisk Tillväxt" (Stockholm: Handelns Utredningsinstitut [Swedish Research Institute of Trade], 2002), 10.

34. Bergström and Gidehag, *Sverige versus USA*, 58.

35. Fredrik Bergström and Robert Gidehag, "EU versus USA" (Stockholm: Timbro, 2004), 12, 13, 16, available at http://www.timbro.se/bokhandel/pdf/9175665646.pdf.

36. Official national debt data made available by the Swedish National Debt Office on their website, https://www.riksgalden.se/templates/RGK_Templates/TwoColumnPage____2749.aspx .

37. See Ludwig von Mises, *Human Action: A Treatise on Economics*; Ludwig von Mises *The Theory of Money and Credit* (New Haven, CT: Yale University Press, ([1912] 1953); and Richard M. Ebeling, *The Austrian Theory of the Trade Cycle and Other Essays* (Auburn, AL: Ludwig von Mises Institute, [1978] 1996).

38. Per L. Bylund, "How the Welfare State Corrupted Sweden," *Mises Daily*, May 31, 2006, available at http://mises.org/daily/2190.

39. Burton A. Abrams and Mark D. Schitz, "The 'Crowding-Out' Effect of Governmental Transfers on Private Charitable Contributions," *Public Choice* 33, no. 1 (1978), 29–39.

40. Bylund, "How the Welfare State Corrupted Sweden."

41. Only 3 percent of preschool children were in public child care in 1963, whereas the 1970s saw a great shortage of such institutions. The system was greatly expanded in the 1970s and 1980s to relieve the shortage. In 1990, between 55 and 65 percent of all two-to-five-year-olds were in public child care; in 2003, the figure stood between 87 and 96 percent. See, for example, Anita Nyberg, "Parental Leave, Public Childcare, and the Dual Earner/ Dual Career-Model in Sweden," discussion paper in *Parental Insurance and Childcare*, 2004, available at http://www.mutual-learning-employment. net/uploads/ModuleXtender/PeerReviews/55/disspapSWE04.pdf.

42. Lundberg writes that "in 1960 the labor force participation percentage of women was 50 percent and in 1980 it was about 75 percent, a record within OECD countries." Lundberg, 21. In 1990, 85.1 percent of all mothers were employed. Nyberg, 9.

43. A Swedish elementary school teacher with long experience brought this example of the state of affairs in the Swedish educational system to this author. A mother to one of the teacher's students came to the teacher furious that she, the mother, rather than the school would have to take care of her own sick son. The mother exclaimed that she had already spent ten years of her life taking care of the child and that it was about time that society did its "fair share." After all, she had a job and a social life that needed her attention.

44. Unemployment among youth (those fifteen to twenty-four years old) stood at 25.2 percent in March 2009, according to seasonally adjusted statistics from Eurostat. The high unemployment rate for younger people reflects Sweden's numerous job-security laws and the overall trend demanding more highly productive workers. "Open unemployment" is the term used for those of working age who are unemployed but not partaking in any of the plentiful government measures to provide job training, educate, or otherwise drive down the unemployment statistic.

45. It should be noted that Swedes are not perfectly disconnected from the morality of the older generations. Swedes generally are very sensitive to people consciously abusing the system and would report on their neighbors for receiving welfare benefits for which they were not eligible. In other words, welfare state dependence does not create a lack of morality but changes the moral view of what is just.

The Origins of the Crisis
Antony P. Mueller

1. See, for example, Richard A. Posner, *A Failure of Capitalism: The Crisis of '08 and the Descent into Depression* (Cambridge, MA: Harvard University Press, 2009).
2. Joseph T. Salerno, *Money: Sound and Unsound* (Auburn, AL: Ludwig von Mises Institute, 2010).
3. Bank for International Settlements, 79th Annual Report (June 29, 2009), 1, available at www.bis.org.
4. Bank for International Settlements, 78th Annual Report (June 30, 2008), 4, available at www.bis.org.
5. Ibid., 8.
6. See, for example, Mark Thornton, "Housing: Too Good to Be True," *Mises Daily*, June 4, 2004. The housing bust came as no surprise to those who had attended the annual Austrian scholars conference at the Ludwig von Mises Institute in Auburn, Alabama, in the late 1990s and early 2000s.
7. For recent comprehensive expositions see Roger W. Garrison, *Time and Money: The Macroeconomics of Capital Structure* (London and New York: Routledge, 2006), and Jesús Huerta de Soto, *Money, Bank Credit, and Economic Cycles* (Auburn, AL: Ludwig von Mises Institute, 2006).
8. Robert Higgs, "Regime Uncertainty: Why the Great Depression Lasted So Long and Why Prosperity Resumed after the War," *Independent Review* 1, no. 4, (Spring 1997), 561–90.
9. Hans-Herman Hoppe, *Democracy: The God That Failed* (Rutgers, NJ: Transaction Publishers, 2001).
10. William A. Niskanen, *Reaganomics: An Insider's Account of the Policies and the People* (New York: Oxford University Press, 1988).
11. David A. Stockman, *The Triumph of Politics: Why the Reagan Revolution Failed* (New York: Harper & Row, 1986).
12. Household liabilities rose by a factor of fourteen since the early 1980s. Data provided by Board of Governors of the Federal Reserve System, Federal Reserve Bank of St. Louis, Economic Research and Data, 2010.
13. Alan Greenspan, *The Age of Turbulence: Adventures in a New World* (New York: Penguin Press, 2007), 108.
14. David B. Sicilia and Jeffrey L. Cruikshank, *The Greenspan Effect: Words That Move the World's Markets* (New York: McGraw-Hill, 2000).

15. Antony P. Mueller, "Bubble or New Era? Monetary Aspects of the New Economy," in *Markets, Information, and Communication: Austrian Perspective on the Internet Economy* (London and New York, Routledge, 2003), 249–61.

16. Guido Hülsmann, "Beware the Moral Hazard Trivializers," *Mises Daily*, June 3, 2008.

17. See, for example, Antony P. Mueller, "Mr. Bailout," *Mises Daily*, September 30, 2004: "Since Alan Greenspan took office, financial markets in the US have operated under a quasi-official charter, which says that the central bank will protect its major actors from the risk of bankruptcy. Consequently, the reasoning emerged that when you succeed, you will earn high profits and market share, and if you should fail, the authorities will save you anyway."

18. John Cassidy, *Dot.com: The Greatest Story Ever Sold* (New York: HarperCollins, 2002).

19. Greenspan, 164.

20. The U.S. central bank targets the federal funds rate as its main policy interest rate. In various waves, this rate was brought down from a height of almost 20 percent at the peak of the anti-inflation stance of the U.S. central bank under Paul Volcker, to 5 percent in the 1990s, and to 1 percent in the early 2000s during Greenspan's chairmanship. Since the beginning of the current crisis, the federal funds rate was brought down to zero bound under the chairmanship of Ben Bernanke. Data for Effective Federal Funds Rate provided by the Board of Governors of the Federal Reserve System, Federal Reserve Bank of St. Louis, Economic Research and Data, 2010.

21. While industrial production barely doubled over the past three decades, bank credit of all commercial banks and the monetary aggregate MZM (money zero maturity) increased almost tenfold during that period. This is my own calculation based on data from the Federal Reserve Bank of St. Louis, Economic Research and Data, 2010, available at http://research.stlouisfed.org.

22. Bank for International Settlements, 80th Annual Report (June 28, 2010), Table V.1, available at www.bis.org.

23. The U.S. current account began to deteriorate in the early 1980s, and after a short recovery around 1990, the U.S. current account deficit increased to more than $800 billion per year before the outbreak of the current crisis. Data from the U.S. Department of Commerce, Bureau of

Economic Analysis, Federal Reserve. Source: Federal Reserve Bank of St. Louis, Economic Research and Data, 2010.

24. As Philip Bagus points out, money not only has a quantitative dimension in terms of the expansion and contraction of monetary aggregates. The use of money, from a subjectivist perspective, also involves a qualitative dimension. In this respect, the current monetary system is characterized by a quantitative debasement of money not only because of its overproduction but also in terms of its quality. See Philip Bagus, "The Quality of Money," *Quarterly Journal of Austrian Economics* 12, no. 4 (2009), 22–45.

25. From the end of the Asian crisis in 1999 until the outbreak of the current financial crisis in mid-2007, the cumulative U.S. current account deficit amounted to $4.6 trillion. See Bank of International Settlements, 79th Annual Report, 5.

26. China devalued its currency against the U.S. dollar from a rate of less than two yuan per dollar in the early 1980s to more than eight yuan per dollar in 1994. The dollar-yuan exchange rate stayed at this level for more than ten years. It was only after 2005 that the yuan was revalued slightly to seven yuan per dollar. Data provided by the Board of Governors of the Federal Reserve System, China/U.S. Foreign Exchange Rate, Federal Reserve Bank of St. Louis, Economic Research and Data, 2010.

27. The Keynesian-monetarist synthesis, which suffers from the neglect of credit growth and debt accumulation, still dominates the thinking at the U.S. central bank. See Ethan S. Harris, *Ben Bernanke's Fed: The Federal Reserve after Greenspan* (Boston: Harvard Business Press, 2008).

28. Ludwig Lachmann, *Capital and Its Structure* (Kansas City: S. Andrews and McMeel, 1978).

29. Fiscal situation and prospects in selected advanced economies, Bank for International Settlements, 80th Annual Report, Table V.1.

30. The U.S. savings rate (gross savings in percent of GDP) fell from 16 percent in 1995 to 11.9 percent in 2008, while the savings rate of China rose from 42.1 percent in 1995 to 59.0 percent in 2008. During the same time period, the Japanese savings rate fell from 30.5 percent to 26.7 percent, in line with the decline of its investment rate, which fell from 28.5 percent to 23.5 percent of GDP. Source: Bank for International Settlements, 79th Annual Report, Table IV.1.

31. U.S. federal debt held by foreign and international investors rose from negligible amounts in the early 1980s to $2 trillion before the beginning

of the current financial crisis; it rose to $3.5 trillion by the end of 2009. This is my own calculation based on sources from the U.S. Department of the Treasury, Financial Management Series; Federal Reserve Bank of St. Louis, Economic Research and Data, 2010; and Economic and Financial Data for the United States, July 2010.

32. See Federal Reserve Statistical Release, "Factors Affecting Reserve Balances," 2010.

33. The external investment position of a country is the balance between the assets held by residents in foreign countries and the domestic assets held by foreigners. Slightly simplified, one can say that a net negative external investment position is the net foreign debt of a country.

34. In the period from mid-2001 up to the end of 2005, the real federal funds in the United States rate was consistently below 1 percent, and for much of this period it was actually negative. Real interest rates in the other major industrial economies were only slightly higher than in the United States. For most of this period, the European Central Bank held short-term interest rates below 1 percent, while in Japan, real interest oscillated between 0 and 1 percent for most of the decade. See Bank for International Settlements, 79th Annual Report, 5. Data from the European Central Bank show that since 2000 the monetary aggregate M3 has almost doubled. See European Central Bank, Monetary Statistics, 2010, available at www.ecb.int.

35. Bank for International Settlements, 80th Annual Report, 38.

The Dangers of Protectionism
Mark Brandly

1. See Murray Rothbard, *America's Great Depression* (Auburn, AL: Ludwig von Mises Institute, 2000), for a thorough explanation of how Federal Reserve monetary policy caused the Great Depression. See pages 241–43 for a brief explanation of the Smoot-Hawley tariff.

2. See Adam Smith, *An Inquiry into the Nature and Causes of the Wealth of Nations* (New York: P. F. Collier Corporation, [1776] 1961), 311–71, for Smith's discussion of free trade.

3. Ibid., 365.

4. Paul Krugman was the leading new trade theorist of the 1980s and 1990s. The new trade theorists developed economic arguments demon-

strating that protectionism could be beneficial. But Krugman asserts that the new trade theorists, including Krugman himself, are "cautious and diffident" regarding any real-world policy conclusions that follow from their theoretical arguments for protection. See Paul Krugman, *Peddling Prosperity* (New York: W. W. Norton and Company, 1994), 266. For a sampling of new trade theorist writing, see Paul Krugman, *Rethinking International Trade* (Cambridge: MIT Press, 1990), and Paul Krugman, ed., *Strategic Trade Policy and the New International Economics* (Cambridge: MIT Press, 1986).

5. Paul Krugman, "Is Free Trade Passe?" *Economic Perspectives* 1, no. 2 (Fall 1987), 131. Krugman is not declaring himself to be a free trader in this passage; he is commenting on the economics profession in general.

6. For a detailed history of U.S. tariff policies from 1789 to 1930, I recommend F. W. Taussig, *The Tariff History of the United States* (New York: Augustus M. Kelley Publishers, [1930] 1967).

7. Paul Krugman makes the Keynesian argument that protection keeps spending in the domestic economy, thereby increasing employment. This argument is based on the Keynesian argument that spending drives the economy. I am not addressing this argument in this essay. For refutations of Keynesian theory, see Henry Hazlitt, *Failure of the New Economics* (New York: D. Van Nostrand and Company, 1959), and Hunter Lewis, *Where Keynes Went Wrong: And Why World Governments Keep Creating Inflation, Bubbles, and Busts* (Mount Jackson, VA: Axios Press, 2009).

8. Henry Hazlitt, *Economics in One Lesson* (San Francisco: Laissez Faire Books, 1996), 60.

9. Ludwig von Mises, *Money, Method, and the Market Process* (Norwell, MA: Kluwer Academic Publishers, 1990), 140.

10. Gottfried Haberler, "Strategic Trade Policy and the New International Economics: A Critical Analysis," in Ronald W. Jones and Anne O. Krueger, eds., *The Political Economy of International Trade: Essays in Honor of Robert E. Baldwin* (Oxford: Basil Blackwell, 1990), 25. Also, Leland B. Yeager and David G. Tuerck, *Foreign Trade and U.S. Policy: The Case for Free International Trade* (New York, Praeger Publishers, 1976), 209–10, discuss this same issue.

11. Henry Hazlitt provides a clear and concise explanation of the negative effect that protection has on wages. Hazlitt, *Economics in One Lesson*, 63–65.

Notes

12. At the other end of an industry's life, we see the "senior industry" argument. Older industries ask for protection against younger, vibrant competitors. The case against protecting senior industries is the same as the case against protecting infant industries. If the senior industry generates benefits over and above its costs, private investors will extend the life of these industries.

13. This positive-externality argument for protection is a subset of the market-failure concept in economics. The central conclusion is that markets fail to produce the optimal amount of a good and the government should recognize this failure and implement policies that correct for the market and lead to the optimal amount of production. One of the strands of thought of the new trade theorists, cited above, is that in cases of externalities, protectionist policies could theoretically improve society's welfare.

14. Yeager and Tuerck, 213–14. Yeager and Tuerck provide a systematic, thorough, compelling case for free trade. If you want to understand international trade theory and trade policies, I recommend that you start with this book.

15. Lou Dobbs, *Exporting America* (New York: Warner Brothers, 2004), 107.

16. See, for example, Charles Schumer and Paul Craig Roberts, "Second Thoughts on Free Trade," *New York Times*, January 6, 2004, available at http://www.nytimes.com/2004/01/06/opinion/second-thoughts-on-free-trade.html; Paul Craig Roberts, "Where Did All the Jobs Go?" *VDare.com*, February 15, 2004, available at http://www.vdare.com/roberts/where_jobs_go.htm; Paul Craig Roberts, "The Offshored Economy," *VDare.com*, March 17, 2010, available at http://www.vdare.com/roberts/100317_offshored_economy.htm; and Paul Craig Roberts, "Cato's Trade Report: Blinded by Ideology," *VDare.com*, October 8, 2007, available at http://www.vdare.com/roberts/071008_cato.htm.

17. Ralph E. Gomory and William J. Baumol, *Global Trade and Conflicting National Interests* (Cambridge: MIT Press, 2000). Roberts discusses the Gomory and Baumol book in "Cato's Trade Report."

18. For a refutation of Gomory and Baumol, see Mark Brandly, "Review Essay: Global Trade and Conflicting National Interests," *Quarterly Journal of Austrian Economics* 10, no. 2 (Summer 2007), 83–92.

19. Schumer and Roberts, "Second Thoughts on Free Trade."

20. Haberler, 27.

21. Gene Grossman, "Strategic Export Promotion: A Critique," in Krugman, ed., *Strategic Trade Policy and the New International Economics*, 48.

22. For a thorough explanation of the difficulties that government officials face in attempting to allocate resources in an efficient manner, see Ludwig von Mises, *Economic Calculation in the Socialist Commonwealth* (Auburn, AL: Ludwig von Mises Institute, 1990). Mises explains the "impossibility" of these types of calculations.

23. Yeager and Tuerck, 218, 220. Yeager and Tuerck published their book in 1976, yet it addresses all of the arguments for protection put forth since then, demonstrating that there is nothing new about the new protectionists.

Entrepreneurship and Government
Dane Stangler

1. Dane Stangler and Robert E. Litan, "Where Will the Jobs Come From?" Kauffman Foundation Research Series: Firm Formation and Economic Growth, November 2009, available at http://www.kauffman.org/uploadedFiles/where_will_the_jobs_come_from.pdf.

2. Tim Kane, "The Importance of Startups in Job Creation and Job Destruction," Kauffman Foundation Research Series: Firm Formation and Economic Growth, July 2010, available at http://www.kauffman.org/uploadedFiles/firm_formation_importance_of_startups.pdf.

3. Michael Horrell and Robert Litan, "After Inception: How Enduring is Job Creation by Startups?" Kauffman Foundation Research Series: Firm Formation and Economic Growth, July 2010, available at http://www.kauffman.org/uploadedFiles/firm-formation-inception-8-2-10.pdf.

4. Carl J. Schramm, "All Entrepreneurship is Social," *Stanford Social Innovation Review*, March 2010, available at http://www.ssireview.org/articles/entry/all_entrepreneurship_is_social/.

5. See, e.g., Frank R. Lichtenberg, "Has Medical Innovation Reduced Cancer Mortality?" National Bureau of Economic Research, Working Paper No. 15880, April 2010, available at http://www.nber.org/papers/w15880; Frank R. Lichtenberg, "Sources of U.S. Longevity Increase, 1960–2001," *Quarterly Review of Economics and Finance* 44, 369–389 (July 2004).

6. See, e.g., Organisation for Economic Cooperation and Development (OECD), "Measuring Entrepreneurship: A Digest of Indica-

tors" (2009), available at http://www.oecd.org/document/31/0,3343
,en_2649_33715_41663647_1_1_1_1,00.html.

7. See Dan Senor and Saul Singer, *Startup Nation: The Story of Israel's Economic Miracle* (New York: Twelve, 2009).

8. See David S. Landes, Joel Mokyr, and William J. Baumol, *The Invention of Enterprise: Entrepreneurship from Ancient Mesopotamia to Modern Times* (Princeton, NJ: Princeton University Press, 2010).

9. See Matt Ridley, *The Rational Optimist: How Prosperity Evolves* (New York: Harper, 2010).

10. The United States has enjoyed a rather steady rate of new firm creation for the past thirty years and, quite possibly, the past century. See Dane Stangler and Paul Kedrosky, "Exploring Firm Formation: Why Is the Number of New Firms Constant?" Kauffman Foundation Research Series on Firm Formation and Economic Growth, paper no. 2, January 2010, available at http://www.kauffman.org/uploadedFiles/exploring_firm_formation_1–13–10.pdf.

11. For narrative ease, this essay treats as fungible the terms "entrepreneur," "startup," and "new firm." Surprisingly, given the overriding importance of the phenomenon of entrepreneurship, there is little scholarly or popular consensus on its precisely delimited definition, on what it *is*, exactly.

12. Joseph A. Tainter, *The Collapse of Complex Societies* (Cambridge: Cambridge University Press, 1988).

13. Ibid., 118.

14. Ibid., 119.

15. Over the past twenty or thirty years, economists have rediscovered the importance of increasing returns in productivity and economic growth. See, e.g., David Warsh, *Knowledge and the Wealth of Nations: A Story of Economic Discovery* (New York: Norton, 2007); and Charles I. Jones and Paul M. Romer, "The New Kaldor Facts: Ideas, Institutions, Population, and Human Capital," National Bureau of Economic Research, Working Paper No. 15094 (June 2009), available at http://www.nber.org/papers/w15094.

16. Tainter, 119, 120 (emphasis original).

17. Ibid., 198.

18. Ibid., 199 (emphasis added). For our purposes here it is also interesting to note how Tainter interprets his theory. He sees the complexity perspective as removing much of the "mysticism" that has grown up around studies of collapse: "It must be admitted that this approach removes much of

the mystery of collapse, and identifies it as a mundane economic matter."

19. See, e.g., Clayton M. Christensen, *The Innovator's Dilemma* (New York: HarperBusiness, 2003); William J. Baumol, *The Free-Market Innovation Machine: Analyzing the Growth Miracle of Capitalism* (Princeton, NJ: Princeton University Press, 2003); Jonathan Hughes, *The Vital Few: The Entrepreneur and American Economic Progress*, 2nd ed. (Oxford: Oxford University Press, 1986).

20. The Kauffman Firm Survey provides an exhaustive breakdown of financing sources for a cohort of firms. See http://www.kauffman.org/kfs.

21. See also http://www.startups.cringely.com. There are exceptions, of course. Biotechnology companies require a high level of financing because of the costs of drug development and clinical trials. New manufacturing companies, too, require some substantial degree of financing, although this varies by the type of manufacturing. The most "expensive" startup on Cringely's tour was a light industry firm that had raised $6 million. Even for firms that require higher levels of financing, venture capital frequently is not the answer: fewer than 16 percent of the companies on the *Inc.* 500 list of fastest-growing firms over the past decade received venture capital. See Paul Kedrosky, "Right-Sizing the Venture Capital Industry," Kauffman Foundation, June 2009, available at http://papers.ssrn.com/s013/papers.cfm?abstract_id=1456431.

22. Nor is its relevance to sectors and companies a recent phenomenon: "Each innovation seems to have a lifespan of its own. . . . As its technological possibilities are realized, its marginal yield diminishes and it gives way to newer, more advantageous techniques." David S. Landes, *The Unbound Prometheus: Technological Change and Industrial Development in Western Europe from 1750 to the Present*, vol. 3 (Cambridge: Cambridge University Press, 1969).

23. See, e.g., Laurence R. Veysey, *The Emergence of the American University* (Chicago: University of Chicago Press, 1970); Roger L. Geiger, *To Advance Knowledge: The Growth of American Research Universities, 1900–1940* (Oxford: Oxford University Press, 1986).

24. Joseph A. Schumpeter, "The Analysis of Economic Change," *Review of Economic Statistics*, May 1935.

25. Venture capital actually provides an illustrative case study of this phenomenon: more and more dollars have been chasing ideas yet experiencing falling returns. See Kedrosky, "Right-Sizing the Venture Capital Industry."

26. These should not be taken as exhaustive; they constitute a descending ladder according to degree of visibility, from the most to the least.

27. I am excluding here the most extreme cases of Cuba and North Korea because there is so little private sector to speak of in those countries, particularly the latter. My point in the text is to look at state encroachment on the private sector where the private sector is allowed to exist. Of course, there is something of a private sector even in North Korea; when the country's currency reforms failed disastrously in recent years, citizens were allowed to engage in some limited market exchange and, of no surprise to anyone except the country's rulers, proved adept at making markets work.

28. See, e.g., Kellee S. Tsai, *Back-Alley Banking: Private Entrepreneurs in China* (Ithaca, NY: Cornell University Press, 2002); Yasheng Huang, *Capitalism with Chinese Characteristics: Entrepreneurship and the State* (New York: Cambridge University Press, 2008).

29. See Amity Shlaes, *The Forgotten Man: A New History of the Great Depression* (New York: Harper Perennial, 2008).

30. William J. Baumol, "Entrepreneurship: Productive, Unproductive, and Destructive," *Journal of Political Economy* 98 (October 1990), 893–94.

31. Rent seeking is not bad per se; it has long been argued that entrepreneurs engage in a form of rent seeking because, when they are the first mover in a certain market, they seek to capture as many gains as they can before competitors enter the market. When she introduced the term (though not the unique idea), Anne Krueger pointed out that rent seeking is a fact of life in mixed economies. Anne Krueger, "The Political Economy of the Rent Seeking Society," *American Economic Review* 64 (1974), 291.

32. See, e.g., Ken Auletta, "The Search Party," *New Yorker*, January 14, 2008.

33. See, e.g., William Voegeli, "Reforming Big Government," *Claremont Review of Books*, Fall 2008; William Voegeli, *Never Enough: America's Limitless Welfare State* (New York: Encounter, 2010).

34. The National Bureau of Economic Research, official keepers of recession and expansion dates, declared the "Great Recession" to have ended in June 2009. See http://www.nber.og/cycles/cyclesmain.html.

35. See http://www.ism.ws/ISMReport/NonMfgROB.cfm?navItem Number=12943.

36. Ross DeVol, Armen Bedroussian, Kevin Klowden, and Candice Flor Hynek, "Best Performing Cities 2009: Where America's Jobs are Created

and Sustained," Milken Institute, November 2009, available at http://
www.milkeninstitute.org/publications/publications.taf?cat=ResRep&fun
ction=detail&ID=38801218. In some ways of course, Washington's movement up the rankings reflects the failing fortunes of other cities. In absolute
terms, though, the D.C. area scores quite well.

37. The *Inc.* 500/5,000 List, available at http://www.inc.com/
inc5000/2009/index.html.

38. See Carl J. Schramm and Dane Stangler, "The Right Way to Regulate," *McKinsey Quarterly: What Matters*, February 2009, available at
http://whatmatters.mckinseydigital.com/credit_crisis/the-right-way-to-
regulate#comment; Jonathan Mahler, "After the Imperial Presidency,"
New York Times Magazine, November 7, 2008.

39. See Carl J. Schramm, "Made in America," *National Interest*, April 2010,
available at http://www.nationalinterest.org/Article.aspx?id=23208.

40. See, e.g., Lewis Lapham, *The Wish for Kings: Democracy at Bay* (New
York: Grove, 1993).

41. Committee on Prospering in the Global Economy of the Twenty-first
Century, "Rising Above the Gathering Storm: Energizing and Employ-
ing America for a Brighter Economic Future," National Academies, 2007,
available at http://www.nap.edu/catalog.php?record_id=11463.

42. See ASTRA, "Riding the Rising Tide: A 21st Century Strategy for
U.S. Competitiveness and Prosperity," December 2007, available at http://
www.aboutastra.org/pdf/ASTRARisingTide121107.pdf; Council on
Competitiveness, "Innovate America," 2005, available at http://www.com-
pete.org/publications/detail/202/innovate-america/.

43. John Kao, *Innovation Nation: How America Is Losing Its Innovation Edge, Why
It Matters, and What We Can Do to Get It Back* (New York: Free Press, 2007).

44. Committee on Prospering in the Global Economy of the 21st Century,
"Rising Above the Gathering Storm."

45. Council on Competitiveness, "Innovate America."

46. ASTRA, "Riding the Rising Tide."

47. Kao, *Innovation Nation*.

48. Carl J. Schramm, "Economic Fluidity: A Crucial Dimension of Economic Freedom," *Index of Economic Freedom* (2008).

49. Harold Evans, *They Made America* (New York: Back Bay, 2004), 5.

50. Joseph A. Schumpeter, "The Creative Response in Economic History,"
Journal of Economic History 7 (1947), 149.

51. Ibid.
52. Ibid.
53. Ibid.
54. Ibid.
55. See also Philip E. Auerswald, *The Coming Prosperity: A Guide to Opportunity in the Age of Entrepreneurship* (New York: Oxford, forthcoming 2011); Dane Stangler, "Creative Discovery: Reconsidering the Relationship Between Entrepreneurship and Innovation," *Innovations* (Spring 2008).

The Cultural Costs of Corporatism: How Government-Business Collusion Denigrates the Entrepreneur and Rewards the Sycophant
Timothy P. Carney

1. See Gabriel Kolko, *The Triumph of Conservatism* (Chicago: Quadrangle Books, 1967), 103; and "Packers Face Report Music," *Washington Post*, June 7, 1906.
2. See John T. Flynn, "Whose Child Is the NRA?" *Harper's*, September 1934.
3. See Robert D. Hershey Jr., "Psychological Lift Seen," *New York Times*, August 17, 1971.
4. See Food and Drug Administration Docket # 00N-1936, vol. 276, c 7153.
5. The Center for Responsive Politics' website, OpenSecrets.org, Lobbying Spending Data, Top Industries, 2009, available at http://www.opensecrets.org/lobby/top.php?showYear=2009&indexType=i.
6. See Tom Hamburger, "Obama Gives Powerful Drug Lobby a Seat at Healthcare Table," *Los Angeles Times*, August 4, 2009; "PhRMA Statement on Senate Health Care Reform Bill," December 24, 2009.
7. OpenSecrets.org, Lobbying Spending Data, Top Spenders, 2009, available at http://www.opensecrets.org/lobby/top.php?showYear=2009&indexType=s.
8. See Daniel Whitten, "Duke Energy, Alcoa, GE Win in Climate Legislation by Signing On," *Bloomberg*, May 22, 2009; Kate Sheppard, "Kerry: Three Big Oil Companies Likely to Back Climate Bill," *Mother Jones*, April 22, 2010; and Amanda Terkel, "Nike Resigns from the U.S. Chamber of Commerce Board of Directors Over Global Warming Disagreements," *ThinkProgress*, September 30, 2009.

9. The White House, "Remarks by the President at the Signing of the Family Smoking Prevention and Tobacco Control Act," June 22, 2009.

10. Samuel Loewenberg, "Smoke Screen," *Slate*, July 25, 2002; data on lobbying expenditures compiled from OpenSecrets.org.

11. PhilipMorrisUSA.com, which cites the IRI/Capstone Total Retail Panel for its figures.

12. Federal Election Commission. Her donation was on October 12, 2008.

13. Karen Delaney, Comment, FDA-2009-N-0294–0338, available at Regulations.gov.

14. Kim Hart, "Apple Secrecy Is Bitter Fruit on Hill," *Politico*, June 14, 2010.

15. John Carey, "Scott and Bill Went Up the Hill: High-Tech Leaders Find That They Can No Longer Afford to Ignore Washington—and Vice Versa," *BusinessWeek*, March 16, 1998.

16. Ibid.

17. See OpenSecrets.org.

18. See Xeni Jardin, "Google, Microsoft Push for 'Net Neutrality' Law," National Public Radio, May 10, 2006.

19. "Wal-Mart Calls for Minimum Wage Hike," *CNN/Money*, October 25, 2005.

20. "Leslie Dach Joins Wal-Mart as Executive Vice President of Corporate Affairs and Government Relations," Wal-Mart press release, July 24, 2006.

21. "Rep. Delahunt: Tourism Pays Price for Post–9/11 U.S. Foreign Policy," US Fed News, April 20, 2005.

22. Jenny Anderson, "Big Money Still Learning to Lobby," *New York Times*, March 13, 2007.

23. Data from OpenSecrets.org.

24. Scott Malone, "GE Teams Up with Geron for Stem-cell Research," Reuters, June 30, 2009.

25. Greenhouse Gas Services, GHGS.com.

26. Data from OpenSecrets.org.

27. Ibid.

28. Ibid.

29. President Barack Obama, "Remarks on a Vision for High-Speed Rail in America," April 16, 2009.

30. Jim Martin, "GE Offers Look at Future," *Erie Times-News*, May 19, 2009.

31. Kate Galbraith, "G.E. Announces New York Battery Factory," NYTimes.com, May 12, 2009, available at http://green.blogs.nytimes.com/2009/05/12/ge-announces-new-york-battery-factory/.

32. "Batteries Buck Downward Investment Trend," NYTimes.com, April 15, 2009, available at http://green.blogs.nytimes.com/2009/04/15/batteries-buck-downward-investment-trend/.

33. "General Electric at Goldman Sachs Fourth Annual Alternative Energy Conference," *Fair Disclosure*, May 21, 2009.

34. Yahoo Finance.

35. Michael Weisskopf, "Auto-Pollution Debate Has Ring of the Past," *Washington Post*, March 26, 1990.

It's Not the Markets, It's the Morals:
How Excessively Blaming Markets Undermines Civil Society
John Larrivee

1. Richard Pipes, *Communism: A History* (New York: Modern Library, 2001), 150.

2. Francis Fukuyama, *The Great Disruption: Human Nature and the Reconstitution of the Social Order* (New York: Touchstone, 1999), 64; Robert Fogel, *The Fourth Great Awakening and the Future of Egalitarianism* (Chicago: University of Chicago Press, 2000), 172.

3. Fogel, 3.

4. Fogel, 170.

5. Fogel, 143.

6. Peter Berger, *The Capitalist Revolution: Fifty Propositions about Prosperity, Equality, and Liberty* (New York: Basic Books, 1988), 99.

7. Fogel, 143–44.

8. Fogel, 3.

9. Fogel, 172.

10. Leszek Kolakowski, "My Correct Views on Everything: A Rejoinder to Edward Thompson's 'Open Letter to Leszek Kolakowski,'" *Socialist Register*, 1974, 5–6; David Horowitz, *The Politics of Bad Faith: The Radical Assault on America's Future* (New York: Free Press, 1998), 85–87.

11. Alexander Yakovlev, *A Century of Violence in Soviet Russia* (New Haven, CT: Yale University Press, 2002), 155–67.

12. Pipes, 66.

13. Quoted in Robert Conquest, *Reflections on a Ravaged Century* (New York: W. W. Norton, 2000), 189.

14. Stéphane Courtois, ed., *The Black Book of Communism: Crimes, Terror, Repression* (Cambridge, MA: Harvard University Press, 1999), 4.

15. Leszek Kolakowski, *Main Currents of Marxism* (New York: W. W. Norton, 2005), 1210.

16. Friedrich Hayek, *The Road to Serfdom* (Chicago: University of Chicago Press, [1944] 1994), 148–67.

17. Yakovlev, 6–7.

18. Paul Craig Roberts, *Alienation and the Soviet Economy: The Collapse of the Socialist Era* (New York: Holmes and Meier, [1971] 1990), 3.

19. John Clark and Aaron Wildavsky, *The Moral Collapse of Communism: Poland as a Cautionary Tale* (San Francisco: Institute for Contemporary Studies, 1990), 170, 330.

20. Alexander Yakovlev, *The Fate of Marxism in Russia* (New Haven, CT: Yale University Press, 1993), 37.

21. Yakovlev, *The Fate of Marxism in Russia*, 15.

22. Nikolai Shmelev and Vladimir Popov, *The Turning Point: Revitalizing the Soviet Economy* (New York: Doubleday, 1989), 167.

23. Clark and Wildavsky, 127–39, 199–200.

24. Pipes, 70.

25. Shmelev and Popov, 75–76. Yakovlev cites the same problems, and likewise attributes this to common ownership and to Marxist theory, which fostered suspicion of the truth and the sources of human mores. Yakovlev, *The Fate of Marxism in Russia*, 72–74.

26. Dierdre McCloskey, *The Bourgeois Virtues: Ethics for an Age of Commerce* (Chicago: University of Chicago Press, 2006).

27. Arthur Brooks, *Who Really Cares: The Surprising Truth about Compassionate Conservatism* (New York: Basic Books, 2006), 120–21.

28. Jonah Goldberg, *Liberal Fascism: The Secret History of the American Left from Mussolini to the Politics of Meaning* (New York: Doubleday, 2008); Francois Furet, *The Passing of an Illusion: The Idea of Communism in the Twentieth Century* (Chicago: University of Chicago, Press, 1999), 175.

Religion, the Market, and the State
Gerard Casey

1. Robert H. Nelson, *The New Holy Wars: Economic Religion vs. Environmental Religion in Contemporary America* (University Park, PA: The Pennsylvania State University Press, 2010), 349.

2. Eric Kaufmann, *Shall the Religious Inherit the Earth?* (London: Profile Books, 2010).

3. A brief note on other religious traditions: Confucianism, Hinduism, and Buddhism are, subject to the usual religious warnings about the dangers of excessive attachment to material goods, positive in their approach to the market. Of the currently popular secular religions, economism is, unsurprisingly, generally favorable to the market while environmentalism is, again unsurprisingly, hostile to it. See Mario Gómez-Zimmerman, "The Capitalist Structures of Hinduism." *Religion & Liberty* 6, no. 3 (1996), 8–10; Fenggang Yang, and Joseph B. Tamney, eds., *State, Market, and Religions in Chinese Societies* (Leiden, Netherlands: E. J. Brill, 2005); and David Hamilton, "Buddhist Economics: P. A. Payutto's Search for a Middle Way in the Market Economy" (2007), available at http://buddhismtaoism.suite101.com/article.cfm/buddhist_economics.

4. Jonathan Sacks, "Judaism's Religious Vision and the Capitalist Ethic," *Religion & Liberty* 11, no. 6 (2001), 1.

5. Scott B. Rae, "Views of Wealth in the Bible and the Ancient World." *Religion & Liberty* 12, no. 6 (2002), 6–7.

6. Sacks, 1; Corinne Sauer and Robert M. Sauer, "Jewish Theology and Economic Theory." *Religion & Liberty* 17, no. 1 (2007), 4–5; Corinne Sauer and Robert M. Sauer, *Judaism, Markets, and Capitalism: Separating Myths from Reality* (Grand Rapids, MI: Acton Institute, 2007).

7. Sacks, 2.

8. Thomas E. Woods Jr., *The Church and the Market: A Catholic Defense of the Free Economy* (Lanham, MD: Lexington Books, 2005); Philip Booth, ed., *Catholic Social Teaching and the Market Economy* (London: Institute of Economic Affairs, 2007).

9. Doug Bandow, "Biblical Foundations for Limited Government," *Religion & Liberty* 7, no. 1 (1997), 5–7.

10. Other examples include 1 Peter 2:13–17 and Titus 3:1. I have derived much of the following analysis from sources I can no longer identify.

11. A similar reading applies to another passage in which St. Paul exhorts his readers to "obey them that have the rule over you" (Hebrews 13:17). From the full passage it is perfectly clear that those "that have the rule over you" are the leaders in the Church, not the secular authorities: "Obey them that have the rule over you, and submit yourselves: for they watch for your souls, as they that must give account, that they may do it with joy, and not with grief: for that is unprofitable for you."

12. Adam Smith, *An Inquiry into the Nature and Cause of the Wealth of Nations*, vol. 2 (Oxford: Clarendon Press, ([1775] [1976]), 788–89; Charles G. Leathers and J. Patrick Raines, "Adam Smith on Religion and Market Structure: The Search for Consistency." *History of Political Economy* 40, no. 2 (2008), 345–63.

13. Laurence R. Iannaccone, Roger Finke, et al., "Deregulating Religion: The Economics of Church and State." *Economic Inquiry* 35, no. 2 (1997), 351–52.

The Road to Cultural Serfdom:
America's First Television Czar
Paul A. Cantor

1. Quoted in Russell Johnson (with Steve Cox), *Here on Gilligan's Isle* (New York: HarperCollins, 1993), 91. For more on this subject, see Sherwood Schwartz, *Inside Gilligan's Island* (New York: St. Martin's, 1994), xv–xvi, 5, 269.

2. Minow's speech is available at http://www.americanrhetoric.com/speeches/newtonminow.htm.

3. According to Mary Ann Watson, *The Expanding Vista: American Television in the Kennedy Years* (New York: Oxford University Press, 1990), 29, the entertainment trade press at the time did in fact refer to Minow as a "cultural czar."

4. Robert Corn-Revere, "Avast Ye Wasteland: Reflections on America's Most Famous Exercise in 'Public Interest' Piracy," *Federal Communications Commission Law Journal* 55 (2003), 481. Corn-Revere develops a devastating critique of Minow's speech and his policies as FCC chairman that supplements my analysis on a number of important points, including issues of law and constitutionality, and questions of technology.

5. According to Watson, Minow's threats were real; in the year following

his NAB speech, "fourteen broadcast stations were put on probation with short-term renewals and local hearings were scheduled in eight renewal cases" (Watson, 34).

6. See Watson, 20, for Minow's own admission: "I think Robert was the basic reason I was appointed to the FCC." Watson quotes a reporter saying: "Minow comes to television armed with a background of no experience."

7. The possibility of syndication, selling first-run programs directly to local stations, did gradually develop, but it remained a minor corner of the overall television market.

8. Quoted in Watson, 51. I have relied heavily on Watson's account of Minow's tenure as FCC chairman, first because it is widely regarded as an authoritative source on the period, and second because she interviewed Minow for the project, and allows him to make his own case for his actions. Moreover, she is a great admirer of the Kennedy administration in general and Minow in particular; she calls him "one of the best and the brightest" (Watson, 19). The book jacket even features an endorsement from Minow. Here is a typical example of how partisan and pro-Kennedy Watson's account is: "For American educational television, the Kennedy years were the most exhilarating of times. Exceptional achievements were made in children's, documentary, and public affairs programming by decade's end. The seeds of innovation and independence in public television—the very qualities that would so threaten Richard Nixon in the early 1970s—were planted with hope and determination during the New Frontier" (Watson, 202). I actually turned to Watson expecting to find an account of Minow's FCC tenure that would contradict Schwartz's. But in fact she assembles all the evidence needed to substantiate Schwartz's account of Minow's harmful effect on the television industry. Coming from an enthusiastic partisan of Minow, this evidence is all the more convincing and powerful.

9. Quoted in Watson, 51.

10. Quoted in ibid., 52–53.

11. Ibid., 53.

12. Quoted in ibid., 52.

13. Ibid.

14. Ibid., 53.

15. For a Hayekian analysis of how popular culture operates, which stresses the elements of contingency and unpredictability in television creativity, see my essay "Popular Culture and Spontaneous Order, or How I Learned

to Stop Worrying and Love the Tube," in William Irwin and Jorge J. E. Gracia, eds., *Philosophy and the Interpretation of Popular Culture* (Lanham, MD: Rowman & Littlefield, 2007), 161–86.

16. Consider in this context remarks made by the famous show business impresario Ed Sullivan in testimony before the FCC at the time of Minow's crusade: "There will always be, of necessity, a TV Wasteland. The three networks must produce 10,950 hours of entertainment per year, in contrast to only 600 hours demanded by the entire moving picture industry of our country and the 125 hours per year demanded by the Broadway theater" (quoted in Watson, 29).

17. Minow's distrust of commercial motives is persistent; when asked in a 2002 interview why television quality is low, he replied: "There are three reasons. The first is money. The second reason is money. And the third reason is money." See Newton N. Minow and Fred H. Cate, "Revisiting the Vast Wasteland," *Federal Communications Law Journal* 55 (2003), 415.

18. Quoted in Watson, 51.

19. In its third and final season (1962–63), *The Untouchables* went from the number-eight show on television to number forty-one. See Tim Brooks and Earle Marsh, *The Complete Directory to Prime Time Network and Cable TV Shows, 1946–Present*, 6th ed. (New York: Ballantine Books, 1995), 1088.

20. Quoted in Watson, 53.

21. Perhaps the most disagreeable aspect of Minow was the way he combined rather conventional taste in television with a contempt for the American public's viewing habits. Watson quotes Minow writing to Congressman Abner Mikva: "Now I know who is watching westerns and crime shows: I knew that the rating samples depended on relative cultural illiterates." Even Watson admits that "Minow's playful reply revealed a touch of the snobbism he was accused of by network defenders" (Watson, 42). One wonders what the American people, whose welfare Minow was supposedly concerned about, would have thought if they knew that he referred to them as "relative cultural illiterates."

22. Watson, 22.

23. For evidence of Minow's actual influence on television executives, see Watson, 53–54: "A survey conducted by the research firm of Trendex . . . concluded Minow 'exerted a definite influence' on the thinking of leading television producers in New York and Hollywood. Close to 50 percent of the forty-three producers surveyed said the Chairman's public statements

influenced their program ideas. . . . [The article] from *Variety* which detailed the Trendex study . . . began, 'Television programming has been completely Minowized. . . . Minow's pronouncements, especially criticism of undue violence, has had direct and sharp effect on TV programming. A majority of execs admit that they have consciously tailored shows to conform with FCC recommendations." Minow proudly sent a copy of this article to Robert Kennedy. Having brought *The Untouchables* to justice, Minow may have thought of himself as a Junior G-Man. There is some irony in the fact that a television show about one disastrous intervention by the federal government in American life (*Prohibition*) became the target of another do-gooder out of Washington. In his NAB speech Minow had the impudence to "suggest that we change the name of the FCC to The Seven Untouchables."

24. See Watson, 57–70. Note particularly her statement: "It was as if, when President Kennedy firmly aligned himself with the righteousness of the cause [of civil rights], prime-time television did too" (Watson, 58). Like Minow, Watson clearly identifies quality in television programming with political correctness. She praises shows purely for their political message and not for any aesthetic characteristics.

25. Watson, 189.

About the Contributors

Thomas E. Woods Jr., Ph.D., is the *New York Times* bestselling author of *Meltdown*, *Nullification*, *The Politically Incorrect Guide to American History*, *How the Catholic Church Built Western Civilization*, and several other books. He holds a bachelor's degree in history from Harvard and graduate degrees from Columbia University. A senior fellow at the Ludwig von Mises Institute, he has received the Templeton Enterprise Award, the O. P. Alford III Prize for Libertarian Scholarship, and an Olive W. Garvey Fellowship from the Independent Institute. Woods live in Topeka, Kansas, with his wife and four daughters.

Brian Domitrovic, Ph.D., is the author of *Econoclasts*, the first history of supply-side economics. He holds a Ph.D. in history from Harvard University, where he also did graduate work in the economics department. He earned his bachelor's degree at Columbia University, studying history and mathematics. An assistant professor of history at Sam Houston State University, he has written for the *Wall Street Journal*, *Investor's Business Daily*, *CNN.com*, the *New York Daily News*, *Roll Call*, the *Washington Times*, and many other popular and scholarly publications. Domitrovic lives near Houston with his wife and three daughters.

Carey Roberts, Ph.D., is associate professor of history at Arkansas Tech University. He holds both a master's degree and a doctorate from the University of South Carolina. Dr. Roberts lectures extensively on American political economy.

Per Bylund, a native of Sweden, is a doctoral candidate in applied economics and a graduate researcher at the University of Missouri. He holds master's degrees in both political science and computer science, and an undergraduate degree in business administration. Bylund writes frequently for the popular website LewRockwell.com.

Antony P. Mueller, Ph.D., is the founder and president of the Continental Economics Institute. He is an adjunct scholar of the Ludwig Von Mises Institute (USA) and the academic director of the Instituto Ludwig von Mises Brasil. A former Fulbright scholar, he holds a doctorate in economics from the University of Erlangen-Nuremberg (Germany). Dr. Mueller is currently a professor of economics at the Federal University of Sergipe in Brazil.

Mark Brandly, Ph.D., is an assistant professor in the College of Business at Ferris State University in Michigan. His articles have been published in the *Wall Street Journal*, the *Journal of Commerce*, *Public Finance Review*, the *Free Market*, and many other newspapers and websites. He holds a doctorate in economics from Auburn University and a bachelor's degree in mathematics from Colorado State University.

Dane Stangler is research manager at the Ewing Marion Kauffman Foundation, the world's largest foundation devoted to entrepreneurship. He initiated and manages the Kauffman Foundation Research Series on Firm Formation and Economic Growth. Stangler has written for the *Wall Street Journal*, *City Journal*, *The American*, and other publications, and he contributes to the blog Growthology.org. He and his family live near Kansas City.

Timothy P. Carney, the lobbying editor and a columnist at the *Washington Examiner*, is the author of *Obamanomics* and *The Big Ripoff: How Big Business and Big Government Steal Your Money*. He has received both the Templeton Enterprise Award and the Lysander Spooner Award for the best book on liberty. A protégé of veteran columnist Robert Novak, Carney was senior reporter and later editor at the *Evans-Novak Political Report*. His work has appeared in the *Wall Street Journal*, the *New York Post*, the *American Spectator*, the *American Conservative*, the *Huffington Post*, *National Review Online*, *Human Events*, and many other publications. He and his family live in Maryland.

John Larrivee, Ph.D., is associate professor of economics at Mount St. Mary's University. He holds a bachelor's degree and master's in public policy from Harvard and a doctorate from the University of Wisconsin. He lectures extensively on economics and has written for such publications as the *Journal of Markets and Morality*. Dr. Larrivee lives in Emmitsburg, Maryland.

Gerard Casey, Ph.D., is associate professor in the School of Philosophy at University College Dublin (Ireland) and adjunct professor at the Maryvale Institute (UK). He previously taught at the University of Notre Dame and at the Catholic University of America. Casey holds a doctorate from Notre Dame as well as a Bachelor of Laws (LLB) from the University of London and a Master of Laws (LLM) from University College Dublin.

Paul A. Cantor, Ph.D., is the Clifton Waller Barrett Professor of English at the University of Virginia. He has written on issues as varied as Shakespeare, sitcoms, Oscar Wilde, and economics, and has been described as "a preeminent scholar in the field of American popular culture studies." Dr. Cantor has been a member of the National Council on the Humanities and the director of the National Endowment for the Humanities Summer Seminar in Shakespeare.

Index

Adams, John, 28
"adaptive response," 108–9
aesthetics and politics, 182–85
Age of Greatness, 37–39
alienation of people, 141
American economic growth, 4–8,
    12–15
American Revolution, 18–19, 22, 24
antimarket ideologies, 131–32, *135*,
    135, 145, 151–52
Apple, 116–17
Arthur Andersen, 146
Articles of Confederation, 19, 22
Astor, John Jacob, 29
Austrian School of economics, ix, xii,
    58, 65–66

bailouts
    of 2008–2009, 14, 73, 112–13, 126
    consequences of, 29–33, 61–62
    economics of, 61–63, 89
    and government intervention,
        182–85
    and Hamiltonianism, 19–25
    and Wall Street, 62, 104, 113

Baker, Richard, 120
Balkin, Jack, 104–5
Bank for International Settlements,
    56, 57, 69–70
Bank of England, 20–21
Bank of the United States, 22–26, 29
banking crisis, 55–57. *See also* crisis
    origins
Barbour, Philip, 30–31
Bastiat, Frédéric, x, 30, 128
Baumol, William, 86, 98, 102
Bergh, Andreas, 37–39, 41, 44–45
Bergström, Fredrik, 46
Best Performing Cities, 104
Beverly Hillbillies, The, 180
biblical passages, 163–65
Biden, Joe, 124, 126
big business
    and big government, xii, 111–30
    consequences of, 114–15
    and government intervention, 111,
        122
    and lobbyists, 121–24
big government
    and big business, xii, 111–30

225

big government *(continued)*
  and entrepreneurship, xii, 111–30
  growth of, 102–3
  and lobbyists, 114–18, 121–24,
    129–30
Bing Crosby Special, The, 183
booms and busts, 29–33
bottom-up culture, 177, 180–82
Brandly, Mark, xii, 73
Branting, Hjalmar, 39
Brazil, 105
Bretton Woods conference, 11, 59, 67,
  69
Brooks, Arthur, 150
Bryan, William Jennings, 6
Burke, Edmund, 24
Bush administration, 73, 80
Bush, George W., 77, 105, 112
business–government collusion,
  111–30. *See also* big business
BusinessWeek, 117, 118
busts and bailouts, 29–33. *See also*
  bailouts
"busy-ness era," 14–15
"Buy American" policies, 74–76
Bylund, Per, xi, xii, 35

"canal mania," 29
Cantor, Paul A., xiii, 171
capital flows, 85–89
capitalism
  and consumerism, 144–46
  and corporatism, 129–30
  crisis of, 9
  critiques of, 133–34, 142
  and dishonesty, 146–47
  "failure" of, 55
  future of, 151–53
  and human relationships, 143–44,
    150–51
  and localism, 114
  and markets, 131–53
  and materialism, 144–46

  and moral decay, 148–49
  and selfishness, 135, 136
  and totalitarian disasters, 131–32
Capone, Al, 182
Carnegie, Andrew, 7
Carney, Timothy P., xii, 111
Casey, Gerard, xiii, 155
Cato's Letters, 21
CBS Reports, 183
central banks, 55–60, 64, 67–70
Central Intelligence Agency (CIA), 1, 2
central planning, viii–ix, 73, 95, 147,
  173, 181
charitable obligations, 160–63
charity activities, 133–34, 149–51,
  160–63
Charles II, King, 20
China, 61–65, 73, 101–2, 105, 185
Christensen, Clayton, 98
Christianity, 156–62, 166
civil society, 132, 134–37, *135*, 144,
  151–53
Civil War, 4–6
Clark, John, 144, 147
classical economics, 55, 60, 80
classical liberalism, 30
Clay, Henry, 30, 77
Cleveland, Grover, 6
Clinton, Bill, 112
Cold War, 1, 185
Collapse of Complex Societies, The, 95
collectivism, 1–4, 15, 147
Communism
  and dishonesty, 147–48
  and exploitation, 142–43
  and human relationships, 143–44
  and markets, 131–32, 135, 151
  and religion, 156
  and scarcity, 144
  and totalitarian disasters, 131, 132,
    152
competitiveness strategy, 105–9
complexity, 95–101

complexity curve, *96*, 96–109, *97*
Conrad, Joseph, 183
conservatism, 30, 32–33
consumerism, 144–46
Continental Congress, 19
Contract with America, viii
Cooper, James Fenimore, 30
Corn-Revere, Robert, 174
corporatism. *See also* big government
  and capitalism, 129–30
  costs of, 111–30
  and localism, 114
  names for, 112
  and Obama administration, 113
  roots of, 114–15
Council on Competitiveness, 106
"creative response," 108–9
Cringely, Robert, 99
"crisis of capitalism," 9
crisis origins, 55–71
cultural conservatism, 30
cultural creativity, 180–82
cultural serfdom, 171–87
"culture czar," 171–87

Dach, Leslie, 119
Darwin, Charles, 180
Darwinism, 156
Daschle, Linda, 125
Daschle, Tom, 125
day-care system, 50–51
debt expansion, 19–21, 25–28, 67–70
debt-to-GDP ratio, 103
deflation, 9–10, 70
Delahunt, Bill, 119
Delaney, Karen, 116
Desilu Studios, 181
dishonesty, 146–48
distorted incentives, 102
Dobbs, Lou, 86
Dodd-Frank financial reform bill, 104
Doing Business rankings, 101
Domitrovic, Brian, vii, xi, xii, 1

Easterly, William, 2
economic crisis, 55–71
economic development, 30, 96–97
economic growth, 4–8, 12–15
economic law, 37
economic policy
  Keynesian economic policy, 56–60
  new economic policy, 60, 101
  and politics, 107
  and serfdom, 1–15
  in Sweden, 45–47
economic power, 104–5
economic prosperity, 25, 30, 94
economic renewal, 95–101
Economics: An Introductory Analysis, 1
economism, 156
Edison, Thomas, 126
education, 49–50, 99–100
egalitarianism, 39, 137–38
Eisenhower, Dwight D., 12
Embargo Act, 29
entertainment industry, 108, 109,
  171–87
entrepreneurship
  assisting, 109–10
  and big government, xii, 111–30
  and complexity, 93–110
  disappearance of, 130
  and government intervention, 95,
    106, 110, 114–15
  and government regulation, 104,
    111–12, 115
  and innovation, 95–109
environmentalism, 156
equality and inequality, 137–39, 142,
  159–60
European economy, 46, 61, 68–69
Evans, Harold, 107
exploitation and markets, 142
externalities, 83–84

factories, tale of, 124–27
"failure of capitalism," 55

fascism, 131, 135, 147–48, 151–52, 156
Fed News, 119
Federal Communications Commission (FCC), 171–81, 184–85
Federal Reserve, 7–13, 60–62, 65
Federalist, 27
Federalists, 22–24, 28, 32
film industry, 108, 109
financial crisis origins, 55–71
financial reform bill, 104
fiscal policy, 8–15
Fisher, Irving, 57
Fogel, Robert, 134, 137, 140
Foggy Bottom Land Company, 24
Food and Drug Administration (FDA), 116
Ford, Gerald, 102
foreign debt, 22, 63, 67–69
Foreign Policy, ix
foreign trade, 23, 73–91
Foreign Trade and U.S. Policy, 84
Fox, William, 108
fractional-reserve lending, 23, 25
France, 67
Fred Astaire Show, The, 183
free market, vii–viii, xiii, 130
free trade, xii, 40–41, 73–91
Freudianism, 156
Friedman, Milton, 60, 152

Gallatin, Albert, 26, 28
Garnett, James M., 31
gas turbines, 107, 109
Gates, Bill, 98, 117–18
General Electric, 120–29
George III, King, 28
Germany, 1, 3, 67, 69, 185
Gidehag, Robert, 46
Giles, William Branch, 26
Gilligan's Island, 171, 187
global imbalances, 63–65
global population, ix

God as creator, 157–58
"Goldilocks economy," 58, 60
Gomory, Ralph, 86
Good Samaritan, 161, 163
Goodhart's Law, 105–6
Goodson, Mark, 178–79
Gorbachev, Mikhail, 145
Gordon, Richard, 21
Gouge, William M., 30
"Government Electric," 120–29
government interference, 101–5. *See also* welfare state
government intervention. *See also* interventionism
  and big business, 111, 122
  and entrepreneurship, 95, 106, 110, 114–15
  and Friedrich Hayek, 172–73, 184–85
  and innovation, 117–18
  inviting, xiii
  and Keynesian economics, 56
  and monetary system, 59, 70–71
  and protectionism, 73
  in television, 172–73, 182–85
  and wealth, 114
government intrusion, 9, 168–69
government investments, 102–3
government regulation
  and entrepreneurship, 104, 111–12, 115
  and reset economy, 121
  and television industry, 172
government subsidies, 124–29
government–business collusion, 111–30. *See also* big government
Great Britain, 3, 38, 67
Great Depression, 9, 59, 73–74
Great Moderation, 13, 14, 69
Great Recession, 13, 105
Great Unraveling, The, 36
Greece, 46, 67, 68
Greenspan, Alan, 61–62

Gregory VII, Pope, 166
Gripenstedt, Johan August, 39
gross domestic product (GDP), 10–11, 13, 36, 63, 103
Grossman, Gene, 89

Haberler, Gottfried, 80
Hamilton, Alexander, xi, 17–33, 77
Hamiltonianism, 17–33
Hatch, Orrin, 117
Hayek, Friedrich A.
    and Austrian School, 58
    on capitalism, 2
    on central planning, viii–ix, 73, 143
    on collectivism, 3
    on government intervention, 172–73, 184–85
    on government power, 37, 152
    on social engineering, 187
Hazlitt, Henry, 78
health-care system, ix, 113, 119
hedge funds, 120
Henry, Patrick, 24
Hierta, Lars Johan, 39
Higgs, Robert, 59
Hoover, Herbert, 10, 77
Huggins, Roy, 177
human relationships, distorting, 143–44, 150–51
Hume, David, 105
Humphrey, Hal, 179

Iannaccone, Laurence, 168
Illusion of a Conservative Reagan Revolution, The, viii
Immelt, Jeffrey, 120–21
imports, 78–80
incentives
    distorted incentives, 102
    loss of, 48–49, 129–30
    market incentives, 35
    structures for, 48–53

income inequalities, 137–39, 142, 159–60
India, 85, 105
individualism, 3, 144, 148
Industrial Revolution, 6, 29, 38, 134
infant industries, 81–83
inflation
    beginnings of, 4
    and Hamiltonianism, 19–20, 23–24
    high inflation, 8–14, 68–70, 102, 128
    and stagnation, 59–60
    "under control," 57–60
innovation
    and economic renewal, 95–101
    and government intervention, 117–18
    and startups, 95–109
    strategies for, 105–9
"innovation-based economy," 109
Innovation Nation, 106
interest rates, low, 56, 58–59
international debt, 22, 63, 67–69
international monetary system, 64–65
international trade, 43, 66–67, 73–90
interventionism, 55–56, 59–60, 64–65, 70. *See also* government intervention
Ireland, 68
Irving, Washington, 30, 32
Italy, 67, 68

Japan, 1, 61–67
Jefferson, Thomas, xi, 17–18, 25–28
Jeffersonian reaction, 25–28
Jeffersonian tradition, 30–32
jet propulsion, 107, 109
job exporting, 85–89
Jobs, Steve, 98
Johnson administration, 184
Johnson, Lyndon B., 12
Journal of Economic Literature, 40

Judaism, 156–62
Judeo-Christian tradition, 151,
    156–58, 169

Kane, Tim, 93
Kao, John, 106
Kaufmann, Eric, 156
Kennedy administration, 172, 175,
    184–85
Kennedy, John F., 1, 12, 171, 175
Kennedy, Robert F., 175
Keynesian economics, 12, 42–43, 56,
    59–60, 63
Klasmeier, Coleen, 116
Korean War, 12
Krugman, Paul, 36, 46, 76

Laemmle, Carl, 108
Lapham, Lewis, 105
Larrivee, John, xiii, 131
lawmakers and lobbyists, 119–20
Leave It to Beaver, 186
Lee, Henry, 24
liberalism, 30, 135
libertarianism, 137
life expectancies, 94, 138
Lincoln, Abraham, 77
lobbying game, 111–12
lobbyists
    and big business, 121–24
    and big government, 114–18,
        121–24, 129–30
    elevating, 114–15
    and lawmakers, 119–20
    and state governments, 20
localism, 114
Locke, John, 158
London School of Economics, ix
Louis XIV, King, 105
low interest rates, 56, 58–59
Lundberg, Erik, 40, 42, 44, 50

Macon, Nathaniel, 26
macroeconomic era, 14–15
macroeconomic history, 6, 13–14
macroeconomic performance, 4–6
macroeconomic policy, 6–9, 13–15
macroeconomic theory, 44, 59–63, 66
Madison, James, 18, 25, 26, 105
Maltsev, Yuri, 2
man as procreator, 157–58
Mandeville, Bernard de, 135, 136
Manhattan Project, 108
market crash, 7, 61
market entrepreneurs, 112, 116
market incentives, 35
markets
    antimarket ideologies, 131–32,
        135, *135*, 145, 151–52
    blaming, 140–49
    and capitalism, 131–53
    and civil society, 132, 134–37, *135*,
        144, 151–53
    and exploitation, 142
    free market, vii–viii, xiii, 130
    future of, 151–53
    and morals, 131–53
    and oppression, 141–42, 146
    and religion, 132, *135*, 135–37,
        163–69
    and "spiritual resources," 134,
        137–40
    and state, 155–69
    and virtues, 133–34, 149–51
Marshall Plan, 108
Marx, Karl, 142
Marxism, 145
materialism, 144–46
McCloskey, Deirdre, 149
McCord, Susanna Cheves, 30
McKenna, Regis, 117–18
McKinley, William, 6, 77
Medicare, x, 112–13
microeconomics, 80
Microsoft, 117–18

Minow, Newton, 171–87
Minsky, Hyman, 57
Mises, Ludwig von, xiii, 58, 80
modern liberalism, 135
modern welfare state, 35–53. *See also*
    welfare state
monetarism, 60, 63
monetary expansion, 58–59, 68
monetary policy, 8–15, 61, 69–70, 88
Monroe, James, 26
moral decay, 148–49
morality, new, 49–52
Morgan, J. P., 7–9
Morris, Robert, 24
Mueller, Antony, xii, 55

"nanny state," 48, 50
National Association of Broadcasters,
    171, 175, 177–78, 183–86
national debt, 19–21, 25–28
national innovation strategy, 105–9
National Recovery Act, 112
National Recovery Administration, 102
National Socialism, 131, 135, 151–52
nationalism, 26–32, 124, 132
Nazism, 147–48
Nelson, Robert, 156
neomercantilistic system, 22
Ness, Eliot, 181
New Deal, viii, 10, 112
New Economy, 62, 126
New Frontier, 172–73, 176–77, 180,
    184–85
New Frontiersmen, 176–77
New Holy Wars, The, 156
new morality, 49–52
New Russians, The, xi
New York Times, 36, 120, 125
Nixon, Richard M., 12, 59, 112
Non-intercourse Act, 29

Obama administration, 73, 76, 77,
    113

Obama, Barack
    and corporatism, 113
    economic advisers of, 5–6
    and economic power, 104
    and health care, 119
    and protectionism, 77
    and railway industry, 124–25
    "remaking" America, 120
    and stem-cell research, 122
    and tobacco industry, 115–16
oppression and markets, 141–42, 146
Oracle, 117
outsourcing, 85–89

Panic of 1792, 24
Panic of 1819, 30
Panic of 1837, 30
Panic of 1873, 5
Panic of 2008, vii
Parable of the Good Samaritan, 161,
    163
Parable of the Talents, 159
Parable of the Workers in the Vine-
    yard, 159, 160, 161
Patterson, David, 125
Pax Americana, 18
perestroika, 141
Peter Pan, 183
pharmaceutical industry, 113
Philadelphia Gazette, 30
Philip Morris, 115–16
Pierce, Franklin, 30
Pipes, Richard, 147
Playhouse 90, 183
political entrepreneurs, 112, 116,
    120–21
Politico, 116–17
politics
    and aesthetics, 182–85
    and economic policy, 107
    and religion, 157, 166–69
Popov, Vladimir, 148–49
population of world, ix

positive externalities, 83–84
poverty, alleviating, 160, 162
poverty, destroying, 186–87
poverty levels, 36–37, 49, 137–39
power, access to, 142–43
power, economic, 104–5
productivity slowdown, 98
property and religion, 158–60
property rights, 38, 158–61
protectionism dangers, 73–91, 124
protectionism, opposing, 90–91
protectionist theories, 89–90
public day-care system, 50–51
public debt, 19–21, 27–28, 33
public retirement pension, 42
public schools, 49–50

R. J. Reynolds, 115–16
radios, 108, 109
railway industry, 124–25
Rand, Ayn, 135, 136
Randolph, Edmund, 25
Reagan, Ronald, 13, 60
Reaganomics, 60
recessions
    of 1907, 7
    of 1913, 8
    of 1919–21, 8
    of 1953–60, 12
    of 1981–82, 103
    of 2008–10, 13, 105, 120
Reformation, 166–67
"regulatory certainty," 129
religion
    and government intrusion, 168–69
    and markets, 132, *135*, 135–37,
        163–69
    and politics, 157, 166–69
    and state, 157, 163–69
    types of, 156
religious leaders, xiii
renewal, 95–101
"Report on Public Credit," 22

reset economy, 121
retail, revolutionizing, 98, 100
retirement, x, 39, 42–44, 51
Revolutionary War, 18–19, 22, 24
Rice, John, 123
"Rising Above the Gathering Storm,"
    106
Road to Serfdom, The, viii, ix, 2–4, 37,
    73, 143
"Roaring '20s," 9–10
Robber Barons, 5, 10, 14
Roberts, Carey, xi, xii, 17
Roberts, Paul Craig, 86–88
Romer, Christina, 5, 7, 13
Roosevelt administration, 10
Roosevelt, Franklin D., 10, 102, 112
Roosevelt, Theodore, 112
Russia, 1, 185

Sacks, Jonathan, 157, 158, 161
Samaritan parable, 161, 163
Samuelson, Paul A., 1
Schramm, Carl J., 107
Schumer, Chuck, 120
Schumpeter, Joseph, 100, 108, 109,
    112
Schwab, Larry, viii
Schwadron, Steven, 119
Schwartz, Sherwood, 171–73, 175–76,
    187
Scott, Lee, 118–19
secular religion, 133, 156
serfdom. *See also* welfare state
    accepting, 53
    facing, x, 1–15, 91
    results of, 3, 95, 113, 187
Shall the Religious Inherit the Earth?,
    156
Shays, Daniel, 19
Shmelev, Nikolai, 148–49
Simms, William Gilmore, 30
"skunk works," 99
Smith, Adam, 74, 167–68

Index

Smith, Hedrick, xi
Smoot-Hawley Act, 9, 73–74
social alienation, 141
Social Security, x, 80, 149
socialism, 35–43, 131, 135, 151–52
society, collapse of, 95–97
"soft planning," 102
"Solow residual," 97
Soviet Union, 1–4, 134, 141, 145
"space race," 108
Spain, 67, 68
"spiritual resources," 134, 137–40
SS *Minnow*, 171
"stagflation," 13, 59–60, 63
Stalin, Joseph, 141
Stangler, Dane, xii, 93
Stanton, Frank, 178
startups. *See also* entrepreneurship
    and complexity, 93–110
    and innovation, 95–109
    interference in, 101–5
state
    and dishonesty, 146–48
    encroachment by, xii
    interference from, 101–5
    lobbying, 20
    and markets, 155–69
    origins of, 17–33
    and religion, 157, 163–69
state power, x, 56, 141, 144
statism, resurgence of, vii, xi, xii
stimulus policies, 56, 59, 73–74, 103,
    118, 125–26
stock market boom, 60–61
stock market plunge, 7, 61
Stockholm School, 42
Studio One, 183
subprime mortgages, 55, 57
subsidies, 124–29
Sun Microsystems, 117
sweatshops, 142
Swedish financial crisis, 45–47
Swedish "golden years," 37–39, 41

"Swedish model," xi, 36–37, 40–45,
    49, 52–53
Swedish welfare state, xi, 35–53
Swift, Gustavus, 94
Swift, Jonathan, 21
sycophancy, rewarding, 111–30

Tainter, Joseph, 95–97
Tariff of 1816, 29–30
TARP bailouts, 112–13
Taylor, John, 26, 27, 28
technology, benefits of, 138–39
technology companies, 116–18
technology startups, 98–99
television
    and "culture czar," 171–87
    power in, 172–73
    self-regulation of, 176–80
    threat against, 173–76
television networks, 174–78, 181–82
Ten Commandments, 158–61
They Made America, 107
tobacco industry, 115–16
top-down culture, xiii, 172–73, 176,
    180–82
totalitarian disasters, 131–32, 152
"toxic assets," 23
trade barriers, 73–91
trade deficits, 56, 61, 64–68, 85–87
transportation, 98, 124–25
Trenchard, John, 21
Troubled Asset Relief Program
    (TARP), 113
Truman, Harry, 12
truth, distorting, 146–48
Tuerck, David G., 84, 90
Twilight Zone, The, 183
Tyler, John, 30

unemployment, 4–14, 42–51, 59–60,
    78
"unintended consequences," 102,
    109–10, 172

Index

United Kingdom, 3, 38, 67
Untouchables, The, 181–82
U.S. Treasury Department, 10, 65
utopianism, 186–87

variation era, 8–14
Victory, 183
virtues, 133–34, 149–51
Volcker, Paul, 13, 60

wages and protectionism, 80–81
Wall Street, 62, 104, 113
"Wall Street greed," 55
Wal-Mart, 114, 118–19
Walpole, Robert, 21
Walton, Sam, 98, 100
War for Independence, 18–19, 22, 24
War of 1812, 29
Washington, D.C., 24
Washington, George, 17–18, 25–26
Washington Post, 129
"watershed of 1913," 1–15
Watson, Mary Ann, 178, 179, 183, 184

Wealth of Nations, 74, 167–68
welfare state
    consequences of, 47–53
    constructing, 39–40
    expansion of, 37, 47, 56
    mindset of, 47–53
    and religion, 169
    Swedish welfare state, xi, 35–53
Whittle, Frank, 107
Whonder, Carmencita, 120
Wildavsky, Aaron, 144, 147
Wilson, James, 24
Woods, Thomas E., Jr., vii
World Bank, 2, 101
world population, ix
World War II, 10–11, 18

Yakovlev, Alexander, 145, 146
Yazoo land schemes, 24
Yeager, Leland B., 84, 90

Zaslavskaya, Tatyana, 141
Zuck, Jonathan, 117